CONCENTRATED

INVESTING

CONCENTRATED INVESTING

TRATEGIES OF THE WORLD'S GREATEST ONCENTRATED VALUE INVESTORS

.LEN C. BENELLO • MICHAEL VAN BIEMA
TOBIAS E. CARLISLE

WILEY

Cover design: Wiley

Published by John Wiley & Sons, Inc., Hoboken, New Jersey.
Published simultaneously in Canada.

For general information on our other products and services or for technical support, please contact our Customer Care Department within the United States at (800) 762-2974, outside the United States at (317) 572-3993 or fax (317) 572-4002.

Wiley publishes in a variety of print and electronic formats and by print-on-demand. Some material included with standard print versions of this book may not be included in e-books or in print-on-demand. If this book refers to media such as a CD or DVD that is not included in the version you purchased, you may download this material at http://booksupport.wiley.com. For more information about Wiley products, visit www.wiley.com.

Library of Congress Cataloging-in-Publication Data:

Names: Benello, Allen C., author. | Biema, Michael van. | Carlisle, Tobias E., 1979- author.
Title: Concentrated investing : strategies of the world's greatest concentrated value investors / Allen C. Benello, Michael van Biema, Tobias E. Carlisle.
Description: Hoboken : Wiley, 2016. | Includes index.
Identifiers: LCCN 2016002290|
ISBN 9781119012023 (hardback) | ISBN 9781119012054 (ePDF) |
ISBN 9781119012047 (ePub)
Subjects: LCSH: Capitalists and financiers--Biography. | Investments. | Portfolio management.
Classification: LCC HG172.A2 .B454 2016 | DDC 332.6—dc23 LC record available at http://lccn.loc.gov/2016002290

Printed in the United States of America

10 9 8 7 6 5 4 3 2 1

To my wife Julie, and to my daughters Sophie and Avery.

—Allen Carpé Benello

To Lavinia, Fiamma, and Tristan—my earth, my flame, and my hunter.

—Michael van Biema

For Nick, Stell, and Tom.

—Tobias E. Carlisle

Contents

Preface

Michael and I came up with the idea for this book while riding in a taxi on the way to a meeting with an investment manager. Michael interviews managers of value oriented funds regularly for his fund of funds business, and has met with at least a few hundred during the course of his career. On this particular occasion Michael asked me to come along to help evaluate a new manager, and I agreed to join him in between meetings of my own. As unlikely a place as it was to hatch the inspiration for this project, we were both puzzled by a strange paradox that we had observed over many years in the investment business: The returns generated by investors do not always correlate to their ability to analyze and understand companies.

With the initial idea for a book, and a set of interviews, Michael and I reached out to Bill Falloon at Wiley for help. Bill introduced Michael and me to Tobias Carlisle, the author of two other successful investment books, "Quantitative Value" and "Deep Value." We found that they shared a very similar set of ideas about investing in general and about the theme for the book, concentrated investing, in particular. We hit it off immediately. Tobias agreed to come on board as a coauthor along with Michael and me. He has been instrumental in helping to take the raw interviews and put the investors and their flagship investments into their proper historical and theoretical context. He also helped to examine the strategy quantitatively to determine the drivers of outperformance: Was it a matter of selecting the *right* securities, or holding them in the *right* amounts?

I recall one individual, whom we'll call Investor Number One, whose returns were decent, but who seemed to be totally off-base when it came to the highly subjective and trickier job of figuring out whether a company's business and management were fundamentally attractive, or worth skipping over. He had made some notable blunders, on one occasion pounding the table to his colleagues about a soft goods company that was soon destined for bankruptcy. To me and a few others with whom I spoke at the time, it wasn't difficult to comprehend that this company was not attractive and perhaps even precariously situated, so it left me scratching my head when I read his fund's performance results, which seemed to have a way of levitating away from what must have been some costly errors.

On the other hand, another acquaintance whom we will call Investor Number Two was deeply insightful when discussing an industry or company and always grasped the investment case, for or against, with enviable precision and knowledge of the relevant facts. This second person's returns, however, were decidedly lackluster. He somehow never managed to fully capitalize on his insights, which were tremendously valuable and, one would have thought, should have led to very outstanding returns.

This paradox got us thinking about the topics of security analysis and portfolio construction, and how they relate to returns. Apparently, analytical ability alone does not constitute a really good investor. Investor Number Two in the preceding example should have been doing better with his ideas, and just imagine what Investor Number One could have accomplished if he had been more analytically competent.

A lightbulb turned on when I realized the investors I admire the most (and this admiration comes only in part from the amazing success they've achieved) tend to share one characteristic: They are concentrated value investors. That is, they adhere to a concentrated approach to portfolio construction, holding a small number of securities as opposed to a broadly diversified portfolio. We set out to study the mathematical and statistical research that has been done by various academics on the subject of portfolio concentration, and to chronicle the methods and achievements of some of the people who have benefited from being concentrated value investors. Our first task was to approach Lou Simpson and Kristian Siem, two ultra-successful concentrated value investors who had never previously agreed to interviews on the mechanics of their investment style. As we completed their interviews, we began to compile material on the subject of portfolio concentration, a trail that ultimately reached back beyond the Kelly Formula to John Maynard Keynes.

In *Concentrated Investing: Strategies of the World's Greatest Concentrated Value Investors*, we examine some of the methods these extraordinary individuals employ, providing the reader an insight into how they function and how they have managed to accomplish their returns. However, two very important caveats are necessary. First, concentrated investing is not for everyone. As Glenn Greenberg said, Peter Lynch (manager of the Fidelity Magellan Fund during its most successful period, earning truly amazing average annual returns during his tenure) was anything but a concentrated investor, owning a large number of securities in the fund. Furthermore, concentrated investing should only be undertaken by people who are prepared to do intensive research and analysis on their investments. People outside of the investment profession usually don't have the time to do this, and are far better off with an index fund or finding a competent investment manager—preferably one who employs a focused approach.

The second caveat is more important, and applies to investment professionals and non-professionals alike (perhaps even more to professionals). It is summed up in an insightful and humbling quote from legendary martial artist Bruce Lee, which is as follows:

> A goal is not always meant to be reached, it often serves simply as something to aim at.

Coming from one of the most disciplined and exacting athletes in the history of martial arts, this statement is illuminating. One can hardly imagine Bruce Lee trying to break a two-by-four with his fist and accepting, after a failed attempt, that this goal was not reachable. Evidently, beneath his hard-driving exterior, there was a more philosophical side. Similarly, in the context of this book, our intention is not to show that the great individuals profiled in the following chapters constitute the standard against which one should hold oneself, but to provide a road map with some concrete ideas on how to be a better investor. Not everyone should attempt to replicate their style or accomplishments. Rather, these profiles are a guidepost on the journey to successful investing.

With these caveats, we do believe that the average enterprising investor with the ability to perform in-depth fundamental analysis will be better off trimming the number of investments they hold and redistributing their capital into their top 10 or 15 ideas. To quote Bruce Lee a second time:

> The successful warrior is the average man, with laser-like focus.

—Allen Carpé Benello

Acknowledgments

This book would not have been possible without the generous facilitation and support of Louis A. Simpson. In addition, we are the beneficiaries of a great deal of assistance in the production of the manuscript for *Concentrated Investing*. We'd like to thank the interviewees Lou Simpson, Charlie Munger, Kristian Siem, Glenn Greenberg, and Jim Gordon. Finally, we appreciate the assistance of the team at Wiley Finance, most especially Bill Falloon, Susan Cerra, and Meg Freeborn, who provided guidance and advice along the way.

CONCENTRATED
INVESTING

Introduction

Concentrated Investing

Conscientious employment, and a very good mind, will outperform a brilliant mind that doesn't know its own limits.

—Charlie Munger[1]

Concentration value investing is a little-known method of portfolio construction used by famous value investors Warren Buffett, Charlie Munger, long-time Berkshire Hathaway lieutenant Lou Simpson, and others profiled in this book to generate outsized returns. A controversial subject, the idea of portfolio concentration has been championed by Buffett and Munger for years, although it moves in and out of fashion with rising and falling markets. When times are good, portfolio concentration is popular because it magnifies gains; when times are bad, it's often abandoned—after the fact—because it magnifies volatility. Concentration has been out of favor since 2008, when investment managers began in earnest to avoid what they perceive as a risky business practice.

It is time to re-visit the subject of bet sizing and portfolio concentration as a means to achieve superior long-term investment results. We will start by examining some of the academic research on concentration versus diversification on long-term investment results. One central feature of the discussion surrounding concentration is the Kelly Formula, which provides a mathematical framework for maximizing returns by calculating the position size for a given investment within a portfolio using probability (i.e., the chance of winning versus losing) and risk versus reward (i.e., the potential gain versus the potential loss) as variables. The Holy Grail for any investor is a security with a high probability of winning and also a large potential gain compared to the potential loss. Given favorable inputs, the Kelly Formula can produce surprisingly large position sizes, far larger than the typical position size found in mutual funds or other actively managed investment products. In addition, some academic studies point to the diminishing advantages of portfolio diversification above a surprisingly small number of individual investments, provided each investment is adequately diversified (no overlapping industries, etc.). Also, portfolios with a relatively smaller number of securities (10 to 15) will produce results that vary greatly from the results of a given broadly diversified index. To the extent that investors seek to outperform an index, smaller portfolios can facilitate that goal, although concentration can be a double-edged sword.

Investors can employ the traditional value investing methodology of fundamental security analysis to identify potential investments with favorable Kelly Formula inputs (a high probability of winning, and a high risk/reward relationship), in order to maximize the chances of significant outperformance, as opposed to significant underperformance, with a concentrated portfolio.

We have unparalleled access to investors in Warren Buffett's inner circle. Interviews with several highly successful investors who have achieved their success employing a concentrated approach to portfolio management over the long term (at least 10 to 30 years) will be incorporated throughout this book. One common feature of these investors is that they have had permanent sources of capital, which has changed their behavior by allowing them to endure greater volatility in their returns. Most people seek to avoid volatility in general because they perceive increased variance as an increase in risk. The investors we examine, however, tend to be variance seekers. At the same time, however, they are able to produce returns with low downside volatility compared to the underlying markets in which they invest.

This book profiles eight investors with differing takes on the concentration investment style. The investors and the endowment interviewed are contemporary. One of the investors profiled, Maynard Keynes, is now a historical figure, but was the early adopter of many of the ideas that came to be held by his successors. The purpose of the book is to tease out the principles that have resulted in their remarkable returns. Though they operated through different periods of time, all have compounded their portfolios in the mid-to-high teens over very long periods—defined as more than 20 years. The investors in this book are rare in that they all have either permanent or semi-permanent sources of capital. We hypothesize that this is an important factor in allowing them to practice their focused style of investment. The book also puts forward a mathematical framework, the Kelly Criterion, for sizing investment "bets" within a portfolio. The conclusion of both the profiles of these great investors and of the Kelly Criterion is remarkably coincident.

Modern portfolio theory would have us believe that markets are efficient and that attempts to beat market performance are both foolhardy and expensive in terms of return. Yet the fact remains that there is at least a small cadre of active managers who have beaten the market by a significant margin over prolonged periods. This book and the investors profiled in it agree with the proponents of efficient market theory on two points:

1. Markets are mostly efficient.
2. They should be treated as efficient if you are, as Charlie Munger puts it, a "know-nothing" investor.

In other words, it requires a lot of hard work and a significant amount of knowledge to produce market-beating returns. If you do not have this, it is to your benefit to diversify and index. If, however, you possess knowledge and the capability for hard work as well as a few other characteristics outlined in the book, it is to your benefit to focus your energies on a small number of investments. The degree of focus is a stylistic choice and cannot be prescribed for any given individual, but the investors in this book concentrate on anywhere from 5 to 20 individual securities. The larger the number, the more the benefits of diversification, the lower the volatility of the portfolio, but also, in most cases, the lower the long-term returns. The trade-off between larger bets and more volatility is an individual choice, but both the Kelly Formula and the participants in the book point to the advantages of larger bets and more concentrated portfolios. In fact, the reader will probably be quite surprised by how large the bets can be calculated to be. Once again, placing bets of significant size depends on appropriately skewed probabilities, and these types of probabilities are uncommon, but both the mathematics and the investors argue for large bets when situations with unusual risk/return arise. It is important to note that the risk referred to here is the risk of permanent loss of capital and not the more commonly used academic metric of volatility. The investors in this book are willing to suffer through periods of temporary (but significant) loss of capital in an attempt to find opportunities where the probability of the permanent loss of capital is small. In other words, they attempt to find situations that offer a strong margin of safety where one's principal is protected either by assets or by a strong franchise and an unlevered balance sheet.

The investors in this book come from very different backgrounds ranging from an English major to an economist, but somehow they ended up in quite similar places in terms of their general investment philosophy. The singular trait that unites these investors, and separates this group from the herd of investors who try their luck on the stock market is temperament. Asked in 2011 whether intelligence or discipline was more important for successful investors, Buffett responded that temperament is key:[2]

> *The good news I can tell you is that to be a great investor you don't have to have a terrific IQ. If you've got 160 IQ, sell 30 points to*

somebody else because you won't need it in investing. What you do need is the right temperament. You need to be able to detach yourself from the views of others or the opinions of others.

You need to be able to look at the facts about a business, about an industry, and evaluate a business unaffected by what other people think. That is very difficult for most people. Most people have, sometimes, a herd mentality, which can, under certain circumstances, develop into delusional behavior. You saw that in the Internet craze and so on.

. . .

The ones that have the edge are the ones who really have the temperament to look at a business, look at an industry and not care what the person next to them thinks about it, not care what they read about it in the newspaper, not care what they hear about it on the television, not listen to people who say, "This is going to happen," or, "That's going to happen." You have to come to your own conclusions, and you have to do it based on facts that are available. If you don't have enough facts to reach a conclusion, you forget it. You go on to the next one. You have to also have the willingness to walk away from things that other people think are very simple. A lot of people don't have that. I don't know why it is. I've been asked a lot of times whether that was something that you're born with or something you learn. I'm not sure I know the answer. Temperament's important.

Munger says of Buffett's theory:[3]

He's being extreme of course; the IQ points are helpful. He's right in the sense that you can't [teach] temperament. Conscientious employment, and a very good mind, will outperform a brilliant mind that doesn't know its own limits.

In the next chapter we meet Lou Simpson, the man Warren Buffett has described as "one of the investment greats."[4]

NOTES

1. Charles Munger, interview, February 23, 2012.
2. "A Class Apart: Warren Buffett and B-School Students," NDTV, May 24, 2011, https://www.youtube.com/watch?v=4xinbuOPt7c, as discussed in Shane Parrish, "What Makes Warren Buffett a Great Investor? Intelligence or Discipline?" *Farnam Street Blog*, April 19, 2014.
3. Charles Munger, interview, February 23, 2012.
4. Warren Buffett, "Chairman's Letter," Berkshire Hathaway, Inc., 2010.

CHAPTER 1

Lou Simpson: The Disciplined Investor

A Portrait of Concentration

Stop the music.

—Warren Buffett to Jack Byrne, chairman of GEICO, after meeting Lou Simpson in 1979[1]

In 1979, GEICO, an auto insurance company based in Washington, DC, that had been brought close to bankruptcy just three years earlier was searching for a new chief investment officer. The company's recent near-death experience, and the perception of insurance companies' investment efforts as hidebound, and highly risk-averse, had made the search difficult. The recruiter, Lee Getz, vice chairman of Russell Reynolds, did find a candidate who later turned it down because his wife refused to move to Washington.[2] Lamenting his lack of success in filling the position in over a year, Getz told his friend Lou Simpson about the little insurance company with big problems that no one wanted to tackle. He asked Simpson, the chief executive of California-based investment firm Western Asset Management, if he was interested in the job. Simpson was reluctant.[3] Western Asset Management had been a subsidiary of a big California bank holding company. Simpson was sick of politicking within the confines of bank bureaucracy, and didn't have any great desire to repeat the experience in an insurance company. He also knew that GEICO had almost gone belly up just three years earlier.

As a favor, Getz asked Simpson to interview with the company's chairman, John "Jack" Byrne Jr., the man who had almost single-handedly pulled GEICO back from the brink of insolvency.[4] Simpson agreed if only to help out an old friend. He traveled to Washington to meet with Byrne, who Simpson judged as being "a very, very smart guy," but also a micro-manager involved in everything GEICO did.[5] Simpson found the role interesting, but not compelling. He craved autonomy, and Byrne, who had just saved GEICO, seemed unlikely to grant it. Byrne called Simpson back for a second interview. Though he had reservations he dutifully traveled back to Washington. In the second interview, Byrne told Simpson, "We're really interested in you. But the one hoop you're going to have to go through is to meet with Warren Buffett."[6] With about 20 percent of GEICO, Buffett was the largest shareholder through Berkshire Hathaway. Byrne said, "Warren thinks we need a new investment person. The person before was really not up to the job."[7] Though Buffett didn't yet have a high profile, Simpson had read about the Nebraska-based value investor who was just renewing a longstanding interest in GEICO.

"UNSTOPPABLE" GEICO

Buffett has a storied 65-year association with GEICO, beginning in 1951 as a 20-year-old graduate student in Benjamin Graham's value investing class at Columbia. He recounted the first 45 years of that association in his 1995 Chairman's Letter following Berkshire's purchase of the half of GEICO it didn't own.[8] It was then the seventh-largest auto insurer in the United States, with about 3.7 million cars insured (in 2015, it is second, with 12 million policies in force). Buffett attended Columbia University's graduate business school between 1950 and 1951 because he wanted to study under Graham, the great value investor and investment philosopher, who was a professor there. Seeking to learn all he could about his hero, he found that Graham was the chairman of *Government Employees Insurance Company*, to Buffett "an unknown company in an unfamiliar industry."[9] A librarian referred him to *Best's Fire and Casualty* insurance manual—a large compendium of insurers—where he learned that GEICO was based in Washington, DC.

On a Saturday in January 1951, Buffett took the early train to Washington and headed for GEICO's downtown headquarters. The building was closed for the weekend, but he frantically pounded on the door until a custodian appeared. He asked the puzzled janitor if there was anyone in the office the young Buffett could talk to. The man said he'd seen one man working on the sixth floor—Lorimer Davidson, assistant to the president and founder, Leo Goodwin, Sr. Buffett knocked on his door and introduced himself. Davidson, a former investment banker who had led a round of funding for GEICO before joining it, spent the afternoon describing to Buffett the intricacies of the insurance industry and the factors that help one insurer succeed over the others.[10]

Davidson taught Buffett that GEICO was the very model of an insurer built to succeed. Formed in 1936, at the height of the Great Depression by Goodwin and his wife Lillian, GEICO was set up to be low-cost from the get go.[11] Goodwin had been an executive at the United Services Automobile Association (USAA), an auto insurer founded to insure military personnel, and a pioneer in the direct marketing of insurance. He had seen data that showed federal government employees and enlisted military officers tended to be financially stable, and also low-risk drivers. Those two attributes, he surmised, would mean that premiums were paid on time, with lower and infrequent claims. Agents were typically used to provide professional advice for more complex business insurance requirements. Auto insurance, though it was mandatory and expensive, was also relatively simple. Most consumers would know what they required in an auto policy.[12] Goodwin reasoned that GEICO could cut out the agents and market directly to consumers, thereby minimizing distribution costs, just as USAA had. Those two insights—direct selling that bypassed agents to financially secure, low-risk policyholders—put GEICO in a very favorable cost position relative to its competitors. Later, Buffett would write that there was "nothing esoteric" about its success: its competitive strength flowed directly from its position as the industry low-cost operator.[13] GEICO's method of selling—direct marketing—gave it an enormous cost advantage over competitors that sold through agents, a form of distribution so ingrained in the business of these insurers that it was impossible for them to give it up.[14] Low costs permitted low prices, low prices attracted and retained good policyholders, and this virtuous cycle drove GEICO's success.[15] GEICO was superbly managed under the Goodwins. It grew volumes rapidly, and did so while maintaining unusually high profitability. When Leo Goodwin retired in 1958, he named Davidson, the man whom the 20-year-old Buffett had met on that Saturday in January 1951, as his successor.[16] The transition was a smooth one, and GEICO's prosperity continued with Davidson in the chief executive role. Volumes grew such that, by 1964, GEICO had more than 1 million policies in force.[17] Between its formation in 1936 and 1975, it captured 4 percent of the auto market, and grew to be the nation's fourth largest auto insurer.[18] It looked, in Buffett's estimation, "unstoppable."[19]

But GEICO was struck by a double whammy in the 1970s. First, Davidson retired in 1970, and then both Leo and Lillian Goodwin passed away. Without a rudder, it seemed to stray from the principles that had made it successful.[20] When real-time access to computerized driving records became available throughout the United States in 1974, GEICO moved beyond its traditional government employee constituency to begin insuring the general public.[21] By 1975, it was clear that it had expanded far too aggressively during a difficult recession.[22] Actuaries had also made serious errors in estimating GEICO's claims costs and reserving for losses. This faulty cost information caused it to underprice its policies, and lose an enormous amount of money.[23] Weak management, bad investment choices, and years of rapid expansion took their toll.[24] In 1976, GEICO stood on the brink of failure.

It was saved from collapse when Jack Byrne was appointed chief executive in 1976. Byrne took drastic remedial measures.[25] He organized a consortium of 45 insurance companies to take over a quarter of GEICO's policies.[26] To pay the remaining claims, he had GEICO undertake a stock offering that severely diluted existing stockholders.[27] The stock price was savaged. From its peak, it fell more than 95 percent.[28] Believing that Byrne could rescue GEICO, and that, despite its problems, it maintained its fundamental competitive advantage as a low-cost auto insurer, Buffett plunged into the market in the second half of 1976, buying a very large initial interest for Berkshire.[29] Byrne put it on a path to insuring only "government employee"-style policyholders from a much wider pool of potential insureds, and improving its reserving and pricing discipline. Though the company shrank significantly in the first few years of Byrne's tenure, Berkshire kept buying, making purchases at particularly opportune times. By 1979, GEICO had taken a step back from the precipice, but it was only half the size that it had been. While the business maintained its inherent competitive advantage—its rock-bottom operating costs—and Byrne had reserving and pricing under control, it was clear that GEICO needed help on the investment side. After searching for over a year without luck, and being turned down by the first good prospect, Byrne had whittled the field down considerably from the initial candidates. Simpson was one.[30] And a meeting with Buffett stood in the way.

On a Saturday morning in the summer of 1979, Simpson traveled to Omaha to meet with Buffett in his office. In the meeting Buffett said, "I think maybe the most important question is, what do you own in your personal portfolio?"[31] Simpson told him, but Buffett didn't give away whether he was impressed or not. After talking for two to three hours, Buffett drove Simpson to the airport where they met Joe Rosenfield. Rosenfield was a good friend of Buffett's, and an impressive investor in his own right: He would almost single-handedly steer little Grinnell College's $11 million endowment into a $1 billion behemoth, one of the biggest *per student* for any private liberal arts school in the country.[32] Simpson and Rosenfield discovered they were both big-time Chicago Cubs fans, and spent the time chatting about the team (Rosenfield would go on to acquire 3 percent of the Cubs, and, in his seventies, vowed not to die until they won a World Series).[33] After visiting with Buffett and Rosenfield, Simpson flew back to Los Angeles. Evidently Buffett found the stocks in Simpson's personal portfolio acceptable because he wasted no time. He called Byrne straight after the interview, and told him, "Stop the music. That's the fella."[34] Byrne called Simpson to offer him the job, and upped the compensation package.[35] Though his wife was skeptical about leaving California, Simpson persuaded her, saying, "I think this is an interesting opportunity and I really don't want to stay where I am."[36] Simpson accepted, and the family began preparing to move to Washington, DC.

AN EMERGING VALUE INVESTOR

> Lou has never been one to advertise his talents. But I will: Simply put, Lou is one of the investment greats.
>
> —*Warren Buffett, "2010 Berkshire Hathaway Letter to Shareholders"*

Louis A. Simpson was born in Chicago, Illinois, in 1936. He grew up an only child in the Chicago suburb of Highland Park.[37] At the end of his college freshman year at Northwestern University in 1955, he went to see the school guidance counselor. After subjecting Simpson to the usual barrage of tests, the counselor told the 18-year-old that he had an aptitude for numbers and financial concepts.[38] Simpson, who had been studying first engineering and then pre-med, transferred to Ohio Wesleyan with a double major in economics and accounting. Three years later he graduated with high honors and was offered a Woodrow Wilson National Fellowship to study labor economics at Princeton. He received his MA from Princeton in two years, and began to work on his doctorate, researching the market for engineers. Simpson was offered the opportunity to teach full time as an instructor of economics, teaching the basic courses of accounting and finance, even though he had never taken a formal course in finance. At the first faculty meeting, the provost told the junior faculty members that only 10 percent would proceed to get tenure. Now married and with his first child, Simpson realized that the very long odds of tenure meant that teaching was an unlikely path to financial security.

While teaching full time, Simpson started writing letters and interviewing for positions in investment management firms and investment banks. He'd always had an interest in investments and managed his own tiny stock portfolio as a teenager, which was unusual at the time. A firm in Chicago, Stein Roe & Farnham—then perhaps the largest independent investment firm between New York, Boston, and the West Coast (today it has disappeared)—had a partner who was a Princeton graduate who conducted the interviews at the campus. He and Simpson hit it off. The deciding factor for Simpson was that Stein Roe was prepared to offer him $100 a month more than any firm in New York. So in 1962, he dropped out of doctoral studies at Princeton University to return to Chicago.[39] He was 25, and working in his first full-time job as a portfolio manager at Stein Roe.[40]

At Stein Roe, Simpson managed separate accounts, beginning with individuals and gradually moving toward institutions. Stein Roe did offer mutual funds, though Simpson did not work on them. The strategy for the separate accounts was narrowly confined. An investment committee created a model portfolio, and the separate accounts were expected to follow it. Simpson followed the model portfolio, but had a tendency to concentrate the managed accounts more than the model portfolio dictated.[41] He stayed seven-and-a-half years with Stein Roe, and was made a partner. He was concerned that the partners were much more interested in the size of their slice of the pie than in trying to grow the whole pie.[42] He told a good friend from Princeton that he was open to making a change. The friend introduced him to Shareholders Management, a mutual fund management firm in Los Angeles.[43] Shareholders Management was headed by "fund wizard" Fred Carr, a darling of the market during the go-go years in the 1960s, when the fad was for performance mutual funds.[44] Shareholders Management was one of the hottest. Under Carr's guidance, Shareholders' Enterprise Fund had soared 159 percent from 1967 to 1969, and the fund's assets had ballooned more than fiftyfold, to $1.7 billion.[45] Carr was a "gunslinger," a market timer who dove in and out of the shares of small, rapidly growing stocks.[46] A *Business Week* magazine profile in 1969 said of Carr that he "may just be the best portfolio manager in the U.S."[47] Carr offered Simpson a role not managing the hot mutual funds, but the separate accounts. Simpson would have to take a cut in base salary, but received a substantial option package. He accepted, and so in 1969, he became one of the first partners to leave Stein Roe.[48]

Simpson moved his family, now with three children, to Los Angeles to join Shareholders Management under Carr. While Shareholders Management had been for several years regarded by the market as an unusually gifted investment team, all was not as it seemed. Carr had bought a lot of "letter stock"—stock not registered with Securities and Exchange Commission (SEC), which cannot be sold to the public, meaning that it is extremely illiquid—for the Enterprise Fund. This strategy had done very well as the market ran up, but the long bull market soon collapsed, and investors in Carr's Enterprise Fund were slammed, leading to large-scale redemptions. Compounding the problem, there was virtually no market for sales of the unregistered letter stock needed to meet the redemptions. Simpson's timing was unlucky. He had joined in September 1969, the absolute top of Shareholders Management's run. One month after his arrival, the losses in the

Enterprise Fund were so bad that Carr was forced to resign, and cashed in his equity in the funds as he left.[49] Though he had been hired to run managed accounts, Simpson was tasked with managing part of the Enterprise Fund. He quickly found that he didn't fit into the Shareholders' culture. "I viewed myself an investor, and they were trading-oriented," he says.[50] At lunch one day, one of the firm's lawyers asked Simpson, "Do you realize how screwed up this place is? They've done things that are not on the up and up, and, if you want to maintain your reputation, it would be a good idea to leave."[51] Simpson resigned shortly after. He had been at Shareholders' Management for just five months. He was 33, with three children, and he had just moved to Los Angeles. Though he had some opportunities in Chicago, he decided to see what was available on the West Coast.

After a brief search, Simpson settled on United California Bank to help start an investment management business and be second-in-command in the investment area. That new business was eventually spun out into a separate company called Western Asset Management, and became a subsidiary of Western Bank Corporation.[52] Simpson stayed at Western Asset Management for nine years as head of portfolio management, and then director of research.[53] Western Asset Management was successful, but Simpson found it difficult to operate in a big banking environment. The chairman of Western Bank Corporation wanted to make him CEO of Western Asset Management, but said he would only do it if Simpson promised to stay on. The chairman forced the resignation of the former chief executive, and Simpson was made the new chief executive of Western Asset Management. Though he stayed on for three years, he found the management role chafed him. He yearned to do something entrepreneurial. Friends of his wanted to set up some kind of investment management company with him, but he wasn't sure.[54] The experience with Shareholders Management had a transformative effect on Simpson, wholly changing his perspective on investment.[55] Shareholders Management taught him about the importance of business risk, and started him on the road to value investing.[56] During his time at Western Asset Management he was able to think, developing his investment philosophy, both on a personal and a company basis. He began to embrace value investing. His philosophy evolved dramatically when he ran the research department and he moved toward a more concentrated value investment approach. And then GEICO came calling.

BIG, CONCENTRATED BETS

In the 1970s, most insurance companies held a broad portfolio of bonds, counting on diversification to minimize risk, and little in the way of stocks. They also held a high proportion of the portfolio in government bonds, which, during the period of high inflation in the 1970s, had led to sizable losses for most portfolios.[57] Before Simpson arrived in 1979, GEICO was no exception. He would radically change GEICO's course. The agreement Simpson had struck with Byrne allowed the new investment chief to put up to 30 percent of GEICO's assets in stocks.[58] At the time, most property and casualty insurers limited stock holdings to about 10 percent of assets.[59] The agreement also allowed him to hold concentrated positions.[60] Simpson went to work as soon as he arrived, slashing the company's bond holdings and rebuilding the stock portfolio in a limited number of names.[61]

Wary of Byrne's reputation for micromanagement, Simpson had made it clear he was to be solely responsible for managing GEICO's investments. "The more people you have making decisions, the more difficult it is to do well," he said.[62] "You have to satisfy everybody."[63] Neither Buffett nor Byrne were to interfere with the portfolio.[64]

Simpson's instincts about Byrne were right. After he had been at GEICO for more than a year, he went away for a week on vacation. Byrne took the opportunity to buy some stocks for the portfolio. When Simpson returned, he immediately sold Byrne's positions. Byrne asked, "Why would you do that? They were good ideas."[65]

Simpson replied, "If I'm going to be responsible for the portfolio, I'm going to make all the decisions."[66] From then on, Simpson made his own decisions, essentially working autonomously.[67] Describing the arrangement in 2004, Buffett wrote,

> *You may be surprised to learn that Lou does not necessarily inform me about what he is doing. When Charlie and I assign responsibility, we truly hand over the baton—and we give it to Lou just as we do to our operating managers. Therefore, I typically learn of Lou's transactions about ten days after the end of each month. Sometimes, it should be added, I silently disagree with his decisions.* But he's usually right. [*emphasis Buffett's*][68]

Simpson did, however, regularly speak to Buffett about his investing philosophy. Simpson was impressed by Buffett's encyclopedic knowledge of businesses and numbers, and his long list of contacts.[69] In addition to Buffett's view on investing, Simpson would also ask Buffett about companies that he thought he knew something about.[70] Over time, Simpson and Buffett fell into a routine. Buffett would call Simpson, or Simpson would call Buffett. Initially as often as several times a week, as time went on, the men might let a month or two go by before the two talked, but they always stayed in regular contact.[71] Though both operated independently, GEICO and Berkshire did have several common positions. They tended not to overlap because

GEICO had a significant size advantage. Where Buffett needed to take positions of more than $1 billion to generate a return meaningful relative to the Berkshire portfolio worth many billions, GEICO could take much smaller positions given its smaller portfolio size. Simpson found several larger ideas he wanted to buy for GEICO, but if he learned Berkshire was already buying the stock, he stood back to allow Berkshire to complete its buying.[72]

When he first arrived at GEICO, Simpson found a group of investment people who did not share his investment approach but thought he would try to work with them for a while. He asked Buffett to come to GEICO twice a year to spend an hour with the investment team. During one of these talks, Buffett told a story that left an impression on Simpson.[73] Buffett said, "Suppose somebody gives you a card with 20 punches, and each time you make an investment move you have to punch the card. Once you have had 20 punches, you're going to have to sit forever with what you have."[74]

The story stuck with Simpson, helping him avoid trading and to focus on developing a long-term investment perspective.[75] Simpson says, "I never did a lot of trading but the story really did highlight that you need to have a lot of conviction in what you're doing because you only have so many shots and you better be confident on the shots that you take."[76] Heeding Buffett's advice, Simpson gradually concentrated larger and larger sums of money into just a handful of companies. In 1982, GEICO had about $280 million of common stock in 33 companies. Simpson cut it to 20, then to 15, and then, over time, to between 8 and 15 names.[77] At the end of 1995, just before Berkshire's acquisition of GEICO ended separate disclosures of the insurer's portfolio, Simpson had $1.1 billion invested in just 10 stocks.[78] Simpson was willing to concentrate positions in a single sector. At one time GEICO owned five or six electric utilities, which Simpson regarded as a single, big position.[79] In the early 1980s, GEICO took a huge bet on three of the "Baby Bells," the nickname given to the independent regional telephone companies spun out from AT&T, Inc., following the U.S. Department of Justice's antitrust lawsuit filed in 1974. Simpson also regarded those holdings as one position.[80] He took a large position because he assessed the Baby Bells as offering an unusually good risk/reward ratio.[81] Admiring Simpson's bet, Byrne remarked, "It was a very big hit on a very large amount of money."[82]

Simpson would take those big bets only when he thought the odds were well in his favor. He regards GEICO's single biggest winner as the Federal Home Loan Mortgage Corporation, known as "Freddie Mac."[83] Freddie Mac is a government-sponsored enterprise created in 1970 to expand the secondary market for mortgages in the United States. It buys mortgages on the secondary market, pools them, and sells them as a mortgage-backed security to investors on the open market. It operates in a duopoly with the Federal National Mortgage Association, commonly known as "Fannie Mae." When GEICO bought into Freddie Mac, it was not a public company. While Fannie Mae was then public, Freddie Mac was only semi-public, with a small market in its stock, and the bulk owned by savings and loans associations. Simpson found it trading exceedingly cheaply, between three and four times its earnings. In addition to its manifest cheapness, Simpson was attracted to its franchise, which it owed to its status as a duopoly with Fannie Mae. Buffett had already bought up to his limit, and was restricted by regulation from buying more because Berkshire owned Wesco, which was a Thrift Bank. Simpson thought Freddie Mac was one of the best opportunities he'd ever seen, and in the mid to late 1980s, he took an enormous position for GEICO. He finally sold the position during 2004 and 2005, three years before Freddie Mac ran into trouble. GEICO sold out not because Simpson regarded Freddie Mac stock as being "horribly expensive," but because he saw the business "taking on more risk, increasing leverage, and buying lower and lower quality mortgages to make the targets set by Wall Street analysts who thought Freddie Mac should be able to compound its earnings 15 percent a year."[84] Simpson says that, while GEICO's reasons for selling turned out to be correct, he had no idea Freddie Mac would melt down completely. (In 2008, the Federal Housing Finance Agency put both Fannie Mae and Freddie Mac under conservatorship, equivalent to bankruptcy for a privately owned business. The action was described as "one of the most sweeping government interventions in private financial markets in decades."[85] As of the date of writing, they remain in conservatorship.) For GEICO, Freddie Mac was a very successful investment. "After we bought it," says Simpson, "it went on a very, very big run, returning 10 to 15 times GEICO's investment."[86]

Simpson also invested GEICO in a number of merger arbitrage deals, an investment strategy in which an investor, typically, simultaneously buys and sells the stocks of two merging companies in order to profit when the companies actually merge.[87] Simpson, however, chose only to invest on the long side of these deals since he felt he could capture enough of the arbitrage that way. Simpson recalls that the 1980s, with the explosion of contested mergers and acquisition, were a particularly good time for merger arbitrage. GEICO invested in several of the food company takeovers after the deal was announced hoping that another bidder would top the offer. In the heated market, they often did. GEICO's returns from merger arbitrage were excellent, in line with or even a little bit better than the remainder of the portfolio. As the decade wound on, however, Simpson became increasingly concerned that the takeovers were getting too heated, and he didn't know if the market could sustain the torrid pace. Simpson believes he got lucky by declaring victory before GEICO had a disaster. After he stopped investing in merger arbitrage, there were many broken mergers in the lead up to the crash of 1987, and "we were darn lucky that we didn't get a few bum deals."[88] While he disclaims any ability to predict macro factors, he has looked at valuation levels of the market as a whole.[89] In 1987, before the crash, he also moved GEICO's portfolio to approximately 50 percent in cash because he thought the valuation of the market was "outrageous."[90] Simpson says that the huge cash position "helped us for a while and then it hurt us," because "we probably didn't get back into the market as fast as we could have."[91]

SIMPSON'S RESULTS AT GEICO

> [W]e try to exert a Ted Williams kind of discipline. In his book *The Science of Hitting*, Ted explains that he carved the strike zone into 77 cells, each the size of a baseball. Swinging only at balls in his "best" cell, he knew, would allow him to bat .400; reaching for balls in his "worst" spot, the low outside corner of the strike zone, would reduce him to .230. In other words, waiting for the fat pitch would mean a trip to the Hall of Fame; swinging indiscriminately would mean a ticket to the minors.
>
> —*Warren Buffett, "1997 Berkshire Hathaway Letter to Shareholders"*

In 1980, his first year at the helm of GEICO's investment portfolio, Simpson returned 23.7 percent.[92] A great return in almost any other year, that year it was just below the market average, which returned 32.3 percent. Over the next two years, however, he beat the market handsomely, racking up a 45 percent return in 1983, far above the market's 21 percent gain. By then, almost a third of GEICO's portfolio was invested in stocks, up from just 12 percent when Simpson started. Byrne later noted, "We gave him a broad, unfettered pasture to work in, and we allowed him to put an unusual percent of the company's assets into equities. And Lou just knocked the cover off the ball for us."[93] Simpson was head of investments for GEICO for 31 years from 1979 until his retirement from GEICO in 2010, aged 74, by which time he was president and co-chief executive officer of GEICO Corporation.[94] His record over that long period is extraordinary, trouncing market averages and most investment managers' performance. Simpson says of his time at GEICO, "Over the years we put together a good record. At one time we were hitting on all cylinders and I think there was a period of five, six, seven, eight years where we were outperforming by over 15 percent a year. But over a 25-year period, and this was in the Berkshire Report, our over performance was 6.8 percent a year."[95]

Buffett first mentioned Simpson in passing in a letter to the shareholders of Berkshire in 1982, describing him as "the best investment manager in the property-casualty business."[96] From that heady start, he became increasingly effusive about Simpson as time wore on. He detailed Simpson's record in the 2004 report, writing, "Take a look at the facing page to see why Lou is a cinch to be inducted into the investment Hall of Fame."[97] Under the heading "Portrait of a Disciplined Investor *Lou Simpson*," Buffett set out Simpson's extraordinary record, reproduced here in Table 1.1.

Buffett joked in 2010 that he had since omitted updates to Simpson's record only because its performance made Buffett's look bad, quipping, "Who needs that?"[98] For his part, Simpson does not crow about GEICO's performance except to say that "it has been very, very good."[99]

The deal Simpson had struck with GEICO after he had been at the company several years paid him handsomely. Detailing the arrangement he and Byrne had made with Simpson, Buffett wrote in 1996, "In Lou's part of GEICO's operation, we again tie compensation to investment performance over a four-year period, not to underwriting results nor to the performance of GEICO as a whole. We think it foolish for an insurance company to pay bonuses that are tied to overall corporate results when great work on one side of the business—underwriting or investment—could conceivably be completely neutralized by bad work on the other. If you bat .350 at Berkshire, you can be sure you will get paid commensurately even if the rest of the team bats .200."[100] Simpson was paid big bonuses if GEICO's investments outperformed the S&P 500 over a sustained period, which he achieved numerous times during his tenure at GEICO. Evidently, Buffett was happy with the arrangement. When Berkshire acquired the remaining half of GEICO, Buffett kept Simpson, and the deal, in place. While the salary package was very lucrative for Simpson, Buffett noted that he "could have left us long ago to manage far greater sums on more advantageous terms. If money alone had been the object, that's exactly what he would have done. But Lou never considered such a move."[101]

Simpson, associates say, has derived great satisfaction from the recognition that Buffett has bestowed upon him.[102] Buffett has described him as "the class of the field among insurance investment managers."[103] He was also made a part of the so-called Buffett Group, an inner circle of about 50 who gather with Buffett every other year for days of conversation about

TABLE 1.1 "Portrait of a Disciplined Investor *Lou Simpson*" from Buffett's 2004 Berkshire Hathaway "Chairman's Letter"

Year	Return from *GEICO Equities*	S&P Return	Relative Results
1980	23.7%	32.3%	–8.6%
1981	5.4%	–5.0%	10.4%
1982	45.8%	21.4%	24.4%
1983	36.0%	22.4%	13.6%
1984	21.8%	6.1%	15.7%
1985	45.8%	31.6%	14.2%
1986	38.7%	18.6%	20.1%
1987	–10.0%	5.1%	–15.1%
1988	30.0%	16.6%	13.4%
1989	36.1%	31.7%	4.4%
1990	–9.9%	–3.1%	–6.8%
1991	56.5%	30.5%	26.0%
1992	10.8%	7.6%	3.2%
1993	4.6%	10.1%	–5.5%
1994	13.4%	1.3%	12.1%
1995	39.8%	37.6%	2.2%
1996	29.2%	23.0%	6.2%
1997	24.6%	33.4%	–8.8%
1998	18.6%	28.6%	–10.0%
1999	7.2%	21.0%	–13.8%
2000	20.9%	–9.1%	30.0%
2001	5.2%	–11.9%	17.1%
2002	–8.1%	–22.1%	14.0%
2003	38.3%	28.7%	9.6%
2004	16.9%	10.9%	6.0%
Average Annual Gain 1980–2004	20.3%	13.5%	6.8%

value investing, among other subjects.[104] David R. Carr Jr., president of Oak Value Capital Management, an investment management company, and a Berkshire shareholder, said, "He's one of the sainted crowd; he understands and practices value investing."[105] Buffett has noted about Simpson's returns that they "are not only terrific figures but, fully as important, they have been achieved in the right way. Lou has consistently invested in undervalued common stocks that, individually, were unlikely to present him with a permanent loss and that, collectively, were close to risk-free."[106]

SIMPSON, THE VALUE INVESTOR

OUR INVESTMENT PHILOSOPHY

1. Think independently.

We try to be skeptical of conventional wisdom and to avoid the waves of irrational behavior and emotion that periodically engulf Wall Street. Such behavior often leads to excessive prices and, eventually, permanent loss of capital. We don't ignore unpopular companies. On the contrary, such situations often present the greatest opportunities.

2. Invest in high-return businesses run for the shareholders.

Over the long run, appreciation in share prices is most directly related to the return the company earns on its shareholders' investment. Cash flow, which is more difficult to manipulate than reported earnings, is a useful additional yardstick. Companies that cannot earn positive free cash flow (cash flow after capital expenditures and working capital needs) chew up owners' equity and are continually forced to raise new capital. We try to identify companies that appear able to sustain above-average profitability. Most companies cannot because competition prevents it. Many executives have priorities other than maximizing the value of their enterprises for owners, such as expanding corporate empires. We ask the following questions in evaluating management: 1. Does management have a substantial stake in the stock of the company? 2. Is management straightforward in dealings with the owners? (We look for managers who treat us as partners in the business and inform us frankly of problems as well as good news.) 3. Is management willing to divest unprofitable operations? 4. Does management use excess cash to repurchase shares?

The last may be the most important. Managers who run a profitable business often use excess cash to expand into less profitable endeavors. Repurchase of shares is in many cases a much more advantageous use of surplus resources.

3. Pay only a reasonable price, even for an excellent business.

We try to be disciplined in the price we pay for ownership even in a demonstrably superior business. Even the world's greatest business is not a good investment if the price is too high. The ratio of price to earnings and its inverse, the earnings yield, are useful gauges in valuing a company, as is the ratio of price to free cash flow. A helpful comparison is the earnings yield of a company versus the return on a risk-free long-term United States Government obligation.

4. Invest for the long term.

Attempting to guess short-term swings in individual stocks, the stock market or the economy is not likely to produce consistently good results. Short-term developments are too unpredictable. On the other hand, shares of quality companies run for the shareholders stand an excellent chance of providing above-average returns to investors over the long term. Furthermore, moving in and out of stocks frequently has two major disadvantages that will substantially diminish results: transaction costs and taxes. Capital will grow more rapidly if earnings compound with as few interruptions for commissions and tax bites as possible.

5. Do not diversify excessively.

An investor is not likely to obtain superior results by buying a broad cross-section of the market—the more diversification, the more performance is likely to be average, at best. We concentrate our holdings in a few companies that meet our investment criteria in the belief that we have a chance at superior results only if we take risks intelligently, when the risk-reward ratio is favorable to us. Good investment ideas, that is, companies that meet our criteria, are difficult to find. When we think we have found one, we make a large commitment.

Source: Document from Lou Simpson's personal archive (circa 1983).

Buffett has described Simpson as having "the rare combination of temperamental and intellectual characteristics that produce outstanding long-term investment performance."[107] In particular, Buffett admired Simpson's ability to invest in stocks with below-average risk, and yet generate returns that were the best in the insurance industry, a hallmark of Buffett's.[108] Simpson's investing for GEICO often paralleled Buffett's efforts at Berkshire.[109] And students of Buffett's style will recognize his influence in Simpson's process: seek undervalued businesses with proven track records, strong management, a high likelihood of continued steady growth, pricing power, financial strength, and a history of rewarding shareholders. "He has this great ability to understand what's going to be a good business," said Glenn Greenberg, a longtime friend who is now managing partner at Brave Warrior Capital Management. (Simpson considers Glenn an excellent investor and they have ended up owning the same stocks numerous times over the past 30 years.) "And it's concentrated because there aren't that many really good businesses."[110]

Simpson has an unassuming manner and puts people at ease. He has a wide circle of acquaintances, which assists in gaining insights into companies and industries he is researching. He is also a master of understatement, so much so that in conversation the import of his observations aren't understood until long after the discussion is over. Like the man, Simpson's office is unassuming. It is situated in a low-key, nondescript office building in Naples, Florida, an 8- to 10-minute drive from his home. A passerby would have no clue about the business being transacted in it. It is also unusually quiet. He says that he has always tried to block out as much noise as possible.[111] There are no interruptions; no ringing phones, no Bloomberg in the office—Simpson keeps it in the entranceway, separate from the office, so that he has to stand up from his desk to look something up if he needs it. "If I have the Bloomberg on, I find I am looking at what the market is doing," he said. "I really like to be the one who is parsing the information, rather than having a lot of irrelevant information thrown at me."[112] His desk, like the rest of his office, kitchen, and meeting rooms, is clutter free.

His work life is similarly low key. He is disciplined about exercising before work, and arrives at his office long before market hours. Simpson reads everything he can find about companies that have caught his eye.[113] He doesn't search for investments in analyst reports, or by speaking to sell-side researchers. "People on Wall Street tend to be very articulate, highly educated and intelligent, and can be very persuasive," he says. "It's best to just stay away."[114] Simpson worked for the first 12 years of his tenure at the GEICO office in Washington,* rather than closer to Wall Street. "I

* Subsequently, he had offices in southern California and in Chicago.

have always felt I could do a better job in adding value by being somewhat removed from the casino and pari-mutuel atmosphere of the market," he said.[115] At GEICO he worked with a small staff of one to three analysts.[116] He and his analysts would personally visit the companies GEICO invested in. On one occasion, he sent an assistant undercover to the Manpower temporary agency to study its training methods.[117]

Simpson thinks that investment portfolios should be constructed as a collection of pieces of businesses that are reasonably valued, where the investor has confidence that they will be bigger, and more profitable, three to five years from now. He describes himself as a "bottoms up stock picker" who is agnostic to industry, or sector diversification. Those decisions fall out by what he thinks is attractive on a valuation basis and where he has conviction. He recalls that in the 1980s, GEICO at times had 40 percent of the equity portfolio in food stocks and other consumer products companies simply because he assessed that they offered a great risk-to-reward ratio.[118] "His headlights go out further than anybody I know," Mr. Greenberg said. "It's like asking Picasso how he does it. He'll explain it and then you still can't put paint on a canvas like that."[119]

Though he doesn't follow any magic formula for investing, believing that investors should keep an open mind about valuation, his favored metric for valuation is price to free cash flow measured on a per share basis.[120] He seeks out those positions in which he thinks the valuation is reasonable, and there will be continued top and bottom line growth such that there's a better chance of the valuation moving up rather than down over a period of time. While he favors free cash flow, he doesn't like to be restricted to any single metric. He holds to some basic principles that he has refined over time, requiring a discount from intrinsic value, a high-quality company, and high-quality management. In assessing management, he examines their capital allocation record, their integrity, and whether the business is run for owners or whether the managers are hired guns looking to make money for themselves.[121] This distinction often manifests in the chief executive's willingness to undertake buybacks when the stock is undervalued.

Simpson believes that companies should buy back stock where it's appropriate to do so—when the stock is undervalued. He hopes that his positions enjoy a double hit—partially from fundamental growth and partially from buying back stock—leading to an increased valuation on a per share basis.[122] Buffett said to Simpson early in Simpson's tenure at GEICO that, if Buffett talks to a chief executive about a buyback, and its impact on intrinsic value, if they don't get it in two minutes they're never going to get it.[123] Simpson found that to be true in both the companies where he was involved as an outside director, and also in the companies where he was a shareholder. If management doesn't quickly grasp the importance of buybacks on intrinsic value per share, they'll never understand it. It annoys Simpson to see companies announce a share buyback hoping to increase the stock price, and then not follow through and actually buy in stock.[124] While he was at GEICO, the company bought more than 50 percent of its outstanding stock. The buybacks were so extensive that they moved Berkshire's shareholding to the point that, before Buffett made the offer to buy the portion of GEICO it didn't own, Berkshire owned slightly more than 50 percent, up from a third at inception. Simpson asked Buffett to sell into one of GEICO's Dutch auction tenders.* GEICO asked Buffett to sell Berkshire's interest proportionately. Buffett was reluctant to do so, but liked the idea of the buyback, and so agreed to tender on a pro rata basis. In all the companies where Simpson was an outside director, and while he was at GEICO, he argued for a standing authorization to buy in 10 percent of the company's outstanding common stock. That way, if the price ever fell to a point that made sense for a buyback, the authorization was approved, and available to use immediately.[125]

Simpson tries to avoid businesses with political risk, preferring mundane businesses that are under the radar screen, and not dependent on government decisions. Like Buffett, he also tends to avoid technology businesses. "The problem with technology is that, when business models change, it's hard to figure out how it impacts the business."[126] In such a situation, he would stand back and say, "I don't understand."[127] He characterizes American Express as one such business subject to changing technology, believing fewer and fewer people will have credit cards, preferring instead to do financial transactions through mobile devices. American Express has a very strong customer group, but if that customer group continues to shrink, business is "going to be tough."[128] While it has been a very good franchise, and Simpson believes the chief executive is "good," the technology is changing rapidly.[129] Another example he cites that suffers from both technology and political risk is the cable business in the United States. While the stocks are cheap he doesn't believe that they are well run for the non-controlling shareholders, and he can't figure out the impact of those two risks. The technology is changing rapidly. New competition is emerging from streaming services like Netflix, Amazon, and Apple. Additionally, the political risk exists that the government may interfere, which "they've already tried to a certain extent."[130] While the government hasn't yet succeeded, they may try again, and the outcome of that intervention is unpredictable. "The economics appear attractive, but they are ultimately unknowable because of the political risk."[131]

* In a *Dutch auction*, bidders submit bids detailing the number of shares, and the price at which they will sell. The final price is set at the lowest price at which the entire buyback will be complete, and all bidders at or below that price receive that price.

He contrasts American Express with Nike, the sports footwear, apparel, and equipment manufacturer headquartered near Beaverton, Oregon.[132] Simpson says he has a long history with Nike and made "a lot of money for GEICO over a period of time" on it.[133] For GEICO, he bought it, sold it back, bought some more, sold it back, and then bought more than ever. He doesn't believe Nike's product is going to go out of style; they'll continue to sell more shoes and more apparel. How much more? He is yet to figure that out, pointing out that Nike hasn't "even tapped India yet which could be as big a market potentially as China and their business in China is huge and growing like crazy."[134] It has on occasion been cheap because Nike is struggling in other parts of the world, like Europe, and the United States, where its market is much more mature. He found Nike while researching its competitor Reebok in the early 1990s. Simpson bought Reebok for GEICO at a time that Reebok was about the same size, or a little larger than Nike. He traveled to Boston several times to meet with Paul Fireman, who brought Reebok to the United States.[135] He believed that Fireman was unfocused and ran Reebok as a fashion label. He started reading more, and did some field research into sporting goods, and footwear. It became clear to Simpson that Nike had the better product, and the better position in the market, attempting to tie sports and performance with Michael Jordan. He believed that Nike had the "focus of a superior company" and it was in a market with a huge, international runway.[136] Simpson got to know Phil Knight, the founder of Nike, well, even to the point of becoming friends. While he felt the company was conservatively run from a financial standpoint and although they could have been buying in more stock, he liked the fact that they did not get involved in a lot of stupid acquisitions.[137]

The one segment of the athletic shoe market that Nike didn't dominate was the market for soccer shoes, which was the biggest sport globally and a huge market. At that time Adidas had the superior position. Now, Simpson believes that Nike is slightly ahead of Adidas in that market, and they've got the better sponsorship deals. Simpson recalls that Buffett asked him in Sun Valley a number of years ago, "Which company has the better franchise, Coke or Nike?"[138]

"Nike," Simpson responded.[139]

"Why would you say that?" Buffett asked.

"Nike has a much more open-ended chance of growing. They really have just skimmed the surface outside of the U.S. whereas Coca-Cola is powerful all through the world. Their product is not growing that fast, and their prime product is not a healthy product. Coke is a good franchise but Nike has a much better chance of growing. This company could tighten up its financials and they could be more disciplined. They could buy in stock, they could increase their dividend and they really don't need to do a lot of mergers. Also, in the apparel area, which is much bigger on an overall basis than the shoe market, they just have a small share of the market and they've got a great name. I mean China is a huge market for them today, growing rapidly. Latin America is doing very, very well, and, as I said, they haven't really attacked India."[140]

Simpson notes that Nike's valuation was never "super" cheap, but neither was it outrageous.[141] On a free cash flow basis, it traded at a yield of 7 to 7.5 percent.[142] When Simpson bought it, it was approaching an 8 percent free cash flow yield. He liked Nike's opportunity for growth, and the fact that the brand traveled well around the globe.[143]

> *When you watch the French Open and you see a dominant player like Federer and Nadal, they've got Nike swooshes plastered all over them. That's the best advertising in the world.*

As he had done with a number of stocks, Simpson regarded Nike as a long-term holding, but was prepared to trade around the core position. When it got pricey, up to 20 times earnings, and there were alternatives that appeared to be cheaper, Simpson would sell some of GEICO's position. He didn't ever sell the whole position because, though it got very pricey, he had confidence in its continued growth, and he felt that it was a long-term holding. When it traded down to a multiple of 13 times earnings, Simpson would buy more. Over a period of 20 years, GEICO was never out of Nike. At times it was a very large position, and at the end of his time at GEICO it was 16 percent of GEICO's portfolio, which size it grew to because it appreciated. He notes that it is a problem for companies that, as they get bigger and bigger, it becomes harder and harder to have the same kind of percentage growth, but regards Nike as a candidate for sustained long-term growth. He continues to keep Nike in his universe to buy, but maintains discipline on the price. "Over time," says Simpson, "the nice thing about a good business is it becomes worth more and more so you have to constantly evaluate your targets."[144] On this point he agrees with Buffett that the most important thing is to figure out the future economics of the business. This allows an approximate discounted cash flow valuation. While a current valuation based on the past record is a simple matter, it's not easy to figure out the future economics of the business. However, some businesses are easier than others. Coca-Cola, for example, is easier to figure out than those businesses that have to deal with government regulation. While that won't hurt some businesses, particularly those with a strong presence outside the United States, it won't help, and it's not good for overall market valuations.

Simpson has a rule of thumb that it's hard to invest in a company with a market capitalization smaller than the assets an investor has under management. Simpson also believes that sitting on the boards of publicly traded companies has made him a better investor. Shortly after his arrival at GEICO, he was asked to sit on the board of a local bank. He found it interesting, but determined that it was not a very well-run organization. He resigned, and four years later the bank was bankrupt. Since then he has served on over 20 boards, some very large, public companies like AT&T and Comcast, some smaller private company boards, and some very interesting boards. Simpson sat on the Salomon Brothers board for the last five to six years it was public, and was chairman of the audit committee the entire time. This experience served as a graduate course in accounting for a financially complex company. Board positions helped him develop a greater understanding of how businesses really operate. He represented Berkshire several times. In one case, when Buffett asked him to serve on the Bowery Savings Bank board, and represent Berkshire's interest there, Simpson said, "I will do it but you're going to have to sell me some of your stock at the price you paid because I really want to have some skin in the game."[145]

Simpson learned a great deal about business operations when he first arrived at GEICO and was involved in what he describes as an "operating oversight basis."[146] He doesn't regard himself as an expert on insurance, but says that, as a result, he "understands the major factors that make for success."[147]

Being an outside director gave Simpson a different perspective. He realized that there's a lot of dysfunctionality in many companies that analysts miss because they really don't understand the business. Many companies try to spin stories. Having some operational experience made him realize that many outside directors are "pretty ineffective."[148]

> *It's very lucrative to be a director today. If the fees are very important to you, you're going to be beholden to the CEO because that is the person that generally is responsible for you being on the board and staying on the board. Now this is changing somewhat and boards are becoming more independent and shareholders are becoming more and more active and stepping in where things are not being run very well but still, directors will tend to support management.*

It seems that, like Buffett, Simpson believes that he is a better investor because he is a businessman and a better businessman because he is an investor.

CONSERVATIVE, CONCENTRATED

Buffett describes Simpson's investment approach as "conservative, concentrated"—the same approach Buffett takes at Berkshire.[149] Simpson was able to concentrate the GEICO portfolio because of the stable capital base provided by its *float*. Float is money it holds but doesn't own, and may invest on its own behalf. Insurance policy holders prepay premiums, and make claims at a later date. The loss claims must be communicated to the insurer, and then take a period of time to resolve. In the interval between receiving the premium, and paying out the loss claim, the insurer holds large sums of money that it may invest for its own benefit. Though individual policies and claims vary, the amount of float an auto insurer holds remains stable in relation to its premium volume. Simpson had shown a tendency to concentrate portfolio positions at Stein Roe and at Western Asset, but portfolio concentration was the order of the day at GEICO. Influenced by Buffett, and given the flexibility to do so by GEICO's stable capital base, Simpson focused the portfolio on his best investment ideas.[150]

While GEICO's strong operating business, led by Tony Nicely, gave Simpson the latitude to run very large equity positions as a percentage of assets, it was still unusual amongst insurers to do so.[151] Relative to its competitors, GEICO had very conservative operating leverage—the volume of policies written against its assets—and very aggressive investment leverage—the amount of common stock held as a proportion of the portfolio. While most other property and casualty insurers would invest 10 to 15 percent or less of the portfolio in equities, GEICO under Simpson held 35 to 45 percent of the portfolio in equities, and those positions were held in a concentrated manner. This high concentration meant that GEICO's portfolio looked very little like its competitors' portfolios. Insurance companies are institutions that must follow the "prudent man" rule—a legal maxim that precludes certain types of investments, and requires due diligence, and diversification. Most insurers interpreted the rule as requiring very broad diversification across portfolio assets. GEICO was unusual in choosing to interpret it as requiring minimal diversification, allowing it to concentrate instead.[152] When the rating agencies questioned that practice, Simpson responded, "Well, so far it's worked pretty well and hopefully it will continue to work well."[153] Though they were somewhat uncomfortable about the proportion of equities in the portfolio, and the concentration of those equities, the ratings agencies were mollified because the operating leverage of the company was so moderate.[154]

It was not the investment leverage that got GEICO into trouble in the 1970s, but the cost of its float. Lorimer Davidson taught the young Warren Buffett in 1951 that the important metrics for an insurance business are, first, the amount of float it generates and, second, its cost.[155] As Buffett has explained many times in his Chairman's Letters, in the ordinary course, the premiums do not cover the losses and expenses the insurer must pay. That deficit is called an "underwriting loss," and that loss is the cost of float. If its premiums do exceed the total of its expenses and losses, it registers an "underwriting profit" that adds to the investment income that its float produces. If it is able to underwrite profitably in most years, it enjoys the use of free money—and gets paid for holding it—but it is an unusual event. Buffett explains that the attempts of insurers to achieve this result creates intense competition, so vigorous in most years that it causes the industry as a whole to operate at a significant underwriting loss. This loss is what the industry pays to hold its float.

An insurance business will succeed over time if its cost of float is less than the cost it would otherwise incur to obtain funds, but will have a negative value if the cost of its float is higher than market rates for money.[156] In most years, the industry premiums are inadequate to cover claims plus expenses. Consequently, the industry's overall return on tangible equity has mostly fallen far short of the average return realized by the rest of American industry, a sorry performance Buffett believes is certain to continue.[157] An insurer risks failure if its premiums and returns on the float are inadequate to cover claims plus expenses. As Buffett explained in his 2004 Chairman's Letter, most American businesses harbor an "institutional imperative" that rejects extended decreases in volume. Chief executives don't want to report to shareholders that not only did business contract last year but that it will continue to drop. In insurance, the urge to keep writing business is also intensified because the consequences of foolishly priced policies don't become apparent for some time. If an insurer is optimistic in its reserving, reported earnings will be overstated, and years may pass before true loss costs are revealed. It was this "form of self-deception" as Buffett described it, that nearly destroyed GEICO in the early 1970s.[158]

Simpson believes that, when considering active management, the base case for an investor must be a passive index fund, for example an S&P 500 index fund, a total market index fund, or a worldwide market index fund. That base case index fund allows an investor to obtain a market return very cheaply, so unless an active manager can add value over and above that index, the investor is better off in the index fund. For active managers as a whole, investing is a zero sum game, less fees and transaction costs, so most active managers won't do as well as the market because they are the market. Academic studies tend to flatter the active managers due to survivorship bias, which means that because the worst drop out, they aren't counted. How, then, does a manager add value over the market? In Simpson's opinion, a "closet indexer"—an investor who closely follows index components to achieve returns in line with the index without disclosing that they are doing so—and who varies from the index "a little bit here and there and everywhere" won't outperform.[159] A broadly diversified portfolio will likely underperform the market after taking out fees. Simpson concluded that one means of outperforming is to hold a concentrated portfolio of securities where an investor has a lot of conviction. He reached his conclusion through an application of common sense, by reading the academic literature, and under Munger and Buffett's influence. Illustrating his tendency toward understating his own achievements, Simpson says, "Concentration may be the only way I can add value to the process."[160] Simpson is also skeptical that any investor can add value over a longer period of time by trading vigorously. He doesn't believe, for example, that the ease of buying and selling exchange traded funds (ETFs) will help most investors because most investors will trade them, and tend to buy when they are high and sell when they are low. He agrees with John Bogle, who prefers index funds to ETFs, not because they're cheaper—the fees on index funds might be a few basis points more—but because investors are more likely to buy them and put them away. They're not likely to trade them. The ETF's big advantage—that they can be traded throughout the entire day—will turn out to be a negative for most investors, including professional investors, because it will make them more likely to trade the ETF for a few percentage points, which won't work over a long period of time.

Simpson's preference for high concentration means that his portfolios tend to have very little turnover. GEICO's portfolio under Simpson was notable for its low turnover relative to that of its competitors.[161] He says that he has done very well when fully invested, found a new idea, and then sold out of the idea that he had the least confidence in to replace it with the new idea.[162] He argues that, once the portfolio is fully invested, one, two, or three good ideas a year are more than sufficient. He would be very happy to have a couple of ideas a year that he could make into sizable positions. He believes that a record is built as much on what an investor doesn't buy, as it is on what he does buy. "We are sort of the polar opposites of a lot of investors," Simpson said.[163] "We do a lot of thinking and not a lot of acting. A lot of investors do a lot of acting, and not a lot of thinking."[164] If an investor doesn't do anything stupid, they can come out well ahead. Simpson defines this to mean staying within one's circle of competence. It's something he learned by trial and error, and it's an idea reinforced by Buffett. Simpson points to his own mistakes with airline stocks. He believes he has now developed a bias that means he'd never touch one. He also avoids Russian joint ventures, and most Russian stocks. That's not a consideration for most investors. He notes that, when dealing with marketable securities, investors have so many options, and can participate in markets all over the world in ETFs, and that avoiding some markets is fine. The market has become so much broader with more foreign securities available in the local market. In his portfolios today he owns 12 stocks, and 5 of them are domiciled outside of the United States. Simpson feels he has no expertise in some countries like China, India, Brazil, or Mexico, but will invest where he feels he has an understanding of financial reporting and governance standards.[165]

He believes that there are certain people who are good stock pickers, who have a good feel for the market, and who, over a period of time, not every year or every two or three years, but over reasonable periods of time, can add value. His basic premise in starting his new firm is that he offers an alternative that has a good prospect of adding value over the market. How much value is added depends a little on luck, he says. If Simpson's new firm can hit a few home runs he believes it will do well, but acknowledges that not everything is going to do well. He hopes that he'll have a reasonable batting average if he can find a few real winners and avoid some of the real losers. His track record at GEICO would suggest that Simpson will do better than average.

In the next chapter we examine the philosophy of concentration as developed and practiced by economist John Maynard Keynes, as well known for his intellect as his ego.

NOTES

1. Miles Weiss, "Buffett Stock Picker Simpson Opens Florida Firm after Retiring from GEICO," *Bloomberg*, January 20, 2011.
2. Lou Simpson, interview, June 8, 2011.
3. Ibid.
4. Ibid.
5. Ibid.
6. Ibid.
7. Ibid.
8. Warren Buffett, "Chairman's Letter," Berkshire Hathaway, Inc., 1995.
9. Ibid.
10. Ibid.
11. "GEICO's Story from the Beginning," https://www.geico.com/about/corporate/history-the-full-story/.
12. Warren Buffett, "Chairman's Letter," Berkshire Hathaway, Inc., 2004.
13. Warren Buffett, "Chairman's Letter," Berkshire Hathaway, Inc., 1996.
14. Warren Buffett, "Chairman's Letter," Berkshire Hathaway, Inc., 2010.
15. Warren Buffett, "Chairman's Letter," Berkshire Hathaway, Inc., 1996.
16. "GEICO's Story from the Beginning," https://www.geico.com/about/corporate/history-the-full-story/.
17. Ibid.
18. Warren Buffett, "Chairman's Letter," Berkshire Hathaway, Inc., 2004.
19. Ibid.
20. "GEICO's Story from the Beginning," https://www.geico.com/about/corporate/history-the-full-story/.
21. Ibid.

22. David Barboza, "GEICO Chief May Be Heir to an Legend," *New York Times*, April 29, 1997.
23. Warren Buffett, "Chairman's Letter," Berkshire Hathaway, Inc., 2004.
24. "GEICO's Story from the Beginning," https://www.geico.com/about/corporate/history-the-full-story/.
25. Warren Buffett, "Chairman's Letter," Berkshire Hathaway, Inc., 1995.
26. Time (1977). "Insurance: Geico Pulls Through," *Time Magazine*, January 3, 1977.
27. Ibid.
28. Warren Buffett, "Chairman's Letter," Berkshire Hathaway, Inc., 1995.
29. Ibid.
30. David Barboza, "GEICO Chief May Be Heir to an Legend," *New York Times*, April 29, 1997.
31. Lou Simpson, interview, June 8, 2011.
32. Jason Zweig, "The Best Investor You've Never Heard Of," *Money magazine*, June 2000, http://money.cnn.com/2000/06/01/zweig_on_funds/zweig_on_funds/a.htm.
33. Ibid.
34. David Barboza, "GEICO Chief May Be Heir to an Legend," *New York Times*, April 29, 1997.
35. Lou Simpson, interview, June 8, 2011.
36. Ibid.
37. Ibid.
38. Ibid.
39. Ibid.
40. David Barboza, "GEICO Chief May Be Heir to an Legend," *New York Times*, April 29, 1997.
41. Ibid.
42. Ibid.
43. Lou Simpson, interview, June 8, 2011.
44. David Barboza, "GEICO Chief May Be Heir to an Legend," *New York Times*, April 29, 1997.
45. Ibid.
46. Ibid.
47. Scot J. Paltrow, "Enigmatic Fred Carr: Insurance: Junk Bond Troubles Have Put the Spotlight on the Chief of Loss-Plagued First Executive. But Much about Him Remains a Mystery," *Los Angeles Times*, April 8, 1990.
48. Lou Simpson, interview, June 8, 2011.
49. David Barboza, "GEICO Chief May Be Heir to an Legend," *New York Times*, April 29, 1997.
50. Geraldine Fabrikant, "A Maestro of Investments in the Style of Buffett," *New York Times*, April 23, 2007.
51. Lou Simpson, interview, June 8, 2011.
52. Ibid.
53. Ibid.
54. Ibid.

55. David Barboza, "GEICO Chief May Be Heir to an Legend," *New York Times*, April 29, 1997.
56. Ibid.
57. Ibid.
58. Miles Weiss, "Buffett Stock Picker Simpson Opens Florida Firm after Retiring from GEICO," *Bloomberg*, January 20, 2011.
59. Ibid.
60. Ibid.
61. David Barboza, "GEICO Chief May Be Heir to an Legend," *New York Times*, April 29, 1997.
62. Geraldine Fabrikant, "A Maestro of Investments in the Style of Buffett," *New York Times*, April 23, 2007.
63. Ibid.
64. Lou Simpson, interview, June 8, 2011.
65. Ibid.
66. Ibid.
67. Geraldine Fabrikant, "A Maestro of Investments in the Style of Buffett," *New York Times*, April 23, 2007.
68. Warren Buffett, "Chairman's Letter," Berkshire Hathaway, Inc., 1996.
69. Lou Simpson, interview, June 8, 2011.
70. Ibid.
71. Geraldine Fabrikant, "A Maestro of Investments in the Style of Buffett," *New York Times*, April 23, 2007.
72. Lou Simpson, interview, June 8, 2011.
73. Ibid.
74. Ibid.
75. Ibid.
76. Ibid.
77. Ibid.
78. David Barboza, "GEICO Chief May Be Heir to an Legend," *New York Times*, April 29, 1997.
79. Lou Simpson, interview, June 8, 2011.
80. Ibid.
81. Miles Weiss, "Buffett Stock Picker Simpson Opens Florida Firm after Retiring from GEICO," *Bloomberg*, January 20, 2011.
82. Ibid.
83. Lou Simpson, interview, June 8, 2011.
84. Ibid.
85. Zachary A. Goldfarb, David Cho, and Binyamin Appelbaum, "Treasury to Rescue Fannie and Freddie," *Washington Post*, September 7, 2008.
86. Lou Simpson, interview, June 8, 2011.
87. Ibid.
88. Ibid.
89. Ibid.
90. Ibid.

91. Ibid.
92. David Barboza, "GEICO Chief May Be Heir to an Legend," *New York Times*, April 29, 1997.
93. Ibid.
94. Warren Buffett, "Chairman's Letter," Berkshire Hathaway, Inc., 2010.
95. Lou Simpson, interview, June 8, 2011.
96. Warren Buffett, "Chairman's Letter," Berkshire Hathaway, Inc., 1982.
97. Warren Buffett, "Chairman's Letter," Berkshire Hathaway, Inc., 1996.
98. Warren Buffett, "Chairman's Letter," Berkshire Hathaway, Inc., 2010.
99. David Barboza, "GEICO Chief May Be Heir to an Legend," *New York Times*, April 29, 1997.
100. Warren Buffett, "Chairman's Letter," Berkshire Hathaway, Inc., 1996.
101. Warren Buffett, "Chairman's Letter," Berkshire Hathaway, Inc., 2006.
102. Warren Buffett, "Chairman's Letter," Berkshire Hathaway, Inc., 2010.
103. Warren Buffett, "Chairman's Letter," Berkshire Hathaway, Inc., 1983.
104. David Barboza, "GEICO Chief May Be Heir to an Legend," *New York Times*, April 29, 1997.
105. Ibid.
106. Warren Buffett, "Chairman's Letter," Berkshire Hathaway, Inc., 1986.
107. Warren Buffett, "Chairman's Letter," Berkshire Hathaway, Inc., 1984.
108. Ibid.
109. David Barboza, "GEICO Chief May Be Heir to an Legend," *New York Times*, April 29, 1997.
110. Ibid.
111. Lou Simpson, interview, June 8, 2011.
112. Geraldine Fabrikant, "A Maestro of Investments in the Style of Buffett," *New York Times*, April 23, 2007.
113. David Barboza, "GEICO Chief May Be Heir to an Legend," *New York Times*, April 29, 1997.
114. Lou Simpson, interview, June 8, 2011.
115. Geraldine Fabrikant, "A Maestro of Investments in the Style of Buffett," *New York Times*, April 23, 2007.
116. Ibid.
117. David Barboza, "GEICO Chief May Be Heir to an Legend," *New York Times*, April 29, 1997.
118. Lou Simpson, interview, June 8, 2011.
119. David Barboza, "GEICO Chief May Be Heir to an Legend," *New York Times*, April 29, 1997.
120. Lou Simpson, interview, June 8, 2011.
121. Ibid.
122. Ibid.
123. Ibid.
124. Ibid.
125. Ibid.
126. Ibid.

127. Ibid.
128. Ibid.
129. Ibid.
130. Ibid.
131. Ibid.
132. Ibid.
133. Ibid.
134. Ibid.
135. Ibid.
136. Ibid.
137. Ibid.
138. Ibid.
139. Ibid.
140. Ibid.
141. Ibid.
142. Ibid.
143. Ibid.
144. Ibid.
145. Ibid.
146. Ibid.
147. Ibid.
148. Ibid.
149. Warren Buffett, "Chairman's Letter," Berkshire Hathaway, Inc., 1995.
150. Lou Simpson, interview, June 8, 2011.
151. Ibid.
152. Warren Buffett, "Chairman's Letter," Berkshire Hathaway, Inc., 2010.
153. Lou Simpson, interview, June 8, 2011.
154. Ibid.
155. Warren Buffett, "Chairman's Letter," Berkshire Hathaway, Inc., 1995.
156. Ibid.
157. Warren Buffett, "Chairman's Letter," Berkshire Hathaway, Inc., 2010.
158. Warren Buffett, "Chairman's Letter," Berkshire Hathaway, Inc., 2004.
159. Lou Simpson, interview, June 8, 2011.
160. Ibid.
161. Warren Buffett, "Chairman's Letter," Berkshire Hathaway, Inc., 2010.
162. Lou Simpson, interview, June 8, 2011.
163. Geraldine Fabrikant, "A Maestro of Investments in the Style of Buffett," *New York Times*, April 23, 2007.
164. Ibid.
165. Lou Simpson, interview, June 8, 2011.

CHAPTER 2

John Maynard Keynes: Investor Philosopher

The Economics of Concentration

I get more and more convinced that the right method in investment is to put fairly large sums into enterprises which one thinks one knows something about and in the management of which one thoroughly believes. It is a mistake to think that one limits one's risk by spreading too much between enterprises about which one knows little and has no reason for special confidence.

—John Maynard Keynes, "Letter to F. C. Scott," 1934 from John F. Wasik, *Keynes's Way to Wealth: Timeless Investment Lessons from the Great Economist*

From its heady peak at the close on September 3, 1929, the Dow Jones Industrial Average began a progressively violent slide that ushered in the worst financial crisis of the twentieth century. In the optimistic period following the end of the Great War, the Dow had run up 10 times in the near 10-year speculative boom of the Roaring Twenties—the longest bull market ever recorded to that point. Signs of trouble emerged in October 1929, when a spasm of selling left the market down –14.7 percent before it bounced back over the next week, only to resume its slide again on October 11. The herky-jerky, up-and-down dance resolved itself into a dive on "Black Thursday," October 24, when the market slid another –6 percent. Already off –21.6 percent from its peak, the market accelerated over the next few days, closing down another –12.8 percent on "Black Monday," October 28, and then another –11.7 percent on "Black Tuesday," October 29. The panic, which had spread across the Atlantic, and then around the world, induced the London Stock Exchange to crash in sympathy with New York. Finally, on November 13, 1929, the market found what looked like a bottom, down –47.8 percent from its September high. It wasn't to be. After staging a small recovery over the next year, it started to wilt again in the last few months of 1930. 1931 began with the market down –55.4 percent from its peak, and ended with a whimper, down –79.4 percent. The July 8, 1932, bottom, 2 years and 10 months from the peak, found the market down a stunning –89.2 percent (see Figure 2.1).

Through this period, John Maynard Keynes, the British economist whose ideas formed the basis for so-called *Keynesian economics*, managed his own capital, and several portfolios for friends, two insurance companies, and his alma mater, King's College at Cambridge University. Keynes had been speculating in rubber, wheat, cotton, and tin futures when the commodity markets began to turn down in 1929.[1] Notoriously arrogant, he believed that his "superior knowledge" of economic cycles—what he described as "the means of forecasting the future superior to the ordinary"[2]—would keep him one step ahead of other market participants. Instead he found himself

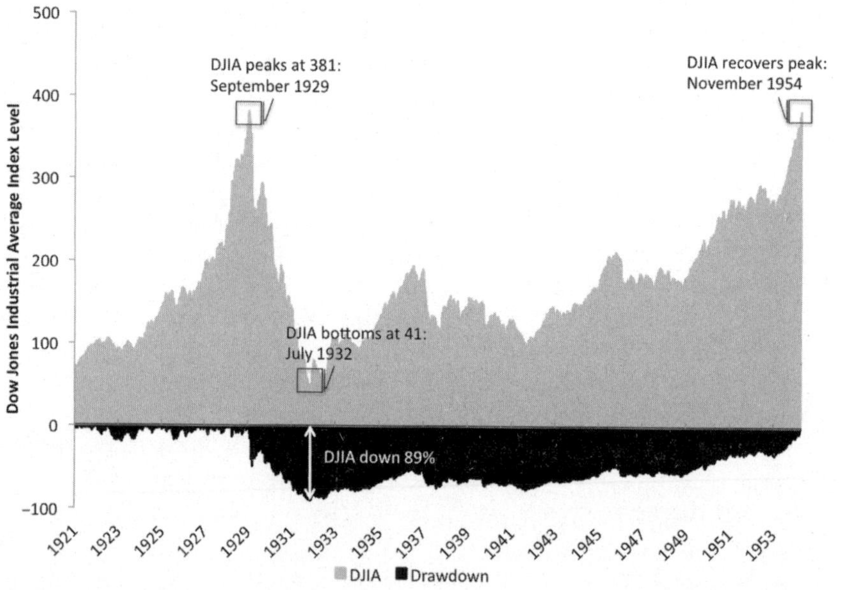

FIGURE 2.1 Annotated Chart of Dow Jones Industrial Average (1921 to 1955)
Data source: Samuel H. Williamson, "Daily Closing Value of the Dow Jones Average, 1885 to Present," MeasuringWorth, 2015.

on the wrong side of the trade when his commodity positions collapsed. Compounding the error, Keynes's idea of "opposed risks"—that losses from one part of portfolio would always be offset by gains in another part of the portfolio—failed, as his speculative equity positions collapsed in the stock market rout along with the commodity positions intended to protect them. Believing that the crash represented the routine end of an ordinary business cycle that would lead into a short-term downturn, Keynes held on to his long positions. By the beginning of the next decade, when it became apparent that the bust was no run-of-the-mill depression, all his commodity positions were total losses. Keynes, who had been wiped out in the early 1920s, was almost wiped out for a second time. From peak-to-trough, Keynes lost 80 percent of his capital. His portfolios' only saving grace were sizable holdings in dividend-paying utilities. The Great Crash had a chastening effect. Humbled, he slowly began to move his process away from top-down macroeconomic speculation, and market timing. Keynes, who by 1932 had gained and lost two fortunes speculating in currencies and commodities, finally transitioned to the value investment philosophy he would pursue for the rest of his life.

Like Benjamin Graham, the great value investor and investment philosopher, Keynes had to contend with several catastrophic market turns through his investment life, including the end of the First World War, the Great Crash, the Great Depression, and World War II.[3] Operating at a remove from Graham, and apparently unaware of Graham's magnum opus, "Security Analysis,"[4] which was published in 1934, with the assistance of David Dodd, Keynes eventually moved to a fundamental investment style that measured a security's market price against its *intrinsic value*—a quantity that could be estimated from its future cash flows. Like Graham, he too made a distinction between speculation and investment, which Keynes called "enterprise," writing in his own magnum opus, *The General Theory of Employment, Interest and Money*, published in 1936:

> *If I may be allowed to appropriate the term speculation for the activity of forecasting the psychology of the market, and the term enterprise for the activity of forecasting the prospective yield of assets over their whole life, it is by no means always the case that speculation predominates over enterprise. . . . In one of the greatest investment markets in the world, namely, New York, the influence of speculation (in the above sense) is enormous. Even outside the field of finance, Americans are apt to be unduly interested in discovering what average opinion believes average opinion to be; and this national weakness finds its nemesis in the stock market. It is rare, one is told, for an American to invest, as many Englishmen still do, "for income"; and he will not readily purchase an investment*

> *except in the hope of capital appreciation. This is only another way of saying that, when he purchases an investment, the American is attaching his hopes, not so much to its prospective yield, as to a favourable change in the conventional basis of valuation, i.e. that he is, in the above sense, a speculator.*

These definitions—investment being the attempt to make "superior long-term forecasts of the probable yield of an investment over its whole life," while speculation being the attempt to foresee "changes in the conventional basis of valuation a short time ahead of the general public"[5]—accord closely with Graham's own definitions. "An investment operation," counseled Graham, "is one which, on thorough analysis, promises safety of principal and a satisfactory return. Operations not meeting these requirements are speculative."[6] He later elaborated on his brief reference to speculation by saying, "Speculative operations are all concerned with changes in price."[7]

Keynes independently developed the idea that the price of a security is distinct from its intrinsic value, which Graham codified in *Security Analysis*. He also seems to have extended beyond Graham to develop his own unique form of value investment. That investment philosophy led Keynes to be described as "one of the most innovative investors ever, inspiring investors and economic thinkers from Warren E. Buffett to Robert J. Shiller."[8] Many investors have acknowledged the influence of Keynes on their own process, including Buffett, George Soros,[9] and David Swensen.[10] Buffett in particular embraced Keynes's philosophy, discussing in detail in his annual *Berkshire Hathaway, Inc.*, Chairman's Letters his own evolution from Grahamite value investor to a value investment strategy that is remarkably similar to the one Keynes finally adopted. In 1991, he said Keynes was a man "whose brilliance as a practicing investor matched his brilliance in thought" before quoting from a letter Keynes wrote to a business associate, the chairman of Provincial Insurance, Francis C. Scott, on August 15, 1934. Buffett, who was endeavoring to describe his own investment philosophy, held that Keynes's letter "says it all:"[11]

> *As time goes on, I get more and more convinced that the right method in investment is to put fairly large sums into enterprises which one thinks one knows something about and in the management of which one thoroughly believes. It is a mistake to think that one limits one's risk by spreading too much between enterprises about which one knows little and has no reason for special confidence. . . . One's knowledge and experience are definitely limited and there are seldom more than two or three enterprises at any given time in which I personally feel myself entitled to put full confidence.*

As his new investment philosophy was being tested in 1938 with a severe drawdown in the lead-up to World War II, Keynes wrote that he advocated the "careful selection of a few investments . . . having regard to their cheapness and potential intrinsic value over a period of years ahead."[12] Keynes, who Buffett noted in 1988 started out "as a market-timer (leaning on business and credit-cycle theory)," had, Buffett wrote, "converted, after much thought, to value investing.[13] More than that, Keynes had embraced a style of value investment that favored holding a few, long-term positions that would grow over time, just as Buffett himself did. From 1932 onward, Keynes was a resolute concentrated value investor. After suffering a third severe setback in 1938, he recouped his assets and died leaving an estate with securities worth just short of £440,000—worth $30 million in 2015, which did not include a tally of his extensive collection of artwork and rare manuscripts. That art collection was valued for a bequest at £30,000 in 1946, and revalued to an extraordinary £17 million in 1988 ($68 million).[14] This chapter examines Keynes's evolution as an investor, and his contribution to the theory of concentrated value investment.

CELEBRITY ECONOMIST

> I don't feel the least humble before the vastness of the heavens.
>
> —*Keynes, "F. P. Ramsey,"* Essays in Biography *(1933), p. 310*

First Baron Keynes, CB, FBA, was born June 5th, 1883, in Cambridge, England to John Neville Keynes, a Cambridge don, who lectured in economics and moral sciences at the University of Cambridge, and Florence Ada Keynes, a social reformer. This was Victorian England under Queen Victoria, a time of straight-laced morality, *Pax Britannica*—the British Peace—and general prosperity. At the same time the United States was enjoying its Gilded Age, and Europe its *Belle Époque*—beautiful era. The eldest of three children, Keynes proved to be a brilliant student. He earned a scholarship to Eton, the all-male private boarding school referred to as the "chief nurse of England's statesman" for its education of royals, British prime ministers, and other notable figures. In 1902, Keynes left Eton, where he had excelled in mathematics, classics, and history, for a scholarship to King's College, Cambridge. His brilliance as a student persisted, and he was awarded a first class BA in mathematics in May 1904. With no clear idea what he planned to do after Cambridge, but supremely confident about his future, Keynes wrote to his friend, Lytton Strachey, in 1905 saying that:[15]

I want to manage a railway or organise a Trust, or at least swindle the investing public; it is so easy and fascinating to master the principles of these things.

In 1906, Keynes sat for the civil service exam, the competitive test to join the British bureaucracy, and was disappointed to come second, still an incredibly impressive showing. He became a junior clerk in the India Office, which was situated in London, and charged with administering the British Raj. He quickly tired of the role, and after two years, returned to study probability theory at Cambridge, working on a project funded by his father and the economist Arthur Pigou. He published his first scholarly article on economics in 1909, and was formally invited to become a lecturer on economics at Cambridge in a course funded by the great Alfred Marshall, author of the predominant English economics textbook of the day, and one of the most influential economists of his time. In 1914, at the outbreak of World War I, Keynes was recruited by the Treasury to aid in financing the war effort.[16] He stayed in that post until May 1919, when he left to write *The Economic Consequences of Peace* over two months in the English summer. The book was heavily critical of the Versailles Treaty—entered into by the Allied powers and the vanquished Germany—which called for crushing reparations from Germany. He predicted in the book that the overly harsh terms of the treaty would lead to catastrophic economic instability in Germany with the potential to set off another world war within 20 years. The book was a best seller throughout the world, and established Keynes as a leading liberal economist. By the time he was ultimately proven correct he was a world-renowned intellectual, and celebrity.

IRRATIONAL MARKETS

Markets can remain irrational a lot longer than you and I can remain solvent.

—*Keynes, A. Gary Shilling,* Forbes 151*, no. 4 (1993), p. 236*

Keynes's public life as an economist and academic has been thoroughly documented. His life as an investor, less so. Financial journalist John F. Wasik tells the story of Keynes's investment accomplishments in his thoroughly researched book *Keynes's Way to Wealth.*[17] Wasik plowed through copious material, including Keynes's 100-year-old lecture notes, from the library of King's College at the University of Cambridge in England to examine Keynes's quarter-century investment record there. He reports that Keynes began speculating in stocks, bonds, currencies, and commodities around the end of World War I in 1919.[18] He had dabbled in investment as a youth, and he began speculating with his own capital in 1919, but wouldn't undertake his first formal role as an investment manager until 1921 at 38 years of age. He had lectured at Cambridge on the stock market in 1910, describing it as "essentially a practical subject, which cannot properly be taught by book or lecture," about which "I myself have no practical experience of the questions involved."[19] He was given his first taste of finance when in 1911, he was appointed to King's College's Estates Committee, which was tasked with managing the college's property and funds. The Estates Committee held King's College's non–real estate assets largely in cash. Keynes pushed to invest the money, which meant, at the time, buying and holding bonds.[20] The stock market was out of the question. It was regarded as the province of the individual investor, and common stocks were not regarded as institutional assets.[21]

Keynes had no inherited wealth, and he was not well paid as a junior clerk. He started making money lecturing and tutoring private students at Cambridge. Royalties from his publication of *The Economic Consequences of Peace* in 1919, and fees from speaking engagements and opinion pieces, boosted his income sufficiently to provide him with a small grubstake—£4,000 or approximately $300,000 today.[22] Keynes's broker allowed him to leverage his capital on margin 10 to 1,[23] and he used the not insignificant sum to begin speculating in the currency markets. He believed that his experience in Treasury, the research that led to *The Economic Consequences of Peace*, his work in probability, and lecturing in economics had provided him with the "superior knowledge" needed to succeed in the nascent currency markets. Foreign exchange rates, which had been fixed prior to the outbreak of war, were now free-floating and, as a result, newly volatile. Keynes used the currency market to express his macroeconomic views about nations' postwar prospects. He expected inflation to destroy the French franc, the German reichsmark, and the Italian lira, and their economies to collapse. He expressed that view by *shorting* those currencies—selling them on the anticipation that they would fall, expecting to profit by buying them back at a lower price—and buying the U.S. dollar.[24] By Easter 1920, the capital in Keynes's account had vaulted to £14,000 ($905,000).[25]

Keynes outlined his macroeconomic investment philosophy in the prospectus of the Independent Investment Company, an investment vehicle he co-founded and floated on the London Stock Exchange in 1924.[26] He called his approach to market timing the *credit cycle theory of investment*.[27] Explaining the theory subsequently, Keynes wrote, "Credit cycling means in practice selling market leaders on a falling market and buying them on a rising one and, allowing for expenses and loss of interest, it needs phenomenal skill to make much out of it."[28] He employed this approach with the King's College endowment, and with two earlier investment vehicles. With a stockbroker friend, Oswald Toynbee "Foxy" Falk, whom he had met at the British Treasury, Keynes had established an informal syndicate in 1920 to speculate in foreign exchange, managing his own capital and some money from his *Bloomsbury Set* friends.[29] (The Bloomsbury Set was an informal group of prominent English writers, intellectuals, and artists, the most famous of whom included Virginia Woolf, E. M. Forster, and Lytton Strachey, all of whom lived, worked, or studied together near Bloomsbury, London.) The syndicate, akin to a modern hedge fund, was a rarity. Institutional managers favored bonds and real estate. The trades worked briefly, and the syndicate showed several quick gains in its first few months of operation. It was short lived. In May 1920, a "spasm of optimism about Germany" drove the wilting European currencies back up, wiping out both the overleveraged syndicate, and the overconfident Keynes.[30] Keynes's margin account, which had peaked at £14,000, now showed a deficit of £13,125 ($850,000).[31] His broker called for another £7,000 ($450,000) to be placed into the account. [32] Keynes couldn't meet the call: He was so broke that he needed his father to support his day-to-day living expenses. Undaunted by the reversal, the supremely confident 37-year old approached the prominent financier Sir Ernest Cassel to back his speculation, telling Cassel, "I anticipate very substantial profits with very good probability if you are prepared to stand the racket for perhaps a couple of months."[33] Cassell was a well-known merchant banker who, as Bernard Baruch once famously claimed, "When as a young and unknown man I started to be successful I was referred to as a gambler. My operations increased in scope. Then I was a speculator. The sphere of my activities continued to expand and presently I was known as a banker. Actually I have been doing the same thing all the time."[34] Despite Keynes's admission that, "I am not in a position to risk any capital myself, having quite exhausted my resources,"[35] Cassel backed him. He dove back into the currency market using Cassel's £5,000 loan, and a £1,500 advance from his publisher to maintain the short positions that had wiped him out at the beginning of the year.[36] His view about the longer-term performance of the economies was borne out. Inflation ravaged Europe after the war, and several currencies fell into what would become a terminal decline. From a negative net worth in mid-1920, after repaying Cassel, Keynes had net assets of £22,558 in 1922—a net worth of approximately $1.8 million today.[37]

He had established a second investment vehicle, A.D. Investment Trust Limited, in July 1921, shortly after the first syndicate was wiped out.[38] The investment trust traded commodities, seeking to profit from the demand for the goods needed to rebuild postwar Europe—rope, metals, oil, food, and cotton—and also invested in stocks. He viewed the market for commodities as inefficient, producing mispricings when supply and demand fell out of balance. He saw commodities speculators fulfilling a role as "risk bearers," who took positions when producers, who sought only to hedge, pushed prices out of equilibrium. Thus he could "earn substantial remuneration *merely* by running risks and allowing the results of one season to average with those of others; just as an insurance company makes profits without pretending to know more about an individual's prospects of life of the chance of his house taking fire than he knows himself."[39] The investment trust also bought stocks, bonds, real estate, and gold. Keynes used the trust's commodities positions to hedge its stock positions in what he described as "opposed risks."[40] He believed that by putting offsetting asset classes into the portfolio—ones that would gain if others fell—he could protect the portfolio from known risks.[41] The "opposed risks" idea required Keynes to hedge out the risk that a stock's profitability might suffer from an increase in the cost of a commodity essential to its business by buying the commodity outright. So, for example, he might buy lead used in the production of car batteries to hedge his holdings in automobile manufacturers, a technology favorite of his. If the price of lead fell, stock in the automaker would rise. If the price of lead rose, Keynes's auto stock holding was protected by his holding in lead commodity contracts. Though the investment strategy was speculative, Keynes's "opposed risks" idea anticipated somewhat the subsequent developments in modern portfolio theory diversification through uncorrelated assets.[42] Keynes remained a director of the investment trust until he resigned in November 1927, and sold all of his shares.[43] The trust performed well from 1923 to 1927, paying out dividends at a rate of 10 percent annually. On his resignation, Keynes's net worth had swollen to £39,550—about $3.6 million today.

Though he had resigned from A.D. Investment Trust, Keynes continued to speculate in commodities in his personal account. He was long a basket of commodity contracts and stocks into the teeth of the Great Crash when the fault in the "opposed risks" idea was revealed in brutal fashion. Where the stock and commodity positions might ordinarily move in opposition, in the indiscriminate selling of the panic both sides of the trade fell at the same time. Keynes, who in addition to the leverage embedded in the commodity contract also invested on margin, was wiped out for a second time. A.D. Investment Trust, with which Keynes now had no association, was also wiped out. It was a humbling moment.

THE INVESTOR

> Even apart from the instability due to speculation, there is the instability due to the characteristic of human nature that a large proportion of our positive activities depend on spontaneous optimism rather than on a mathematical expectation, whether moral or hedonistic or economic. Most, probably, of our decisions to do something positive, the full consequences of which will be drawn out over many days to come, can only be taken as a result of animal spirits—of a spontaneous urge to action rather than inaction, and not as the outcome of a weighted average of quantitative benefits multiplied by quantitative probabilities. Enterprise only pretends to itself to be mainly actuated by the statements in its own prospectus, however candid and sincere. Only a little more than an expedition to the South Pole, is it based on an exact calculation of benefits to come. Thus if the animal spirits are dimmed and the spontaneous optimism falters, leaving us to depend on nothing but a mathematical expectation, enterprise will fade and die—though fears of loss may have a basis no more reasonable than hopes of profit had before.
>
> —*Keynes,* The General Theory, *1936*

Keynes's transition from macroeconomic speculator to fundamental investor was hastened by the 1929 crash, but seems to have begun earlier. Along with his A.D. Investment Trust cofounder "Foxy" Falk, he had established another investment vehicle in 1923 called P.R. Finance Company. While Keynes was only responsible for managing one-third of the capital, P.R. Finance held many of the same positions as A.D. Investment Trust, and was similarly torpedoed in 1928. It struggled through to the mid-1930s before being liquidated.[44] While P.R. Finance was not unique among Keynes's portfolios in showing a definite shift away from commodities and currencies at the beginning of the 1920s to stocks at the beginning of the 1930s, what makes P.R. Finance interesting is that it survived long enough for Keynes's new investment strategy to manifest. Among its faltering commodities positions, P.R. Finance held shares in some U.S. utilities. These stocks paid dividends and didn't swoon as much as the commodities contracts had in the late 1920s. Where the speculative commodities holdings showed increasing losses until P.R. Finance's liquidation in 1936, the portfolio had actually rallied from its low in 1929 on the back of its stock holdings, which by then dominated the portfolio. The assets had "recovered to the neighborhood of par"—what they initially paid for their stakes—at the time of liquidation, and so investors in P.R. Finance were almost made whole, which was unusual given the time period.[45] Wasik observes, "[W]hat had started out looking like an aggressive hedge fund ended up looking like a conservative, dividend-oriented mutual fund."[46]

His investing philosophy evolved as Keynes began to doubt his belief that he could profit from his "superior knowledge" of economic cycles. When he reviewed his investment performance as a macroeconomic speculator employing his *credit cycle investment theory*, Keynes noted, "We have not proved able to take much advantage of a general systematic movement out of and into ordinary shares as a whole at different phases of the trade cycle."[47] The extent of Keynes's philosophical shift was made plain in 1930, when he had to fight his fellow directors who wanted to close out P.R. Finance's stock holdings at the nadir, arguing, "If we get out, our mentality being what it is, we shall never get back in again until much too late and will assuredly be left behind when the recovery does come. If the recovery never comes, nothing matters."[48] By August 1934, Keynes had completely revised his approach to investment. His views had settled sufficiently that by August 15, 1934, he wrote the letter to Scott quoted with approval by Buffett, in which he said, "As time goes on, I get more and more convinced that the right method in investment is to put fairly large sums into enterprises which one thinks one knows something about and in the management of which one thoroughly believes."[49] He attributed his subsequent success managing the King's College endowment to his decision to concentrate on a few core holdings considered cheap relative to their intrinsic value and held for several years. While the fact of the correspondence with Scott occurring in 1934—around the publication of Graham's *Security Analysis* in 1934—leaves open the possibility that he read Graham and Dodd, he seems to have moved to an intrinsic value-based investment approach without contact with Graham or knowledge of *Security Analysis*. In a 1925 paper Keynes cited a 1924 book, E. L. Smith's *Common Stocks as Long-Term Investments*, which advocated buying stakes in U.S. companies to share in the "residual claims on industrial growth."[50] Keynes saw that U.K. companies could also provide a "return premium over bonds, providing 'an investment in real values' and offering an income premium over bonds."[51] In a study of Keynes's investment record published in 2015 by David Chambers, a professor at the Judge School of Business at Cambridge, Elroy Dimson, emeritus professor at the London Business School, and Justin Foo, a postdoctoral fellow of Cambridge, the authors argue based on archival and statistical evidence that the pivotal moment for Keynes occurred in 1932. Up to 1932, he tended to purchase stocks that had run up significantly relative to the market, which then tended to fall after he purchased them. He sold propitiously—the stocks tended to drop after Keynes sold out—but he was undone by the losses he incurred while he held them. His investment performance improved markedly after the 1932 break, when he substantially altered his investment approach. After 1932, Keynes still tended to buy stocks that had run up relative to the market, though they had done so more modestly when compared to the earlier period. These positions then went on to generate significant gains after he purchased them. On Keynes's selling the positions they also continued to run up modestly. Chambers et al. conclude that Keynes had no skill as a market timer. By then, however, the man who had started out as a top-down speculator relying upon his "superior knowledge" to forecast the macroeconomic climate, was behaving more like a bottom-up, fundamental investor who sought solid, dividend-paying stocks with good long-term prospects. His gains came from taking large positions in those securities that had financial statement sheets he could understand, and sold products or services he believed he could assess objectively. Keynes, who noted in the preface to his *The General Theory of Employment, Interest and Money* (1936) that "The difficulty lies, not in the new ideas, but in escaping from the old ones," had finally left behind his market-timing speculations and his theories of macroeconomic credit cycling.

Keynesian Intrinsic Value

> When my information changes, I alter my conclusions. What do you do, sir?
>
> —*Keynes, in response to a criticism during the Great Depression of having changed his position on monetary policy*[52]

While Keynes undertook investment roles at the National Mutual Life Assurance Society from 1919 to 1938, and the Provincial Insurance Company from 1923 to 1946, only at King's College, Cambridge, did he have complete discretion over policy. He was invited to sit on the King's College Estate Committee two years after returning to Cambridge as a lecturer in 1911. After his stint in the Treasury, on his return to Cambridge in November 1919, he was appointed Second Bursar. The First Bursar was responsible for the financial administration of King's College, which might encompass anything from collecting tuition fees to managing assets, and the Second Bursar acted as assistant to the First. Cambridge was subject to a statute and to the Trustee Act, which restricted its investment holdings to high-grade fixed income securities.[53] By mid-1920, Keynes had persuaded the college to carve out from the endowment a separate portfolio not subject to the restrictions of the legislation.[54] The new portfolio would contain common stock, currency, and commodity futures.[55] Though Keynes shifted some of the capital out of long-term government bonds, the endowment maintained its income level, which was important because endowment income was not reinvested in the portfolio, but rather directed to spending. The dividend yield on King's U.K. equity portfolio averaged 6.0 percent from 1921 to 1929, surpassing the 5.2 percent dividend yield on the U.K. equity market and the 4.6 percent yield on government bonds. From 1930 to 1939, the discretionary portfolio's dividend yield averaged 5.9 percent, again exceeding the 4.4 percent dividend yield on the U.K. equity market and the 3.4 percent government bond yield. Again, from 1940 to 1946, the College's discretionary portfolio enjoyed a 5.8 percent dividend yield, higher than the 4.0 percent dividend yield in the U.K. equity market and the 3.0 percent yield available on government bonds.[56] Keynes also favored liquidating King's College's real estate holdings and investing the proceeds in the stock market, a move that was vehemently opposed by many of the college's fellows who viewed stock market trading as "speculation."[57] Keynes countered that he'd rather "speculate" in an asset that had a daily price quotation, and was liquid enough to be bought, and sold, than "invest" in an asset for which the price was largely unknown.[58]

It was in the role as manager of the King's College endowment that Keynes established his reputation as a money manager. When he was appointed First Bursar for King's College in 1924, he consolidated into a single discretionary portfolio the college's endowments, the separate portfolio he had established in 1920, and another discretionary portfolio known as "The Chest" or "Chest Fund."[59] As First Bursar, Keynes made the final investment decisions for both the discretionary portfolio, including the more aggressive Chest Fund, and the restricted portfolio subject to the statutes.[60] His long association with Cambridge—his father was a Cambridge don, he completed his undergraduate studies there, and he lectured there on-and-off from 1911—and obvious regard for the institution, made him more careful with Cambridge's capital than he had been with his own. He avoided margin, and mostly avoided the currency and commodities futures he traded in his own portfolio. [Keynes didn't ever wholly abandon currency speculation at Cambridge, but the sums he dedicated to it became smaller and smaller relative to the size of the discretionary portfolio. By 1933, they were negligible. In only 4 out of 12 years between 1933 and 1945, the Chest Fund made or lost more than £1,000 ($100,000) in currency speculation, and, cumulatively over the full period, it lost just £339 ($21,500).][61] Keynes's equity investments for King's College reflected his own beliefs. Over the full period from 1921 to 1945, at each December year-end, 81 percent by value, and 65 percent by number of Keynes's personal holdings were also held by King's College.[62]

On taking the reins of the discretionary portfolio, Keynes moved aggressively into ordinary shares, as common stock is referred to in Britain. He kept 75 percent of the discretionary portfolio in ordinary shares over the financial years 1922 to 1929, 46 percent from 1930 to 1939, and 69 percent from 1940 to 1946.[63] Keynes also started buying for the discretionary portfolio U.S. common and preference stocks in the 1930s. Including the U.S. common stock, the discretionary portfolio's total holdings in ordinary shares and common stock averaged 57 percent from 1930 to 1939, and 73 percent from 1940 to 1946. The discretionary portfolios also held U.K. preference shares and U.S. preferred stock. From 1922 to 1929, preference shares comprised about 12 percent of the portfolio. From 1930 to 1939, 22 percent of the portfolio was dedicated to U.K. preference shares and U.S. preferred stock, and 20 percent from 1940 to 1946.[64]

Like Lou Simpson would 50 years later in the United States, Keynes revolutionized insurance investment management in the United Kingdom. Before Keynes, institutional investing meant buying and holding bonds and real estate. U.K. institutions had only 3 percent of their assets in stocks in 1920 and only 10 percent by 1937.[65] As he had with King's College's discretionary portfolios, though he held considerably less sway, Keynes pushed two British insurance companies he was involved with to shift into equities. He advocated that institutional portfolios put up to 75 percent of the assets in equities, considerably more than any insurer was prepared to allocate at the time, and more than Keynes would while managing those portfolios.[66]

Keynes relished concentration, focusing as much as half of his portfolio into five holdings.[67] He liked to make colossal, concentrated bets on industries that he thought would appreciate sharply. Chambers et al. found that Keynes concentrated the majority of his U.K. equity holdings in just two sectors—commercial and industrial, and metal mining firms—dedicating to each one-third of his U.K. equity portfolio over the full period.[68] In the metal mining sector, on the basis of his macroeconomic views, Keynes favored tin-mining stocks in the mid-1920s, and gold-mining stocks in the early 1930s. He had assessed that the dual forces of price-inelastic supply and growing demand would cause the price of tin to explode.[69] He expressed this view in his personal account using tin futures, but chose for the endowment the slightly more conservative long position in low-cost Malayan tin miners.[70] Despite referring to gold as a "barbarous relic" in his 1924 book, *Monetary Reform*, Keynes took another mammoth, concentrated bet on gold mining stocks, moving two-thirds of his portfolio into South African gold mining stocks in 1933.[71] Keynes had guessed that the devaluation of the South African rand would cause the earnings of South African gold miners to appreciate.[72] As his huge position in South African gold mining stocks attests, Keynes wasn't afraid to invest in any jurisdiction where he could find cheap stocks. His portfolios were filled with companies from overseas, and also small and mid-capitalization stocks with high dividend yields. This was very unusual for Keynes's time, when even stocks in the top 100 firms were regarded as risky investments. Keynes also focused the portfolio on technology stocks, which in the 1930s meant the automobile and aircraft manufacturing, electricity generation and electrical engineering, and chemicals and pharmaceuticals sectors. He typically avoided the hot technology *floats*—the British term for initial public offerings or IPOs—buying into the stocks when markets were more "subdued."[73] His two biggest holdings, automobile manufacturers Austin Motors and Leyland, accounted for between one-quarter and one-third of the portfolio from 1930 to 1934.

While his positions in mining stocks were driven predominantly by macroeconomic concerns, Keynes was evolving into a fundamental investor. In his correspondence with Francis C. Scott, a portion of which Buffett would later quote in his Chairman's Letter, he outlined the rationale for his investment in Union Corporation, one of the South African gold mining stocks.[74] Union was one of Keynes's largest holdings, representing an average of more than half his gold mining exposure from 1933 to 1946.[75] In a letter to Scott dated June 21, 1934, Keynes said that his main reason for his holding the stock was the fact that it was a "value play," and he held the management in very high regard.[76] Sounding remarkably like Graham, Keynes wrote that a third of Union's "intrinsic value"[77]—a term also used by Benjamin Graham in *Security Analysis* to distinguish a firm's true worth from the price ascribed to it by the stock market—could be found in its cash and government bonds.[78] The shares then traded at a one-third discount to Keynes's estimate of intrinsic value. His investment in Austin Motors offers an insight into his evolving valuation process. Keynes valued Austin Motors shares using the earnings yield—the inverse of the more familiar price-to-earnings ratio—and also *market capitalization per unit produced.*[79] According to his calculations in October 1933, Keynes imputed that Austin traded at a two-thirds discount to General Motors.[80]

Like Graham, Keynes believed it was possible for a stock's price to diverge from this intrinsic value, which could be determined by scrutinizing the financial statements. Much as Graham did, Keynes calculated intrinsic value as the value that private business owners could obtain for the business in a negotiated sale. Though it could deviate from this private intrinsic value, the calculation acted as a tether on the price available in the stock market, and could be exploited when the deviation grew too large. Outlining his view in *The General Theory*, Keynes wrote:[81]

> *Decisions to invest in private business of the old-fashioned type were, however, decisions largely irrevocable, not only for the community*

as a whole, but also for the individual. With the separation between ownership and management which prevails to-day and with the development of organised investment markets, a new factor of great importance has entered in, which sometimes facilitates investment but sometimes adds greatly to the instability of the system. In the absence of security markets, there is no object in frequently attempting to revalue an investment to which we are committed. But the Stock Exchange revalues many investments every day and the revaluations give a frequent opportunity to the individual (though not to the community as a whole) to revise his commitments. It is as though a farmer, having tapped his barometer after breakfast, could decide to remove his capital from the farming business between 10 and 11 in the morning and reconsider whether he should return to it later in the week. But the daily revaluations of the Stock Exchange, though they are primarily made to facilitate transfers of old investments between one individual and another, inevitably exert a decisive influence on the rate of current investment. For there is no sense in building up a new enterprise at a cost greater than that at which a similar existing enterprise can be purchased; whilst there is an inducement to spend on a new project what may seem an extravagant sum, if it can be floated off on the Stock Exchange at an immediate profit. Thus certain classes of investment are governed by the average expectation of those who deal on the Stock Exchange as revealed in the price of shares, rather than by the genuine expectations of the professional entrepreneur. How then are these highly significant daily, even hourly, revaluations of existing investments carried out in practice?

Keynes described his favorite stocks as his "pets,"[82] and, mistakes aside, he seemed loath to part with them once purchased, quipping in *The General Theory* that he would make the purchase of stocks permanent "like marriage."[83]

The spectacle of modern investment markets has sometimes moved me towards the conclusion that to make the purchase of an investment permanent and indissoluble, like marriage, except by reason of death or other grave cause, might be a useful remedy for our contemporary evils. For this would force the investor to direct his mind to the long-term prospects and to those only. But a little consideration of this expedient brings us up against a dilemma, and shows us how the liquidity of investment markets often facilitates, though it sometimes impedes, the course of new investment. For the fact that each individual investor flatters himself that his commitment

> *is "liquid" (though this cannot be true for all investors collectively) calms his nerves and makes him much more willing to run a risk. If individual purchases of investments were rendered illiquid, this might seriously impede new investment, so long as* alternative ways *in which to hold his savings are available to the individual. This is the dilemma. So long as it is open to the individual to employ his wealth in hoarding or lending* money, *the alternative of purchasing actual capital assets cannot be rendered sufficiently attractive (especially to the man who does not manage the capital assets and knows very little about them), except by organising markets wherein these assets can be easily realised for money.*

Keynes eventually became an unusually long-term investor, holding a typical stock for more than five years at a time. The *Wall Street Journal*'s Intelligent Investor columnist Jason Zweig points out by way of comparison, that today the average U.S. stock fund holds onto its typical stock for just 15 months.[84] Chambers et al. find that following Keynes's 1932 intellectual break, he became a much better medium- and long-term investor than he had been in the earlier period. From 1933 to 1946, his medium-term stock picks—those held up to 12 months—beat the market by as much as 14.1 percent when he sold them.[85] By contrast, in the earlier period from 1921 to 1932, his medium-term stock picks tended to underperform by 8.7 percent when he sold them.[86] His long-term stock holdings—those held for more than 12 months—had also returned 3.4 percent more than the market when measured 12 months after purchase, which was the end of the research period.[87] During the period from 1921 to 1932, his long-term stock picks tended to be underperforming the market by 6.8 percent when measured at the 12-month mark. Keynes never became a good market timer. If anything, the timing of his sales in the later period deteriorated. From 1933 to 1946, his long-term holdings continued to rise relative to the market by up to 4.5 percent over 12 months after he sold them. Chambers et al. conclude that the performance of Keynes's stock holdings in the period after 1932 reinforces the view that Keynes exhibited more skill in buying individual stocks, and became a better investor after that point. While he didn't time his initial purchases optimally, Keynes often continued to buy a stock as it fell to lower his cost basis in a process known as "dollar cost averaging." Keynes was also a contrarian investor, purchasing stocks after they had endured significant price falls. Chambers et al. cite the example of his 1939 acquisition of undervalued aircraft manufacturing and armaments stocks following heavy share price falls in the early years of World War II. Next, we examine the returns Keynes's combination of contrarian, concentrated, long-term value investing delivered on behalf of Cambridge's discretionary portfolio.

AN EXAMINATION OF KEYNES'S RETURNS

> I believe now that successful investment depends on . . . a steadfast holding of these in fairly large units through thick and thin, perhaps for several years, until either they have fulfilled their promise or it is evident that they were purchased on a mistake; [and] a balanced investment position. . . . It is true, unfortunately, that the modern organization of the capital market requires for the holder of quoted equities much more nerve, patience and fortitude than from the holder of wealth in other forms.
>
> —*Keynes*[88]

Keynes's longest running position as an investment manager for which we have records was his role managing King's College's discretionary portfolio. His record at the King's College endowment is regarded as being "the purest expression of Keynes'[s] views and skill in an institutional investment context."[89] He began managing the separate portfolio in August 1921, and continued with King's College's endowment until he passed away in 1946. Two academic studies examined Keynes's performance as a money manager. The first, undertaken by finance researchers Jess Chua and Richard Woodward in 1983, examined Keynes's returns managing King's College's Chest Fund from 1928 until 1946. Chua and Woodward found Keynes to be a remarkably skillful investor. Though the period he operated the Chest Fund encompassed the 1929 stock market crash, the Great Depression, and World War II, its capital grew almost fivefold. To put that return in context, the U.K. market was *down* almost 15 percent, and the U.S. market down 21 percent, over the same period. Table 2.1 shows the annual returns and statistics of the Chest Fund, and the U.K. market.

Chua and Woodward observed that the Chest Fund's performance "was clearly superior to that of the market" though it "did not escape the ravages of the market crash in 1929"[90]—dropping –32.4 percent in 1930, and –24.6 percent in 1931, versus –20.3 percent and –25.0 percent for the market in the same years. They further noted that the fund recovered much faster than the market, generating five consecutive years of capital appreciation between 33 percent and 56 percent when the market did not recover at all. The Chest Fund suffered its single worst drop in 1938, falling –40.1 percent as the market fell –16.1 percent. The fund again recovered earlier than the

TABLE 2.1 Chest Fund Returns and Statistics (1927 to 1945)

Year	Chest Fund Index	Chest Fund Return	U.K. Market Return	Treasury Bill Rate	Chest Fund Risk Premium	U.K. Index Risk Premium
1927	100.0					
1928	96.6	–3.4%	7.9%	4.2%	–7.6%	3.7%
1929	97.4	0.8%	6.4%	5.3%	–4.5%	1.1%
1930	65.8	–32.4%	–20.3%	2.5%	–34.9%	–22.8%
1931	49.6	–24.6%	–25.0%	3.6%	–28.2%	–28.6%
1932	71.8	44.8%	–5.8%	1.5%	43.3%	–7.3%
1933	97.0	35.1%	21.5%	0.6%	34.5%	20.9%
1934	129.1	33.1%	–0.7%	0.7%	32.4%	–1.4%
1935	186.3	44.3%	5.3%	0.5%	43.8%	4.8%
1936	290.6	56.0%	10.2%	0.6%	55.4%	9.6%
1937	315.4	8.5%	–0.5%	0.6%	7.9%	–1.1%
1938	188.9	–40.1%	–16.1%	0.6%	–40.7%	–16.7%
1939	213.2	12.9%	–7.2%	1.3%	11.6%	–8.5%
1940	179.9	–15.6%	–12.9%	1.0%	–16.6%	–13.9%
1941	240.2	33.5%	12.5%	1.0%	32.5%	11.5%
1942	238.0	–0.9%	0.8%	1.0%	–1.9%	–0.2%
1943	366.2	53.9%	15.6%	1.0%	52.9%	14.6%
1944	419.2	14.5%	5.4%	1.0%	13.5%	4.4%
1945	480.3	14.6%	0.8%	1.0%	13.6%	–0.2%
Arithmetic mean		13.06%	–0.11%	1.56%	11.50%	–1.66%
Geometric mean		9.12%	–0.89%		7.36%	–2.50%
Standard deviation		29.28%	12.55%		29.87%	12.88%
Beta					1.78%	
Sharpe index		0.385	–0.129			

Source: Jess H. Chua and Richard S. Woodward, "J. M. Keynes's Investment Performance: A Note," *Journal of Finance* XXXVIII, no. 1 (March 1983).

market and went back on a significant run while the market meandered. Over the full 18-year period, the Chest Fund generated an average yearly return of 13.06 percent, and a compound annual return of 9.12 percent, which multiplied the capital in it 4.8 times during which time the general market lost almost –15 percent. Still, "a high level of portfolio risk" accompanied Keynes's outsized returns—a standard deviation of 29 percent, more than double that of the market.[91]

The second study conducted in 2013, by Chambers et al., also examined Keynes's returns as a speculator and investor. The authors examined all of Keynes's portfolios from the 1920s through to his position as First Bursar at the King's College endowment.[92] Through their research, Chambers et al. gained access to the annual investment reports of the King's College's endowment, including lists of security holdings kept in the King's College archives for each financial year ending in August from 1921 until 1946 (with only the 1926 report missing). Though King's had been a large real estate owner since its foundation in 1447, they excluded King's real estate from the analysis because valuations were not undertaken until after Keynes's death. From August 1921 to 1933, the portfolios over which Keynes had investment discretion—those not subject to statute—comprised more than The Chest Fund, the subject of Chua and Woodward's examination.[93] In 1933, the discretionary portfolios under Keynes's remit expanded to include a comingled pool of assets known as "Fund B."[94] As both accounts were managed similarly, Chambers et al., also include in their analysis the returns to Fund B.

Chambers et al. note that Keynes's top-down macro approach to investing generated disappointing returns in the 1920s, and after employing various statistical tests, could find no evidence of any market-timing ability.[95] After this disappointing start, Chambers and colleagues quantify how his record improved as he transitioned to a fundamental value investment approach. In this later period, the performance of his holdings—measured over the first year after purchase relative to the market—improved substantially. Over the period beginning August 1922, through to August 1946, Chambers et al. found that the portfolios over which Keynes had investment discretion returned 16 percent on average, outperforming the equally weighted U.K. stock market's 10.4 percent performance by an average of 5.6 percentage points annually.[96] The restricted portfolio generated an average return of only 6.8 percent, slightly underperforming the 7.1 percent return on U.K. government bonds. Table 2.2, extracted from the work of Chambers et al., shows the annual returns and statistics of Keynes's performance managing the King's College endowment, including all his discretionary portfolios, the restricted portfolios and the total fund, excluding real estate.

TABLE 2.2 King's College Returns and Statistics (1922 to 1940)

Financial Year	Discretionary Portfolio (1)	Restricted Portfolio (2)	Total Fund Ex-Real Estate (3)	U.K. Equity Index (4)	U.K. Govt Bond Index (5)	Relative Performance (1) – (4)
1922	35.33	16.80	18.17	31.40	26.40	3.94
1923	9.55	9.41	9.43	30.66	4.59	–21.11
1924	15.68	5.59	6.47	0.69	2.26	14.99
1925	41.32	4.70	9.62	11.46	3.10	29.87
1926	6.29	5.42	5.61	10.81	2.65	–4.53
1927	1.42	2.70	2.48	26.30	3.08	–24.88
1928	2.96	7.95	6.99	18.78	8.12	–15.82
1929	6.36	3.64	4.14	5.99	–0.31	0.37
1930	–14.21	0.36	–2.19	–18.74	9.13	4.53
1931	–11.53	–6.34	–7.16	–30.89	8.03	19.37
1932	32.65	5.82	9.40	26.15	29.40	6.50
1933	51.43	30.93	34.40	32.13	5.87	19.30
1934	26.60	13.39	17.50	11.38	12.92	15.21
1935	34.02	7.77	17.27	7.21	6.71	26.81
1936	39.57	11.77	23.40	22.83	4.39	16.74
1937	11.30	–1.00	4.26	1.67	–10.15	9.63
1938	–22.58	–8.55	–15.01	–8.71	4.93	–13.87
1939	8.92	–3.93	1.36	–5.57	–10.01	14.50
1940	–5.85	5.83	0.41	–18.84	16.61	13.00
1941	30.45	23.74	26.60	28.52	15.01	1.93
1942	8.39	9.04	8.77	10.85	4.43	–2.46
1943	39.74	7.82	22.04	27.86	–0.49	11.88
1944	15.60	5.24	10.70	12.06	2.87	3.54
1945	13.29	4.42	9.67	5.59	12.33	7.70
1946	22.48	7.84	17.36	19.66	14.58	2.83
AM	15.97	6.81	9.67	10.37	7.06	5.60
Standard deviation	19.08	8.48	10.85	17.11	9.06	13.87
Sharpe	0.73	0.57	0.71	0.49	0.56	n/a

The discretionary portfolios underperformed the market in only 6 out of 25 financial years Keynes managed the portfolio.[97] Four of those six years included 1923, 1926, 1927, and 1928, when the U.K. market put in unusually strong performance. Despite his "superior knowledge" of macroeconomics, Keynes failed to foresee the sharp fall in equities beginning October 1929, and failed to avoid the 14.2 percent decline in 1930. By 1930, the portfolio was a cumulative 12.6 percent behind the equally weighted U.K stock market benchmark since inception, and 40.3 percent behind over a trailing five-year period. After this point, the discretionary portfolio only experienced substantial underperformance once, in the financial year 1938, and never again lagged the U.K. stock market benchmark on either a rolling three-year or five-year basis.[98]

Chambers et al. record that the King's College endowment had a value of £285,000 ($20.1 million) in 1921. Through a combination of investment performance and cash inflows, by 1946, the securities had a value of £1,222,000 ($74 million). Over the quarter-century to 1946, within King's College's endowment, excluding its real estate holdings, the unrestricted portfolios over which Keynes had investment discretion grew from 8 percent to 68 percent of the total value. As decades passed, Chambers et al. found that Keynes turned over the discretionary portfolios less and less. Turnover is defined here as the average of purchases and sales in a given financial year divided by the average U.K. equity portfolio value over that year. In the period from 1921 to 1929, turnover averaged 55 percent of the portfolio each year. From 1930 to 1939, turnover reduced to 30 percent of yearly portfolio value, and from 1940 to 1946, turnover was a mere 14 percent.[99]

Chambers et al. conduct a statistical analysis of Keynes's best and worst performing equities over the full period for which they could find returns—25 years, or 100 quarters from August 1921 to August 1946.[100] They find that, while the results show that there was a substantial margin between his top and bottom five performing holdings over all periods, Keynes added relatively little value in deciding how much to allocate to his best performers. Table 2.3, also from Chambers et al.'s research, shows all listed stocks held at the beginning of each quarter, other than any holding less than 0.01 percent of the equity portfolio, ranked by their total return over the quarter. Panel A shows the average annual return for the entire period from 1921 to 1946, and also the returns for three subperiods. It shows the raw returns of the top five performers, their market-adjusted returns, the sum of the portfolio weights of the top five performers (VW), the sum of their portfolio weights if equally weighted with all other stocks (EW), and the sum of their market adjusted return contributions when value- and equal-weighted respectively. Panel B repeats the analysis for the bottom five performers.

TABLE 2.3 Five Top and Bottom Performing Stocks (1921 to 1940)

%	Raw Return	Market-Adjusted Returns	Weight		Market-Adjusted Weight	
			VW	EW	VW	EW
A: Top Five Performers						
1921–1946	28.5	25.4	16.5	15.6	3	3.3
1921–1929	16.3	12.9	27.6	25.1	3	2.7
1930–1939	37	34.9	13.7	12.4	3.8	4.4
1940–1946	30.9	26.6	7	8.9	1.7	2.4
B: Bottom Five Performers						
1921–1946	−19.2	−21.3	11.7	15.6	−2.1	−3.1
1921–1929	−14.8	−17.6	20.4	25.1	−3.0	−4.1
1930–1939	−25.0	−25.9	6.1	12.4	−2.1	−3.3
1940–1946	−16.0	−18.9	6.1	8.9	−1.1	−1.7

On average in the 1920s and 1930s, Keynes only overweighted his top five performers very modestly, and he underweighted them in the 1940s. He did a little better underweighting his bottom five performers, where he added value in all subperiods. This shows that while Keynes was a concentrated investor, he demonstrated little ability to discern which of his investments would outperform, or, if he could do so, he didn't focus the portfolio on those positions. Next, we examine Keynes's primary contribution, the philosophy of concentrated value investing.

A STUDY IN CONCENTRATION

> There are very few investors, I should say, who eschew the attempt to snatch capital profits at an early date more than I do. I lay myself open to criticism because I am generally trying to look a long way ahead and am prepared to ignore the immediate fluctuations. . . . My purpose is to buy securities where I am satisfied as to assets and ultimate earning power and where the market price seems cheap in relation to these.
>
> —*Keynes, "Letter to F. C. Scott," 1942*[101]

Keynes wrote in his General Theory that successful value investing was "so difficult to-day as to be scarcely practicable:"[102]

> *He who attempts it must surely lead much more laborious days and run greater risks than he who tries to guess better than the crowd how the crowd will behave; and, given equal intelligence, he may make more disastrous mistakes. It needs more intelligence to defeat the forces of time and our ignorance of the future than to beat the gun. Moreover, life is not long enough;—human nature desires quick results, there is a peculiar zest in making money quickly, and remoter gains are discounted by the average man at a very high rate. The game of professional investment is intolerably boring and over-exacting to anyone who is entirely exempt from the gambling instinct; whilst he who has it must pay to this propensity the appropriate toll.*

The reason, wrote Keynes, was that the "[d]ay-to-day fluctuations in the profits of existing investments, which are obviously of an ephemeral and non-significant character, tend to have an altogether excessive, and even an absurd, influence on the market."[103] The investor able to ignore those day-to-day fluctuations had a huge advantage over those seeking to profit from them. The corollary of the long-term focus was the risk of underperforming the market in the short term. Chambers et al. report that the *tracking error* of Keynes's portfolio—the extent to which it deviated from the performance of the market—ran to 13.9 percent, almost four times higher than is typical at institutional funds today.[104] When the tracking error is positive, the manager is beating the market, and when the tracking error is negative, as it must necessarily be on occasion for the manager to outperform, the manager is underperforming. In either case, wrote Keynes, he would be regarded as "eccentric, unconventional and rash in the eyes of average opinion:"[105]

> *If he is successful, that will only confirm the general belief in his rashness; and if in the short run he is unsuccessful, which is very likely, he will not receive much mercy. Worldly wisdom teaches that it is better for reputation to fail conventionally than to succeed unconventionally.*

Keynes knew what he was talking about. He had two very different experiences with the boards of the institutions in which he managed portfolios. Those experiences illustrate both the opportunities available to investors prepared to swim against the tide, as well as the perils of doing so, and the importance of having investors prepared to stick through thick and thin.

Keynes benefited from an administrative arrangement at King's College that allowed him to invest for the long term and ride out any periods of market volatility. He had a free hand to make investment decisions, to change his investment approach when necessary, and to construct a highly focused portfolio, all to the benefit of King's performance.[106] This allowed him to take highly unusual positions for the portfolio. Chambers et al. regard Keynes's uncontested authority to invest as he wished as one of the biggest advantages he had as an investor. King's College's discretionary portfolio suffered its single worst drop in 1938, falling 22.6 percent as the market fell 8.7 percent, yet the college allowed Keynes to continue unmolested in his investment role there. The discretionary portfolio recovered and then some by the end of the following year, and, though it was down again in 1940, it never again touched the 1938 low. It surpassed its 1937 peak by the end of 1941, and then proceeded to double over the next five years, Keynes last managing the portfolio before he passed away in 1946. From the 1938 low, Keynes compounded the King's College discretionary portfolio at 13 percent per year. (Even the Chest Fund, a more volatile sub-portfolio in the discretionary portfolio, which fell 40.1 percent, had by 1943 surpassed its 1937 peak. Like the rest of the discretionary portfolio, it never looked back, returning 12.4 percent per year compound from the 1938 low.) The market was less volatile through this period, but its slide persisted until it bottomed in 1940. It would not recover its 1937 high until 1942, compounding from the low at 6.5 percent, half the rate Keynes achieved in the discretionary portfolio.

The atmosphere at King's College, so conducive to long-term returns, stood in stark contrast to Keynes's experience in the investment management roles he had taken on along with the chairmanship of the insurer National Mutual Life Assurance Society. Keynes had been appointed to the board of the National Mutual, one of the oldest institutions in the city, in 1919.[107] He had served as chairman of the insurer, and helped manage its investment portfolio from 1921. That portfolio lost £641,000 ($61 million), an enormous sum of money in 1937. While Keynes was recuperating from a heart attack, F. N. Curzon, the acting chairman of the insurer called him to account for the loss.[108] Curzon and the board criticized Keynes's investment policy of remaining invested in his "pet" stocks during the decline.[109] In a response to Curzon in March 1938, Keynes wrote:[110]

> *1. I do not believe that selling at very low prices is a remedy for having failed to sell at high ones. . . . As soon as prices had fallen below a reasonable estimate of intrinsic value and long-period probabilities, there was nothing more to be done. It was too late to remedy any defects in previous policy, and the right course was to stand pretty well where one was.*

> *2. I feel no shame at being found owning a share when the bottom of the market comes. I do not think it is the business, far less the duty, for an institutional or any other serious investor to be constantly considering whether he should cut and run on a falling market, or to feel himself open to blame if shares depreciate on his hands. . . . An investor is aiming, or should be aiming, primarily at long-period results, and should be solely judged by these. . . . The idea that we should all be selling out to the other fellow and should all be finding ourselves with nothing but cash at the bottom of the market is not merely fantastic, but destructive of the whole system.*
>
> *3. I do not feel that we have in fact done particularly badly. . . . If we deal in equities; it is inevitable that there should be large fluctuations.*

With the world on the brink of a second world war, the board wanted Keynes to sell and retreat to "safer" assets like gold or government bonds.[111] Keynes refused to comply, and in October 1938, he resigned the chairmanship in disgust.[112] His experience at the Provincial Insurance Company, which was a smaller family-run insurer, managed by Francis Scott, was similar to his experience at King's College. He was appointed a director in 1923, and served until his death in 1946. Through frequent correspondence with Scott, he was able to persuade him of the advantages of remaining invested through the downturn.

Though London was under bombardment, and the United States seemed reluctant to enter the war, Keynes stood fast in his own portfolio.[113] He was convinced that Britain would prevail against Germany. Wasik points out how extraordinarily optimistic this was in 1940: The French Army had collapsed, the British expeditionary forces at Dunkirk had been evacuated, and German U-boats had destroyed 1.5 million tons of British shipping. Keynes may have reflected on the parallels to 1929, that, like the markets failing to recover then, if Britain didn't prevail in this second world war, "nothing matters."[114] His earlier missive, that, "some of the things which I vaguely apprehend are, like the end of the world, uninsurable risks and it is useless to worry about them," was never more appropriate.[115] As we saw earlier, both his personal portfolio, and the discretionary portfolio he managed on King's College's behalf, did eventually recover from the low, but Keynes had to ride out a stomach-churning plunge in the interim. He felt the 1938 drop more keenly in his personal portfolio, which fell two-thirds from £506,222 ($52 million) at the end of 1936 to £181,244 ($18 million) at the end of 1938.[116] He would never again achieve the 1936 high-water mark in his personal portfolio: On his death in 1946, that portfolio was worth £440,000 ($30 million).[117]

In May 1938—two months after his letter to Curzon—Keynes outlined his investment policy in a memo distributed to the Estates Committee of King's College. The King's College discretionary portfolios, and in particular the Chest Fund, had taken substantial losses—the discretionary portfolios would end the year down 22.6 percent, and the Chest Fund would be down a staggering 40.1 percent—in each case, the worst performance in its history. His tone was more conciliatory than the combative posture he struck in the letter sent to Curzon, and this may also account for the different response he received, but the principles he outlined were clearly not open to negotiation. In the letter, Keynes gives the clearest exposition on the rationale of long-term, concentrated value investment. As he had demonstrated in the early 1930s wrestle with the board of the P.R. Finance Company, Keynes began by explaining why he no longer believed in market timing driven by his credit cycling theory:[118]

> *We have not proved able to take much advantage of a general systematic movement out of and into ordinary shares as a whole at different phases of the trade cycle. Credit cycling means in practice selling market leaders on a falling market and buying them on a rising one and, allowing for expenses and loss of interest, it needs phenomenal skill to make much out of it.*
>
> . . .
>
> *As a result of these experiences I am clear that the idea of wholesale shifts is for various reasons impracticable and indeed undesirable. Most of those who attempt to sell too late and buy too late, and do both too often, incurring heavy expenses and developing too unsettled and speculative a state of mind, which, if it is widespread has besides the grave social disadvantage of aggravating the scale of the fluctuations.*

(In a note to his student Richard Kahn that accompanied the letter sent, Keynes mourned the failure of market timing strategies based on credit-cycling, writing, ". . . I have seen it tried by five different parties . . . over a period of nearly twenty years. . . . I have not seen a single case of success.")[119] He went on in the letter to King's College to describe the core of his philosophy in three principles that he believed would result in sound investing. He proposed:[120]

1. *A careful selection of a few investments (or a few types of investment) having regard to their cheapness in relation to their probable actual and potential intrinsic value over a period of years ahead and in relation to alternative investments at the time;*

2. *A steadfast holding of these in fairly large units through thick and thin, perhaps for several years, until either they have fulfilled their promise or it is evident that they were purchased on a mistake;*
3. *A balanced investment position, i.e., a variety of risks in spite of individual holdings being large, and if possible, opposed risks.*

Finally, he says that the "ideal investment portfolio is divided between the purchase of really secure future income (where future appreciation or depreciation will depend upon the rate of interest) and equities which one believes to be capable of a large improvement to offset the fairly numerous cases which, with the best skill in the world, will go wrong."[121] It was highly original thought, hard won from almost twenty years managing through the 1929 crash and the Great Depression, and it presaged by more than 10 years the comparable philosophy outlined by Graham in *The Intelligent Investor* (1949).

Keynes shunned the idea of extremely broad diversification that would develop later as modern portfolio theory, and heavily concentrated his core positions. Under modern portfolio theory, a portfolio is fully diversified only if it contains a share of every stock listed on the stock market (or, in purely academic terms, a share of every asset on earth). At the other end of the scale, a portfolio might be considered concentrated only if it contains a single asset. Investors must make a trade-off as they build a portfolio between maximizing the return through concentration, and minimizing the risk through diversification, and the extent to which an investor leans toward one end of the scale or the other depends on a number of considerations. Over time, the performance of the value investor's portfolio turns on the value investor's ability to identify—and, importantly, hold—undervalued securities, those Graham described as having the widest margin of safety. As the number of stocks in the portfolio swells, the degree of undervaluation, and hence the margin of safety, for each additional stock shrinks. Viewed in isolation, this might suggest that the optimal portfolio contains only a single stock—the most undervalued one—but of course this exposes the investor's whole portfolio to the peculiar risks associated with that single stock. Investors must therefore balance the desire to maximize return by holding only the most undervalued stocks with the desire to minimize the risk associated with any single stock. What, then, is the optimal number of stocks to hold in a portfolio? The answer depends on the skill of the investor.

Skilled investors can maximize their *long-term* performance by maximizing the margin of safety of each stock held in the portfolio, which is to say by concentrating on the best ideas. To be "skilled," an investor must be able to identify which stocks are more undervalued than others, and construct a portfolio containing only the most undervalued stocks. In doing so, investors take on the risk that an unforeseeable event leads to an unrecoverable loss in the intrinsic value of any single holding, perhaps through financial distress or fraud. This unrecoverable diminution in intrinsic value is referred to in the value investing literature as a *permanent impairment of capital*, and it is the most important consideration for value investors. Note that value investors seek to avoid a permanent impairment of capital in portfolio holdings, but accept that the fluctuation of portfolio holdings in market price around the intrinsic value is unpredictable and beyond control. Thus value investors distinguish the partial or total diminution in the firm's underlying value, which is a risk to be considered, from a mere drop in the share price, no matter how significant the drop may be, which is an event to be ignored or exploited. The extent to which the portfolio value is impacted by a portfolio holding suffering a permanent impairment of capital will depend on the size of the holding relative to the portfolio value—the bigger the holding, the greater the impact on the portfolio. Thus the more concentrated an investor becomes, the greater the impact on the portfolio from adverse events on individual holdings. Keynes wrote that he viewed the risk as follows:[122]

> [*My*] *theory of risk is that it is better to take a substantial holding of what one believes in than scatter holdings in fields where he has not the same assurance. But perhaps that is based on the delusion of possessing a worthwhile opinion on the matter.*

Keynes continued that he believed a fully diversified approach was more suitable for investors who did not possess skill in value investing, saying that:

> *The theory of scattering one's investments over as many fields as possible might be the wisest plan on the assumption of comprehensive ignorance. Very likely that would be the safer assumption to make.*

Keynes believed that unskilled investors could maximize their long-term return by limiting the risk to the portfolio of any individual portfolio holding. Today, they can achieve this by diversifying into the market portfolio and minimizing costs through a market index-tracking fund. Skilled value investors limit their risk of a permanent impairment of capital by assessing the risk of financial distress or fraud in each portfolio holding, and sizing the position accordingly.

A risk distinct from the risk that a portfolio suffers as a permanent impairment in capital is the risk that the portfolio capital varies through fluctuations in the share prices of portfolio securities, either in absolute terms, or relative to the market. Absolute variability, or a swing in price, is known as *volatility*, and deviation from the market's performance is known as *tracking risk*. Keynes's stock portfolios exhibited high tracking error, and greater volatility than the comparable market index. This allowed him the opportunity to express his skill, and outperform, but the trade-off was periodic underperformance and portfolio volatility. At King's College, this wasn't a problem, but it led directly to his resignation from National Mutual. Investors need to consider the extent to which they can tolerate these risks. The more concentrated an investor becomes, the greater the portfolio volatility, and performance diverges from the market's performance. Full diversification leads to market performance, and minimizes tracking risk. A concentrated holding in a single stock ties the investor's portfolio wholly to the performance of that stock, and maximizes tracking risk. Modern portfolio theory holds that, as it's impossible to beat the market other than by chance, the investor's best option is the most broadly diversified portfolio, perhaps one based on a market index. Value investment theory holds that mispricings do exist, and investors able to identify those mispriced securities can outperform the market to the extent that the portfolio contains proportionately more undervalued securities, and proportionately fewer overvalued securities, than the market.

Perhaps the most impressive attribute of Keynes was his ability to learn from his own mistakes and adapt his investment philosophy. As the Chambers et al. research demonstrates, Keynes's performance for King's College was not always stellar. He did not chart an unhindered course of investment success from beginning to end. To his credit, he did eventually abandon his top-down macroeconomic market-timing speculations after observing disappointing returns, statistical tests of which (conducted by Chambers et al.) confirm Keynes's view that he had no skill in market timing. This must have been an extraordinarily difficult conversion because his public reputation was tied to his skill as an economist, and he had to acknowledge semi-publicly that his macroeconomic ideas didn't provide him with any "superior knowledge." His investment performance improved after his 1932 intellectual shift. Chambers et al. note that his subsequent improvement in returns was a result of his "no longer having to make top-down asset allocation decisions which compromised his stock-picking instincts" because "he could now take greater care in timing the purchases of those stocks he liked." The portfolio he managed for King's College outshone the market throughout the 1930s, except for the crash of 1938, when he lost two-thirds of his fortune. It quickly recovered. His shift to long-term buy-and-hold value investing allowed him to maintain his commitment to his holdings when the market fell sharply in 1938, his final test. In so doing, he provides an excellent example of the natural advantages that accrue to investors with a long-term focus, who are able to behave in a contrarian manner during economic and financial market downturns.

Under Keynes's tenure as First Bursar of King's College—a period that encompassed the 1929 market crash, the Great Depression, and World War II—the discretionary portfolio of the King's College grew through Keynes's investment prowess and cash inflows from just over £20,000 to £820,000. Keynes's investment performance on behalf of the King's discretionary portfolio generated over the quarter-century to 1946 an annualized return of 16 percent, outperforming the comparable U.K. equity market by 5.6 percent per year. He achieved this return with a very high tracking error relative to the U.K. equity index, almost four times higher than contemporary U.S. university endowments. Keynes's investment record at King's College is extraordinary given that he had many other interests competing for his time and attention, including as an academic and in public service. While Keynes concentrated his portfolios, he did so in ad hoc fashion. The Chambers et al. research found he had little ability to identify stocks that were more mispriced than others, and to capitalize on that intuition by focusing the portfolio on those positions. In the next chapter, we examine the mathematical extension of Keynes's intuition and the remarkable men who conceived of it and implemented it.

NOTES

1. John F. Wasik, *Keynes's Way to Wealth: Timeless Investment Lessons from the Great Economist* (New York: McGraw-Hill, 2014).
2. John F. Wasik, *Keynes's Way to Wealth: Timeless Investment Lessons from the Great Economist* (New York: McGraw-Hill, 2014).
3. Jason Zweig, "The Intelligent Investor: Keynes: One Mean Money Manager," *Wall Street Journal*, April 2, 2012, http://online.wsj.com/news/articles/SB10001424052702304177104577313810084976558.
4. Howard Gold, "What Keynes Can Teach Us about Investing," *MarketWatch*, December 6, 2013, www.marketwatch.com/story/what-keynes-can-teach-us-about-investing-2013–12–06.
5. John Maynard Keynes, *The General Theory of Employment, Interest, and Money* (London: Palgrave Macmillan, 1936).
6. Benjamin Graham and David Dodd, *Security Analysis* (New York: McGraw-Hill, 1934).
7. Janet Lowe, *The Rediscovered Benjamin Graham Lectures: Selected Writings of the Wall Street Legend* (New York: John Wiley & Sons, 1999).
8. John F. Wasik, "John Maynard Keynes's Own Portfolio Not Too Dismal," *New York Times*, February 10, 2014, www.nytimes.com/2014/02/11/your-money/john-maynard-keyness-own-portfolio-not-too-dismal.html.
9. George Soros, "My Philanthropy," in *The Philanthropy of George Soros: Building Open Societies*, ed. C. Sudetic (Philadelphia: Perseus Books, 2011). As discussed in Chambers, Dimson, and Foo, 2015; see note 14.

10. David Swensen, *Unconventional Success: A Fundamental Approach to Personal Investment* (New York: Simon & Schuster, 2005); also, David Swensen, *Pioneering Portfolio Management, 2nd ed.* (New York: Free Press, 2009). As discussed in Chambers, Dimson, and Foo, 2015; see note 14.)
11. Warren Buffett, "Chairman's Letter," Berkshire Hathaway, Inc., 1991.
12. Howard Gold, "What Keynes Can Teach Us about Investing," *MarketWatch*, December 6, 2013, www.marketwatch.com/story/what-keynes-can-teach-us-about-investing-2013–12–06
13. Warren Buffett, "Chairman's Letter," Berkshire Hathaway, Inc., 1988.
14. David Chambers, Elroy Dimson, and Justin Foo, "Keynes the Stock Market Investor: A Quantitative Analysis, *Journal of Financial and Quantitative Analysis* 50 (2015): 843–868. doi:10.1017/S0022109015000186.
15. Ibid.
16. John F. Wasik, *Keynes's Way to Wealth: Timeless Investment Lessons from the Great Economist* (New York: McGraw-Hill, 2014).
17. Ibid.
18. Ibid.
19. Ibid.
20. Ibid.
21. David Chambers, Elroy Dimson, and Justin Foo, "Keynes the Stock Market Investor: A Quantitative Analysis," *Journal of Financial and Quantitative Analysis* 50 (2015): 843–868. doi:10.1017/S0022109015000186.
22. Calculated using the Bank of England's "Inflation Calculator," www.bankofengland.co.uk/education/pages/inflation/calculator/flash/default.aspx.
23. R. F. Harrod, *The Life of John Maynard Keynes* (London: Macmillan, 1951), as discussed at www.maynardkeynes.org/.
24. John F. Wasik, *Keynes's Way to Wealth: Timeless Investment Lessons from the Great Economist* (New York: McGraw-Hill, 2014).
25. R. F. Harrod, *The Life of John Maynard Keynes* (London: Macmillan, 1951), as discussed at www.maynardkeynes.org/.
26. David Chambers, Elroy Dimson, and Justin Foo, "Keynes the Stock Market Investor: A Quantitative Analysis," *Journal of Financial and Quantitative Analysis* 50 (2015): 843–868. doi:10.1017/S0022109015000186.
27. Ibid.
28. Ibid.
29. John F. Wasik, *Keynes's Way to Wealth: Timeless Investment Lessons from the Great Economist* (New York: McGraw-Hill, 2014).
30. Ibid.
31. R. F. Harrod, *The Life of John Maynard Keynes* (London: Macmillan, 1951), as discussed at www.maynardkeynes.org/.
32. Ibid.
33. John F. Wasik, *Keynes's Way to Wealth: Timeless Investment Lessons from the Great Economist* (New York: McGraw-Hill, 2014).
34. Carter Field, *Bernard Baruch, Park Bench Statesman* (New York: McGraw-Hill, 1944). Additional information gathered from Garson O'Toole of Quoteinvestigator.com.

35. John F. Wasik, *Keynes's Way to Wealth: Timeless Investment Lessons from the Great Economist* (New York: McGraw-Hill, 2014).
36. R. F. Harrod, *The Life of John Maynard Keynes* (London: Macmillan, 1951), as discussed at http://www.maynardkeynes.org/.
37. John F. Wasik, *Keynes's Way to Wealth: Timeless Investment Lessons from the Great Economist* (New York: McGraw-Hill, 2014).
38. Ibid.
39. Ibid.
40. Ibid.
41. Howard Gold, "What Keynes Can Teach Us about Investing," *MarketWatch*, December 6, 2013, hwww.marketwatch.com/story/what-keynes-can-teach-us-about-investing-2013–12–06.
42. John F. Wasik, *Keynes's Way to Wealth: Timeless Investment Lessons from the Great Economist* (New York: McGraw-Hill, 2014).
43. Ibid.
44. Ibid.
45. Ibid.
46. Ibid.
47. David Chambers, Elroy Dimson, and Justin Foo, "Keynes the Stock Market Investor: A Quantitative Analysis," *Journal of Financial and Quantitative Analysis* 50 (2015): 843–868. doi:10.1017/S0022109015000186.
48. John F. Wasik, *Keynes's Way to Wealth: Timeless Investment Lessons from the Great Economist* (New York: McGraw-Hill, 2014).
49. David Chambers, Elroy Dimson, and Justin Foo, "Keynes the Stock Market Investor: A Quantitative Analysis," *Journal of Financial and Quantitative Analysis* 50 (2015): 843–868. doi:10.1017/S0022109015000186.
50. Ibid.
51. Ibid.
52. Paul Samuelson, "The Keynes Centenary," *The Economist* 287 (1983).
53. David Chambers, Elroy Dimson, and Justin Foo, "Keynes the Stock Market Investor: A Quantitative Analysis," *Journal of Financial and Quantitative Analysis* 50 (2015): 843–868. doi:10.1017/S0022109015000186.
54. Ibid.
55. Jess H. Chua and Richard S. Woodward, "J. M. Keynes's Investment Performance: A Note," *Journal of Finance* XXXVIII, no. 1 (March 1983).
56. David Chambers, Elroy Dimson, and Justin Foo, "Keynes the Stock Market Investor: A Quantitative Analysis," *Journal of Financial and Quantitative Analysis* 50 (2015): 843–868. doi:10.1017/S0022109015000186.
57. R. F. Harrod, *The Life of John Maynard Keynes* (London: Macmillan, 1951), as discussed at www.maynardkeynes.org/
58. Ibid.
59. Ibid.
60. Jess H. Chua and Richard S. Woodward, "J. M. Keynes's Investment Performance: A Note," *Journal of Finance* XXXVIII, no. 1 (March 1983).
61. Ibid.

62. David Chambers, Elroy Dimson, and Justin Foo, "Keynes the Stock Market Investor: A Quantitative Analysis," *Journal of Financial and Quantitative Analysis* 50 (2015): 843–868. doi:10.1017/S0022109015000186.
63. Ibid.
64. Ibid.
65. Howard Gold, "What Keynes Can Teach Us about Investing," *MarketWatch*, December 6, 2013, www.marketwatch.com/story/what-keynes-can-teach-us-about-investing-2013–12–06.
66. John F. Wasik, *Keynes's Way To Wealth: Timeless Investment Lessons From The Great Economist* (New York: McGraw-Hill, 2014).
67. Jason Zweig, "The Intelligent Investor: Keynes: One Mean Money Manager," *Wall Street Journal*, April 2, 2012, http://online.wsj.com/news/articles/SB10001424052702304177104577313810084976558.
68. David Chambers, Elroy Dimson, and Justin Foo, "Keynes the Stock Market Investor: A Quantitative Analysis," *Journal of Financial and Quantitative Analysis* 50 (2015): 843–868. doi:10.1017/S0022109015000186.
69. Ibid.
70. Ibid.
71. Jason Zweig, "The Intelligent Investor: Keynes: One Mean Money Manager," *Wall Street Journal*, April 2, 2012, http://online.wsj.com/news/articles/SB10001424052702304177104577313810084976558.
72. David Chambers, Elroy Dimson, and Justin Foo, "Keynes the Stock Market Investor: A Quantitative Analysis," *Journal of Financial and Quantitative Analysis* 50 (2015): 843–868. doi:10.1017/S0022109015000186.
73. Ibid.
74. Ibid.
75. Ibid.
76. Ibid.
77. Ibid.
78. Ibid.
79. Ibid.
80. Ibid.
81. John Maynard Keynes, *The General Theory of Employment, Interest, and Money* (London: Palgrave Macmillan, 1936).
82. John F. Wasik, *Keynes's Way To Wealth: Timeless Investment Lessons From The Great Economist* (New York: McGraw-Hill, 2014).
83. John Maynard Keynes, *The General Theory of Employment, Interest, and Money* (London: Palgrave Macmillan, 1936).
84. Jason Zweig, "The Intelligent Investor: Keynes: One Mean Money Manager," *Wall Street Journal*, April 2, 2012, http://online.wsj.com/news/articles/SB10001424052702304177104577313810084976558.
85. David Chambers, Elroy Dimson, and Justin Foo, "Keynes the Stock Market Investor: A Quantitative Analysis," *Journal of Financial and Quantitative Analysis* 50 (2015): 843–868. doi:10.1017/S0022109015000186.
86. Ibid.
87. Ibid.

88. Ibid.
89. Ibid.
90. Jess H. Chua and Richard S. Woodward, "J. M. Keynes's Investment Per formance: A Note," *Journal of Finance,* XXXVIII, no. 1 (March 1983).
91. Howard Gold, "What Keynes Can Teach Us about Investing," *Market Watch*, December 6, 2013, http://www.marketwatch.com/story/what-keynes-can-teach-us-about-investing-2013–12–06.
92. David Chambers, Elroy Dimson, and Justin Foo, "Keynes the Stock Market Investor: A Quantitative Analysis," *Journal of Financial and Quantitative Analysis* 50 (2015): 843–868. doi:10.1017/S0022109015000186.
93. Ibid.
94. Ibid.
95. Ibid.
96. Ibid.
97. Ibid.
98. Ibid.
99. Ibid.
100. Ibid.
101. John F. Wasik, *Keynes's Way To Wealth: Timeless Investment Lessons From The Great Economist* (New York: McGraw-Hill, 2014).
102. John Maynard Keynes, *The General Theory of Employment, Interest, and Money* (London: Palgrave Macmillan, 1936).
103. Ibid.
104. David Chambers, Elroy Dimson, and Justin Foo, "Keynes the Stock Market Investor: A Quantitative Analysis," *Journal of Financial and Quantitative Analysis* 50 (2015): 843–868. doi:10.1017/S0022109015000186.
105. John Maynard Keynes, *The General Theory of Employment, Interest, and Money* (London: Palgrave Macmillan, 1936).
106. Howard Gold, "What Keynes Can Teach Us about Investing," *MarketWatch*, December 6, 2013, http://www.marketwatch.com/story/what-keynes-can-teach-us-about-investing-2013–12–06
107. John F. Wasik, *Keynes's Way to Wealth: Timeless Investment Lessons from the Great Economist* (New York: McGraw-Hill, 2014).
108. David Chambers, Elroy Dimson, and Justin Foo, "Keynes the Stock Market Investor: A Quantitative Analysis," *Journal of Financial and Quantitative Analysis* 50 (2015): 843–868. doi:10.1017/S0022109015000186.
109. John F. Wasik, *Keynes's Way to Wealth: Timeless Investment Lessons from the Great Economist* (New York: McGraw-Hill, 2014).
110. Ibid.
111. Ibid.
112. Barton Biggs, *Hedgehogging* (Hoboken, NJ: John Wiley & Sons, 2008), as discussed in John F. Wasik, *Keynes's Way to Wealth: Timeless Investment Lessons from the Great Economist* (New York: McGraw-Hill, 2014).
113. John F. Wasik, *Keynes's Way to Wealth: Timeless Investment Lessons from the Great Economist* (New York: McGraw-Hill, 2014).
114. Ibid.

115. Ibid.
116. Ibid.
117. Ibid.
118. Jess H. Chua and Richard S. Woodward, "J. M. Keynes's Investment Performance: A Note," *Journal of Finance* XXXVIII, no. 1 (March 1983).
119. David Chambers, Elroy Dimson, and Justin Foo, "Keynes the Stock Market Investor: A Quantitative Analysis," *Journal of Financial and Quantitative Analysis* 50 (2015): 843–868. doi:10.1017/S0022109015000186.
120. Jess H. Chua and Richard S. Woodward, "J. M. Keynes's Investment Performance: A Note," *Journal of Finance* XXXVIII, no. 1 (March 1983).
121. John F. Wasik, *Keynes's Way to Wealth: Timeless Investment Lessons from the Great Economist* (New York: McGraw-Hill, 2014).
122. David Chambers, Elroy Dimson, and Justin Foo, "Keynes the Stock Market Investor: A Quantitative Analysis," *Journal of Financial and Quantitative Analysis* 50 (2015): 843–868. doi:10.1017/S0022109015000186.

CHAPTER 3

Kelly, Shannon, and Thorp: Mathematical Investors

Concentration Quantified

I continued to buy Emerson. My broker asked, "What shall I do tomorrow for your account if it drops again?" The question jolted me. My loss was now $1,500. How much further could it fall?

Early in 1958 Emerson rose, and I sold out at a profit of $500. A year later Emerson tripled in price. The enormous profit that escaped and the sharp price fluctuations tantalized me.

—Thorp and Kassouf, *Beat the Market: A Scientific Stock Market System*, 1967

In 1983, a former professor in mathematics with an odd craft in convertible arbitrage pulled off the New York Stock Exchange's all-time largest dollar-value block trade in the stock of the largest corporation in American history.[1] Curiously, he executed the huge two-thirds of $1 billion trade—long $330 million in *Ma Bell*, and short $332.5 million in "when-issued" *Baby Bells*—for an insignificant $2.5 million gain. Even more curious, his fund had just $15 million in assets. How did such a tiny fund have the audacity to enter into such a colossal trade? Better yet, why was such an insignificant fund even *permitted* to enter into the trade? Ma Bell, the nickname given to American Telephone & Telegraph (AT&T), founded in 1877, to exploit inventor Alexander Graham Bell's patent, was to be broken up. The Justice Department had filed under the *Sherman Antitrust Act* in 1974 that AT&T had stifled competition, and should be brought to heel. AT&T fought a rearguard action until 1982, when it capitulated and entered into a consent decree agreeing to split out its 22 local exchange service companies. The local exchanges were divided into seven independent operating companies—the so-called Baby Bells—which were to be spun off in 1983 to Ma Bell shareholders. Ma Bell would retain its interest in Bell Labs, Western Electric, and its long-distance business. Each holder of a share in the old Ma Bell would receive a package of securities representing the new Ma Bell plus the seven Baby Bells. Though old Ma Bell and the package of new securities represented the same mix of businesses, greater investor interest in the Baby Bells had pushed the price up 0.76 percent—76 cents per $100—relative to Ma Bell shares. For most investors that tiny fissure wasn't worth the time or effort. For Edward O. Thorp, whose bread-and-butter was convertible arbitrage, this was a rare opportunity. To make it worthwhile he would need to drive a bus through that tiny crack. He would need to lay down $662.5 million dollars to collect just $2.5 million. How could he justify risking such a titanic sum for such a minuscule payoff? Thorp had a secret. He employed a little-known formula for optimal position sizing—the mysteriously named *Kelly Criterion*. However he plugged the details of the trade into Kelly's formula, the answer was unavoidable: Bet the farm.

CLAUDE SHANNON AND ED THORP

While working as a post-doctoral researcher at the Massachusetts Institute of Technology (MIT) in November 1960, Thorp submitted an abstract for a talk to the annual meeting of the American Mathematical Society. The abstract, *Fortune's Formula: The Game of Blackjack*, described a method for beating the casino at blackjack. It was slated for rejection by the selection committee.[2] Every year the American Mathematical Society received submissions from an "endless parade of cranks" who claimed they had done the mathematically impossible. Winning gambling systems for *negative expectation games*, those that lose money in the long run, were popular submissions.[3] The society's selection committee would have rejected Thorp's talk along with the others but for the intercession of a member of the committee, number theorist John Selfridge. Selfridge persuaded the skeptics that he knew Thorp from the University of California, Los Angeles, where he had studied for his PhD in mathematics. He told them Thorp was no crank.[4] The committee relented, and Thorp delivered his talk to the American Mathematical Society in January 1961. That talk formed the basis for *Beat the Dealer*, a book that inspired scores of other books and hundreds of technical articles, and is today considered a classic in gambling literature.

In his wonderful book *Fortune's Formula*, William Poundstone recounts that Thorp's key insight was that blackjack was played in casinos using only one deck, which was not shuffled between hands. To a mathematician like Thorp, this meant that blackjack hands were not "independent" of each other. Information from earlier hands could be applied in later hands before the deck was shuffled. All that a player needed to do was keep track of the discarded cards, and keep a "count." When the count indicated that the deck was more or less favorable, the player adjusted his or her betting accordingly. The player would wait patiently until the count indicated that the deck was stacked in his or her favor, and then bet heavily. Sure, there would be swings up and down, but over a large number of hands, that edge, properly exploited, would probably allow the player to beat the game. But how heavily should the player bet when he held an edge? And how should he bet when the deck was stacked against him?

Thorp discussed his blackjack findings with MIT colleague Claude Shannon, the brilliant mathematician whose 1948 master's thesis single-handedly invented *information theory* and ushered in the age of the digital circuit and computer. Shannon's thesis dealt with the transmission of a signal over a noisy line. The problem: Boosting a signal also boosts the noise. How then to transmit a message without losing its meaning due to the signal being misheard or unheard? In grappling with the problem, Shannon's paper, described as "possibly the most important, and also the most famous master's thesis of the [twentieth] century,"[5] proposed the *binary digit*, or *bit*, as the basic unit of information. A bit could have only two values—0 or 1, which could be interpreted as *true* or *false*; *yes* or *no*; or *on* or *off*—allowing the application of Boolean algebra to resolve any logical relationship. An implication of Shannon's thesis was that an electrical switch could perform logic functions, and this created the practical foundation for all digital circuits and computers. Outside of his academic work, Shannon had a number of unusual pastimes, including juggling, unicycling, and tinkering with electrical devices. Whatever grabbed his attention, Shannon pursued with unusual vigor, until, having exhausted its possibilities, he moved on. When Thorp discussed with him the blackjack bet-sizing issue in 1960, Shannon was intrigued, and pursued the idea with customary force. He recalled a five-year-old paper written by a Bell Labs colleague based on his 1948 master's thesis that dealt with precisely that question.

In one of his earlier flights of fancy, Shannon had begun an intensive study of the stock market in the late 1950s.[6] He wanted to know if his information theory could help him decode the market's random walk. His research led him to fill three library shelves with books, including Adam Smith's *Wealth of Nations*, John von Neumann and Oskar Morgenstern's *Theory of Games and Economic Behavior*, Paul Samuelson's *Economics*, and Fred Schwed's *Where Are the Customer's Yachts?* In a notebook Shannon recorded a varied list of thinkers, including French mathematician Louis Bachelier, Benjamin

Graham, and Benoit Mandelbrot. He took notes about margin trading; short selling; stop-loss orders; the effects of market panics; capital gains taxes and transaction costs. The only surviving document from Shannon's research is a mimeographed handout from one of the lectures he delivered at MIT in the spring term of 1956, in a class called *Seminar of Information Theory.* According to the handout, the lecture, called *The Portfolio Problem*, covered *The $64,000 Question*, a wire service giving horse tips, and the *Kelly Criterion.* Nothing else remains.

The lecture's title, and references to *The $64,000 Question*, and the wire service make it likely that the lecture was about bet sizing. *The $64,000 Question* was an American game show broadcast from 1955 to 1958, in which contestants answered questions in a category chosen by them, and in which they were experts. They won money for correct answers. The first question answered correctly resulted in a prize of $1. The second question answered correctly doubled the contestant's winnings to $2, the third doubled to $4, then $8, $16, $32, and so on until the grand prize of $64,000. A contestant could quit at any time if they had won $512 or more, and retire with their winnings. If they chose to continue, however, they risked all they had won to that point. Each successive question was more difficult than the last. An incorrect answer meant a total loss of all winnings, other than a consolation prize if the contestant had won $512, which resulted in them keeping the $512. If they had made it to $4,000, they could keep a Cadillac. The show was an enormous success, capturing as much as 85 percent of the viewing audience when it was shown.[7] *The $64,000 Question* is an example of the *parlay* or *bet-it-all* bet-sizing strategy. In each round of betting, the bettor wagers the entire bankroll. Winning means increasing the bankroll by the offered odds—in the case of *The $64,000 Question* 1:1, or 100 percent—and, losing means reducing the bankroll to nil—or, in *The $64,000 Question*, to the consolation prizes if enough questions had been answered correctly.

John Kelly, a gun-slinging, chain-smoking Texan physicist who worked at Bell Labs with Shannon, learned about a scam involving the show. It was produced in New York and aired live on the East Coast. It was then rebroadcast three hours later on the West Coast. A West Coast gambler found out the winners by telephone and was able to bet on the outcome before the show aired on the West Coast.[8] Kelly was intrigued by the possibility of betting on inside information like the West Coast gambler. He wondered how much a gambler should wager in such a situation. It would be tempting to bet everything, but Kelly was worldly enough to know that in reality "sure things" were sometimes less than sure, and a bettor gambling everything risked ruin. A small bet would avoid a catastrophic loss, but would also fail to capitalize on a rare advantage. What was the optimal bet size to maximize the bettor's return? Kelly wondered if he could apply Shannon's information theory to the problem. He discussed it with Shannon, who urged him to publish the work. Kelly's paper appeared in the 1956 issue of the *Bell System Technical Journal* under the anodyne title, *A New Interpretation of the Information Rate.* Kelly had wanted to call the paper *Information Theory and Gambling*, but some AT&T executives feared that the title and his discussion of a "private wire" would remind readers that AT&T used to lease wires to organized crime figures who ran wire services reporting racetrack results to bookies. Under pressure from AT&T, Kelly changed the title.[9]

In his paper, Kelly likened the problem to a gambler betting on baseball games—not horse racing, as it is often reported—with a "noiseless" private wire that enabled him to get perfectly accurate results before they became common knowledge. If the baseball teams were evenly matched, the gambler could obtain even money bets—1:1—though he knew the outcome of the game. In this theoretical example, with the gambler receiving perfect information, the amount of money he could win would depend only on how much he chose to bet. How much would he bet? Everything he had. If he did so, his capital would grow exponentially and after N bets he would have 2^N times his original bankroll. So, for example, if he started with $100, it would double to $200, then $400, $800, $1,600, $3,200 and so on. After 10 rounds of betting, the original stake would be worth $\$100 \times 2^{10}$, or $102,400. Noting that exponential growth of capital was not uncommon in economics, Kelly argued the value of the gambler's betting, if done on a weekly basis, was equivalent to the value of an investment paying 100 percent interest per week compounded weekly. This allowed him to derive an equation for a quantity, G, he called the *exponential rate of growth of the gambler's capital.*

Kelly now considered a "noisy" private wire where the outcome of each baseball game transmitted to the gambler had a probability p of error and q of correct transmission. Now if gambler still bet his entire bankroll each time, the same equation would still maximize the *expected* value of his capital, but he would likely go broke. Any error in transmission on the noisy wire would lead to ruin, and, if he used the wire indefinitely, he was certain to receive a transmission with an error. Kelly now considered what would happen if the gambler instead bet only a fraction of his capital. How much should he bet? The optimal bet size was one that maximized G, the *exponential rate of growth of the gambler's capital.* Kelly employed Shannon's *rate of transmission* theorem used in his information theory paper, which Kelly simplified to the following:

$$f^* = \frac{bp-q}{b} = \frac{p(b+1)-1}{b}$$

where: f^* is the fraction of the current bankroll to wager
b is the net odds received on the wager ("b to 1"); that is, you could win \$$b$ (and get a return of your \$1 wagered) for a \$1 bet
p is the probability of winning
q is the probability of losing, which is $1 - p$, the probability of winning

While the equation might appear formidable, it can be further simplified to *edge/odds*, which is intuitive in operation. If the Kelly bettor is offered an even-money bet with no edge—for example, a coin flip where the bettor can double, or lose, whatever money is wagered—the optimal bet is zero. The Kelly Criterion won't allow a bettor to take an even money bet with no edge. If the outcome is certain, the Kelly Criterion recommends an optimal bet size of 100 percent of the bankroll. For anything in between, the criterion varied by the offered odds and the edge, or chance of winning. Better odds, or a bigger edge increased the optimal bet size. Poorer odds, or a smaller edge decreased it. Kelly's gambler followed a different criterion from the classical gambler. At every bet Kelly's gambler sought to maximize the expected value of the logarithm of his capital—the compound return—which assumed repeated bets. In his paper Kelly suggested that the model could apply to certain other economic situations. It required only that the possibility of reinvestment of profits and the ability to vary the amount of money invested or bet.

Let's apply the Kelly Criterion to figure out how much of our bankroll to bet. In an even money bet, with odds of 1:1, and a 51 percent chance of winning, the Kelly Criterion recommends an optimal bet size of 2 percent, or \$2 out of a \$100 bankroll:

$$f = (bp - q)/b$$
$$f = (1 * 0.51 - 0.49)/1$$
$$f = 0.02 \text{ or } 2 \text{ percent}$$

We can also rearrange the Kelly Criterion to determine how confident a contestant on *The \$64,000 Question* needed to be to continue to each successive question. If we are forced to bet our entire stake on an even-money bet, Kelly theory dictates that we need to be certain of winning to take the bet. Given sufficient rounds of betting, with any chance of winning short of a 100 percent, the contestant will eventually lose the bankroll. Under these conditions, the contestants on *The \$64,000 Question* really needed to know their stuff. Interestingly, the consolation prizes significantly altered the odds offered once a contestant had won a minimum of \$512, and including them into the equation makes for a remarkable change to the game play. All the questions up to the \$512 question were straight up even-money bets. At \$512, the next question offered no risk of loss for the chance to double

$512 to $1,024. The Kelly Criterion recommends that the contestant take such a bet. The next bet risked $512 ($1,024 – $512) of the $1,024 bankroll to win $976 ($2,000 – $1,024), and the Kelly Criterion would recommend it if the contestant estimated her or his chance of correctly guessing at 67 percent or greater—that is to say if they thought they'd guess correctly 2 times out of 3. The next bet risked $1,488 ($2,000 – $512) of the contestant's $2,000 bankroll to win $2,000 ($4,000 – $2,000). But it also offered an opportunity at the next question, worth $8,000 if he or she got it correct, and a Cadillac valued at about $4,000 if it was answered incorrectly. That opportunity at the next question further improved the odds in their favor. Excluding the opportunity at the Cadillac or the $8,000, the Kelly Criterion would recommend attempting the question only if the contestant thought his or her chance of getting it correct was 85 percent or greater. Including the opportunity at the Cadillac or the $8,000 slightly lowered the hurdle to attempting the question to 81 percent or greater, which is about 4 times in 5. It required confidence, but not certainty, and changed the dynamics of the game play enough to encourage contestants to continue to higher stakes, making for a more exciting game.

Kelly's obscure paper passed by unheralded in his lifetime. He died of a stroke on the sidewalk in 1965 at the age of 41. Legend has it that he never used his own criterion to make a bet. He must have known, however, that it was being used to make bets, not on baseball or horse racing, but on blackjack. In 1960, Thorp figured out how to combine his card-counting system and Kelly's Criterion to beat the dealer—not just one, but many of them. He and Shannon would visit casinos, sometimes in costume—a fake beard or sunglasses—to avoid detection, and play hand after hand of blackjack. Poundstone says that Thorp was so successful in Las Vegas that the casinos started taking "counter-measures" against him, which meant adding more decks, shuffling the cards more frequently, using dealers who cheated by manipulating the deck, threatening Thorp with injury, and then simply banning him from the casinos. In short order, Thorp no longer found blackjack fun or profitable. He had found a new preoccupation in the stock market. Thorp saw the game of blackjack as a model for the efficiency of capital markets, writing, "There is limited inefficiency available to be exploited by those with the best information or the most superior skills."[10] He started hunting in the stock market for that important edge.

It was no great leap for Thorp to apply the same criterion to bet sizing in investing rather than gambling. After all, Kelly derived his original formula using the equation to calculate the value of compound interest, and had left open the possibility the model might apply to other economic situations. Kelly's only requirement was that it allow for reinvestment of profits and variability in the amount of money invested. In 2005, Elwyn Berlekamp, a professor of mathematics at the University of California at Berkeley who had served as Kelly's research assistant in 1960 and 1962, and coauthored Shannon's last paper on information theory in 1967, wrote about the application of the Kelly Criterion to investing:[11]

> *In the idealized model, the portfolio manager has an accurate probability distribution on the future performance of each asset in the universe of potential investments. Kelly's methodology then provides a quantitative specification of how big a position to take in each of the candidate assets. Not surprisingly, the fraction of one's portfolio to be invested in any asset that has a negative expected rate of return will be zero. Most assets with positive expected rates of return will merit the investment of some positive fraction of the portfolio. Among assets with similar expected rates of return, those whose returns are relatively stable will be weighted more heavily than those whose future returns have significant risks of substantial losses, even when these risky investments also have some chance of large gains.*

As Thorp began his investigation of the stock market he spoke again to Shannon, who by the mid-1960s had become something of a guru on the subject following his intensive research in the late 1950s. Shannon got his first taste of blood in the market by investing in high technology start-ups helmed by his MIT and Bell Labs contemporaries.[12] His first big win came from a shareholding in Harrison Laboratories, Inc., started in 1954 by Charles William "Bill" Harrison, a former Bell Labs scientist, and his wife, Gwen. The company made parts for the nascent field of color television cameras. When Hewlett-Packard acquired it in 1962, Shannon received stock as part of the merger, and was struck by the size of the gain.[13] He also invested in Teledyne, Inc., a new venture started by Henry Singleton, a close friend and alumnus from MIT's graduate school. Shannon bought in 1960 at the $1 initial public offer price.[14] By 1967, the stock traded for $24. None other than Warren Buffett would later describe Singleton as a "managerial superstar,"[15] with "the best operating and capital deployment record in American business."[16] Shannon would go on to sit on the board of Teledyne, and would conduct technical and business diligence on potential acquisitions at Singleton's behest. In 1963, Shannon backed another technology group from MIT, Codex Corporation, which made modems.[17] The company eventually became Motorola, and was another hugely successful investment. He also bought Xerox, but sold too early, and made only a small gain.[18]

Like Keynes, Shannon started out as a market timer. True to his tinkering ways, he built an electric device that mimicked the flow of money into and out of the stock market.[19] It turned bearish in 1963 or 1964, and Shannon turned defensive, but the bull market continued on until 1966. The Dow Jones Industrial Average did pull back in 1966 fully 25 percent to a price it first reached in 1963, but Shannon evidently felt that machine hadn't anticipated the timing or the magnitude of the pullback, and stopped using it. By then he was making money investing in hot technology IPOs. Poundstone recounts a story about Thorp visiting Shannon and his wife at their house, and seeing on blackboard in Shannon's study the notation $2^{11} = 2{,}048$.[20] When he asked Shannon what it meant, Shannon paused, and then explained that he had been doubling his money on a monthly basis, and wanted to know how much each initial dollar would be worth after 11 doublings. Shannon didn't maintain that torrid rate of growth over his entire 30-plus year investment career, but he did produce a noteworthy record. From the late 1950s through 1986, Shannon's portfolio returned 28 percent compound.[21] To put that return in context, thirty years of compounding at 28 percent per year multiplies the initial investment 1,645 times, not quite the number Shannon had written on his blackboard, but still incredibly impressive.

As his renown as an investor spread, Shannon became a sought-after lecturer on the stock market. In the mid-1960s, he started giving talks at MIT on the subject of *scientific investing*.[22] Scientific investing did not mean technical analysis. Shannon had tinkered with technical charting in the early 1960s, but had rejected it, describing the price charts used by technicians as "a very noisy reproduction of the important data."[23] Rather, Shannon lectured on statistical methods for profiting from a stock's random walk. One such method was what Poundstone named *Shannon's Demon*. The idea was to form a portfolio of equal parts cash and a stock, and rebalance regularly to take advantage of the stock's randomly jittering price movements. Shannon's Demon worked as follows: Let's say we begin with a portfolio of $10,000: $5,000 will be held in cash, and $5,000 will be invested in a stock at noon. At noon the next day, the portfolio is rebalanced. If the stock is down by, say, half, the portfolio is now worth $7,500 ($5,000 in cash, and $2,500 in stock), and $1,250 of the cash is used to buy more stock to bring the portfolio back into balance. After rebalancing, the portfolio is now holding $3,750 in cash, and $3,750 in stock. At noon the following day, the stock has doubled, and so the portfolio is now worth $11,250, with $7,500 in stock, and $3,750 in cash. Over the two trades, the portfolio has gained $1,250, though the underlying stock has gone nowhere (it halved, and then doubled, returning to its starting price). Figure 3.1 shows the progression of Shannon's Demon portfolio and the stock price over 80 days.

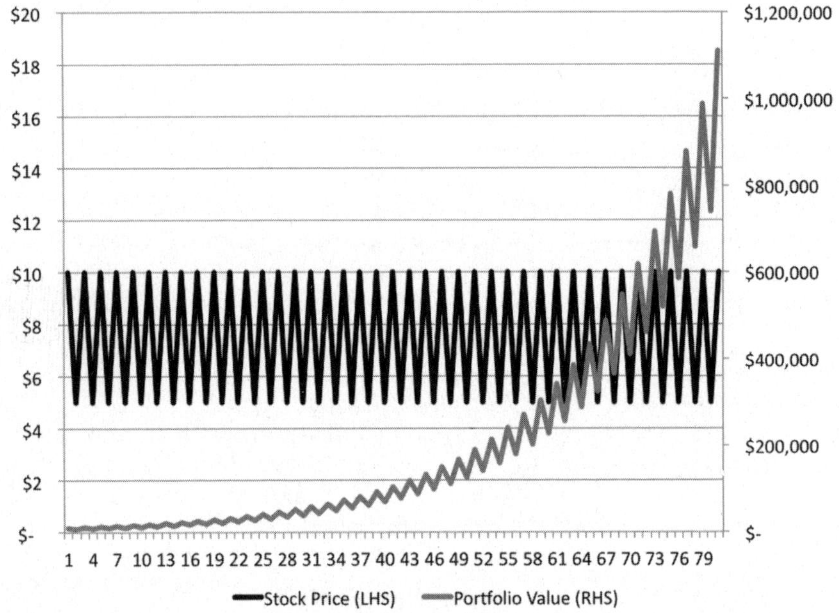

FIGURE 3.1 Shannon's Demon Portfolio and Stock Price
Source: Carbon Beach Asset Management, LLC.

If we continue to rebalance daily, and the stock continues to halve, and double day after day, at the end of 80 days the portfolio will be worth more than $1.1 million. This occurs though the stock hasn't budged—it's still at its starting price—and a buy-and-hold investor in the stock would have no gain. How is this possible? The key to Shannon's Demon is the constant rebalancing of two more *uncorrelated* assets. (Correlated assets move together, uncorrelated assets do not move together.) The rebalancing forces the investor to buy stock at the low, and sell at the high. Investors who dollar-cost average into a position are taking advantage of this phenomenon. As the stock falls after the initial position is purchased, the dollar-cost averaging strategy forces the investor to buy more at the lower position. Value investors like Lou Simpson who trade around a long-term position to pare it back when it exceeds intrinsic value, or build it up when it drops below intrinsic value are employing another variation of the strategy. Shannon's Demon is a special case of the Kelly Criterion because a fixed percentage of the investor's bankroll is bet each period. Shannon was asked at the end of one of his talks if he used the system for his own investments. Poundstone reports that he responded, "Naw. The commissions would kill you."[24] What, then, did Shannon do?

Although he had been a prolific scientific researcher and writer, none of Shannon's study of the stock market translated into a paper. Poundstone reports that he had long thought about publishing something on his investment methods, but couldn't find anything sufficiently original in his process. The only source of contemporaneous notes was an interview conducted in 1986 by Phillip Hershberg, an investment adviser and former engineer. Poundstone read the notes to the article and interviewed Hershberg in an effort to learn Shannon's secret. Poundstone discovered that, far from using his Demon, Shannon was a committed buy-and-hold value investor. Believing that stock prices would "in the long run, follow earnings growth," Shannon sought to "extrapolate . . . the growth of earnings in the next few years from our evaluation of the company management and the future demand for the company's products."[25] The key data was, therefore, "not how much the stock price has changed in the last few days or months, but how the earnings have changed in the past few years."[26] Shannon plotted company earnings on logarithmic paper, and then extrapolated the trend out into the future. He then thought about what factors might allow the trend to continue. Shannon and his wife visited start-up technology companies to meet with management. They also liked to test the products of companies selling to the public. Poundstone recounts how the Shannons, when conducting diligence on Kentucky Fried Chicken, bought and served fried chicken to their guests. "If we try it, and we don't like it, we simply won't consider an investment in the firm."[27] (He doesn't let us know whether the Shannons went on to invest.) Shannon was also one of the first investors to download stock prices. By 1981, he was subscribing to a stock price service and using his Apple II to download the prices into a spreadsheet, which automatically calculated the value of Shannon's portfolio. Hershberg's notes included a computer printout dated January 1981, which contained the snapshot of Shannon's portfolio shown in Table 3.1.

Shannon's $582,717.50 portfolio would be worth approximately $1.5 million in 2015. This figure excludes the value of another stock Shannon held, Datamarine International, which Shannon told Hershberg was the worst-performing stock in the portfolio.[28] Purchased in 1971, it had averaged *only* 13 percent per year since.[29]

There are two striking aspects of Shannon's portfolio observable in the 1981 snapshot. The first is the extreme concentration. Fully 81 percent of the portfolio was dedicated to his biggest position, Teledyne. His second-largest holding, Motorola, made up another 12 percent of the portfolio, and Hewlett-Packard, the third-largest holding, accounted for a further 5 percent. The other seven positions made up just 2 percent of his holdings. The reason for the extreme concentration is the second striking feature of Shannon's portfolio: He didn't trim positions. Shannon simply remained

TABLE 3.1 Shannon's Portfolio Returns and Statistics

Company	Shares	Purchase Price	1981 Price	Value	Return
Baxter International	30	$42.75	$50.00	$1,500.00	17%
Crown Cork & Seal	50	$8.00	$31.75	$1,587.50	297%
Hewlett-Packard	348	$0.13	$82.00	$28,536.00	62,977%
International Flavors and Fragrances	70	$26.50	$22.00	$1,540.00	–17%
John H. Harland	1	$30.00	$39.00	$39.00	30%
Masco	120	$1.63	$28.88	$3,465.00	1,672%
M.I.L.I	40	$32.00	$28.13	$1,125.00	–12%
Motorola	1,086	$1.13	$65.00	$70,590.00	5,652%
Schlumberger	22	$44.00	$108.75	$2,329.50	147%
Teledyne	2,428	$1.00	$194.38	$471,942.50	19,338%
Total				$582,717.50	

invested in each as they grew. This allowed Motorola to compound his initial investment 57 times. Teledyne, his largest investment, grew an incredible 194 times. Hewlett-Packard, his second-largest holding, multiplied his capital an astonishing 630 times from his average purchase price. Even Shannon's smaller positions were evidence of his preference for holding onto positions while they grew. Masco, a near 1 percent position in the portfolio, compounded 17 times. Crown Cork & Seal, which accounted for a *de minimis* 0.3 percent of the portfolio, was up a very respectable three times from his initial investment. Shannon's concentration and unwillingness to sell was a conscious choice on his part. He commented to Hershberg that he had not, at any time in the past 30 years, attempted to balance his portfolio:

> *I would have liked to have done so were it not for tax considerations. I am willing to borrow on our investments if necessary, rather than sell our stocks and convert to interest-bearing instruments.*[30]

Shannon's three biggest gainers, which accounted for 98 percent of his portfolio, were all investments sourced through his MIT and Bell Labs connections. Teledyne was from MIT classmate Singleton, Motorola was the new name for MIT start-up Codex Corporation, and Hewlett-Packard had taken over his Bell Labs' colleague Harrison Laboratories. Shannon commented to Hershberg, "In a way, this is close to some of the work I have done relating to communication and extraction of signals from 'noise'."[31] He continued, saying that a smart investor should "understand where he has an edge and invest only in those opportunities."[32] He seemed to be implying that he used the Kelly Criterion to invest. While Shannon intuitively understood that the Kelly Criterion could be applied to the stock market, his own portfolio suggests that he didn't in fact apply it there. That distinction would fall to Ed Thorp.

EDWARD THORP AND APPLIED KELLY THEORY

In November 1969, Thorp founded what he believed to be the world's first market-neutral hedge fund, *Convertible Hedge Associates* (renamed *Princeton-Newport Partners* in 1974).[33] The fund used warrants, over-the-counter (OTC) options, convertible bonds, preferred stock, and common stock to construct a *delta-neutral* portfolio—one that was unaffected by changes in the underlying common stock. Like Shannon, he too sought to exploit the random walk phenomenon, not through Shannon's Demon, but through convertible arbitrage. Thorp's strategy, though it was considerably more sophisticated, shared with Shannon's Demon the use of constant rebalancing to eke out tiny profits from changes in the prices of matched securities as they reverted to the mean. In his 1967 book *Beat The Market,* his follow-up to *Beat the Dealer*, Thorp also described his investment process as a "a scientific stock market system" perhaps as a nod to Shannon's *scientific investing* lectures. The difference was that Thorp's strategy sought arbitrage opportunities between baskets of securities that by implication should have traded at the same price. For example, in 1974, American Motors convertible bonds were selling for the same price as the stock underlying them and paying 8.3 percent. Thorp shorted the stock while buying the bonds, and pocketing the coupons. He later commented about the trade, "Situations that simple and clear are few and far between, but we made a large part of our living off scenarios just like that."[34] Those situations were about as close to riskless as any investment can get. If the stock, which Thorp was short, rallied, he was protected by his long position in the convertible bond, which would rally in sympathy with the stock. If it failed to do so, and the spread between the two widened to the point that Thorp would get a margin call on the short, he could simply convert the bonds into stock and close out the position. If the price of his long bond position fell, he would be protected by the short in the equity, which would fall along with the bond. If it didn't, and the gap widened, he could simply close out the position for no loss, or continue to collect the coupon. And so Thorp spent his days searching for little arbitrages to clip in obscure, thinly traded securities.

He had been plying his trade in arbitrage for more than a decade by the time Ma Bell announced its breakup. Like every arbitrage scenario Thorp had entered into prior to Ma Bell, this situation called for a very large position under Kelly. Typically, the limiting factor on a position's size was not the Kelly Criterion but the liquidity of the security. Warrants? OTC options? Convertible bonds? Most investors had never even heard of them, let alone understood the relationship of one to the other. This was the reason why the little arbitrages existed in the first place. The securities were unusual, and difficult to trade. Ma Bell would be different. It was the largest corporation on the stock exchange, and it was heavily traded. If the "when issued" securities were unusual, it wasn't reflected in the price. They traded at a thin premium to the old Ma Bell, even though they represented exactly the same mix of businesses. Thorp spotted a rare opportunity: a huge, highly liquid, riskless situation. Kelly told him to back up the truck, and that's exactly what he did. He filled his portfolio with as much of each security as the brokers would let him take—fully two-thirds of $1 billion—and squeezed out of that razor-thin margin a risk-free $2.5 million for his fund. The scale of the deal was enough to make Wall Street sit up and take notice. When the details of the trade leaked out—a former math professor who had been a professional blackjack player used convertible arbitrage to make a riskless profit—Thorp became a mini-celebrity for the second time, and the Kelly Criterion finally got its day in the sun.

Not everyone was enamored of the criterion. Economist Paul Samuelson, the first American to win the Nobel Memorial Prize in Economic Sciences, and considered by the *New York Times* the foremost American economist of the twentieth century, was so maddened with the idea that he wrote a paper seeking to refute it. The paper, "Why We Should Not Make Mean Log of Wealth Big Though Years To Act Are Long," appeared in a 1979 edition of the *Journal of Banking and Finance.* It was a highly unusual entry for such an eminent publication because Samuelson wrote it all, save for the last word—"syllable"—in prose of single-syllable words, presumably so that his intellectual opponents could understand it. It contained such gems as the following:[35]

> *Why then do some still think they should want to make mean log of wealth big? They nod. They feel 'That way I must end up with more. More sure beats less.' But they err. What they do not see is this:*
>
> *When you lose—and you sure can lose—with N large, you can lose real big. Q.E.D.*

Samuelson's point was that the desirability of a maximal gain at the risk of a large loss varied from person to person. A maximal gain, for example, might not be attractive for an already wealthy individual if it risks a loss large enough to affect his or her lifestyle. The purpose of the Kelly Criterion is to maximize the expected value of the logarithm of wealth period by period, but its suggested bets are often very large, and it can be very volatile in the short term. Seeking to avoid the big swings of the Kelly bet, some investors halve the size of the bet recommended by the criterion. This so-called *half-Kelly bet*, achieves three-quarters of the compound return of Kelly with half the volatility.[36] It never pays to bet more than Kelly. Kelly is already the maximal bet for any given edge and odds. Overbetting does not increase the return, but increases the risk to such a degree that it's likely to reduce growth. Figure 3.2, taken from a paper cowritten by Thorp in 2010, shows the probability of doubling and quadrupling before halving and relative growth rates versus fraction of wealth wagered for blackjack (2 percent advantage, $p = 0.51$ and $q = 0.49$).

This elucidates the main disadvantage of the Kelly Criterion. It is very aggressive, recommending bigger and bigger bets as the odds become more favorable. Few have the stomach for it. Even Thorp, who bet so ferociously

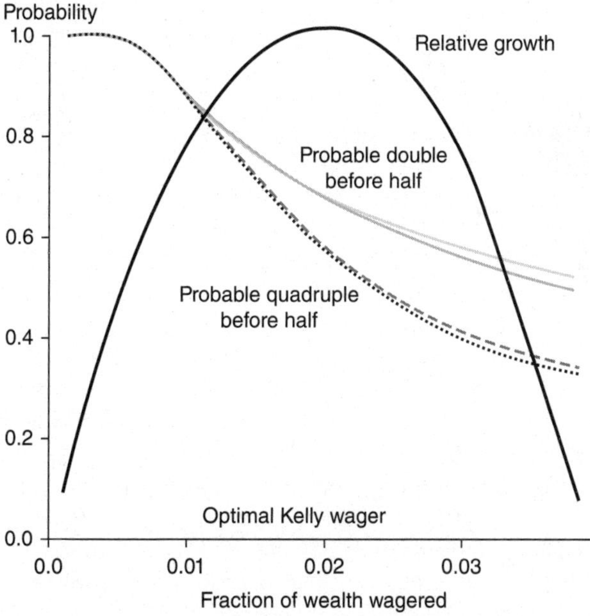

FIGURE 3.2 Probability of Doubling and Quadrupling before Halving
Source: Leonard MacLean, Edward O. Thorp, and William T. Ziemba, "Good and Bad Properties of the Kelly Criterion," *Wilmott Magazine*, January 1, 2010.

on the Ma Bell breakup, recommended *fractional* Kelly betting—betting anything less than full Kelly—in many other scenarios. In the 2010 paper, Thorp recounted the story of how he and Bill Ziemba, the other author, used the Kelly Criterion to size a bet on the inaugural 1984 Breeders' Cup Classic $3 million race, which is considered by many to be the premier thoroughbred horse race of the year in the United States. Kelly recommended the optimal fractional wager on the 3–5 shot *Slew of Gold* to be 64 percent of the bankroll. Thorp and Ziemba made a place and show bet. (In a *place* bet the horse must finish first or second for the bettor to collect and a *show* bet requires the horse to finish first, second, or third to collect. Each pays out at lower odds than a straightforward *win* bet, even in the event that the horse wins.) Thorp and Ziemba won using "a low fractional Kelly wager."[37] Slew finished third but the second-place horse *Gate Dancer* was disqualified and placed third, leading Ziemba to note that "[l]uck (a good scenario) is also nice to have in betting markets."[38]

The intuition of the Kelly Criterion is simple enough: Bet big when you hold an edge; don't bet when you don't hold an edge. Keynes has been described as a "Kelly-type bettor."[39] He embraced that insight, but he shied away from attempting mathematical precision because "our existing knowledge does not provide a sufficient basis for a calculated mathematical expectation."[40] The elegance of Kelly's method of calculating optimal position sizing is that it accounts for precisely that risk. The Kelly Criterion seeks to maximize the compounded return and explicitly captures the possibility that the expected outcome doesn't manifest. Thus the Kelly Criterion never risks ruin. It strikes a balance between maximizing return when the probabilities lie in the investor's favor, and avoiding loss when they do not. The downside to Kelly betting is that favorable odds and a good chance of success lead it to call for huge bets proportionate to the bankroll, making its swings too much for many investors. The solution for many investors has been the fractional Kelly bet. Kelly should be viewed as the maximum bet size. Bets beyond Kelly don't increase the likely return, but do increase the risk of loss. All of these qualitative features of Kelly's Criterion correspond with our intuition about how to bet. Kelly advanced the theory of betting by bringing to it mathematical rigor. He showed that in the very long run, the bankroll of a Kelly betting investor would eventually surpass the bankroll of anyone following any other strategy.

Thorp, who popularized the Kelly bet, and was the first to apply it as a gambler and investor, was no value investor. He wrote in the introduction to *Beat the Market* that he tried value investing:[41]

> *My line of attack was to seek "value." This is called the fundamental approach to the stock market. Members of this school believe*

> *that every stock has an "inherent" value (also called intrinsic value), very often distinct from its market price. The future stream of earnings and dividends determines inherent value.*
>
> . . .
>
> *A fundamentalist studies financial statements, industry and firm prospects, managerial ability, government policy, and whatever else he believes will affect future earnings. This leads him to an estimate of the future income stream of a share of stock which he then converts into inherent value. If the market price of the stock is less than his computed inherent value, then it is attractive; if the market price is more, the stock is to be avoided.*

Thorp ultimately rejected value investing before moving into arbitrage because he found that he couldn't make money:[42]

> *The more I used fundamentals the less money I made, while some friends who were very successful gave little thought to their investments. . . . My attraction to fundamental analysis weakened further as practical difficulties appeared. It is almost impossible to estimate earnings for more than a year or two in the future. And this was not the least difficulty. After purchasing an undervalued stock it is essential that others make similar calculations so that they will either purchase or wish to purchase it, driving its price higher. Many "undervalued" stocks remain bargains for years, frustrating an owner who may have made a correct and ingenious calculation of the future prospects.*

Warren Buffett would be the first to apply Kelly theory to value investing. In the next chapter, we examine how he used Kelly to build Berkshire Hathaway, Inc.

NOTES

1. Ken Kurson, "What a Card!," *Worth*, September 1999.
2. Edward O. Thorp, "The Legacy of Beat the Dealer," Wilmott.com, September 24, 2002.
3. Ibid.
4. Ibid.
5. Howard Gardner, *The Mind's New Science: A History of the Cognitive Revolution* (New York: Basic Books, 1987.
6. William Poundstone, *Fortune's Formula: The Untold Story of the Scientific Betting System That Beat the Casinos and Wall Street* (New York: Hill and Wang, 2006).

7. http://home.williampoundstone.net/Kelly.htm.
8. Ibid.
9. Ibid.
10. Edward O. Thorp, "The Legacy of Beat the Dealer," Wilmott.com, September 24, 2002.
11. Elwyn Berlkamp, "Bettor Math," *The American Scientist*, November-December, 2005.
12. William Poundstone, *Fortune's Formula: The Untold Story of the Scientific Betting System That Beat the Casinos and Wall Street* (New York: Hill and Wang, 2006).
13. Ibid.
14. Ibid.
15. Warren Buffett, "Chairman's Letter," Berkshire Hathaway, Inc., 1982.
16. John Train, *The Money Masters* (New York: HarperBusiness, 1994).
17. William Poundstone, *Fortune's Formula: The Untold Story of the Scientific Betting System That Beat the Casinos and Wall Street* (New York: Hill and Wang, 2006).
18. Ibid.
19. Ibid.
20. Ibid.
21. Ibid.
22. Ibid.
23. Ibid.
24. Ibid.
25. Ibid.
26. Ibid.
27. Ibid.
28. Ibid.
29. Ibid.
30. Ibid.
31. Ibid.
32. Ibid.
33. Edward Thorp, "A Mathematician on Wall Street: What I Knew and When I Knew It—Part 2," *Wilmott Magazine*, August 3, 2013.
34. Ken Kurson, "What a Card!," *Worth*, September 1999.
35. Paul A. Samuelson, "Why We Should Not Make Mean Log of Wealth Big though Years to Act Are Long," *Journal of Banking and Finance* 3 (1979): 305–307.
36. http://home.williampoundstone.net/Kelly.htm.
37. Leonard MacLean, Edward O. Thorp, and William T. Ziemba, "Good and Bad Properties of the Kelly Criterion," Unpublished, January 1, 2010.
38. Ibid.
39. Ibid.
40. John Maynard Keynes, *The General Theory of Employment, Interest and Money* (London: Palgrave Macmillan, 1936).
41. Edward O. Thorp and Sheen T. Kassouf, *Beat the Market: A Scientific Stock Market System, First Edition* (New York: Random House, 1967).
42. Ibid.

CHAPTER 4

Warren Buffett: The Kelly-Betting Value Investor

Portfolio Concentration for Value Investors

The strategy we've adopted precludes our following standard diversification dogma. Many pundits would therefore say the strategy must be riskier than that employed by more conventional investors. We disagree. We believe that a policy of portfolio concentration may well decrease risk if it raises, as it should, both the intensity with which an investor thinks about a business and the comfort-level he must feel with its economic characteristics before buying into it. In stating this opinion, we define risk, using dictionary terms, as "the possibility of loss or injury."

—Warren Buffett, 1993[1]

The Allied Crude Vegetable Oil Company in New Jersey, run by Anthony "Tino" De Angelis, was a wholesaler and commodities trader who bought and sold vegetable oil futures contracts. What set Allied Crude apart was its ability to sell soybean oil, used in salads, at prices far below those offered by any of its competitors. De Angelis's low, low prices saw his business grow at a phenomenal rate until, in November 1963, the entire empire abruptly collapsed. Receivers inspecting the ruins of Allied Crude seeking to recover assets for creditors found his oil tanks bereft of salad oil, and filled instead with seawater or air. It soon became apparent that the source of De Angelis's low prices was the sale of salad oil Allied Crude didn't own, and wasn't even in existence. De Angelis claimed 1.8 billion pounds of soybean oil—more than existed in the entire world at the time[2]—though he held only 110 million pounds in his tanks. In all, Allied Crude had sold $175 million in imaginary salad oil. How did he do it? De Angelis had figured out what every primary school-aged child knows: Oil floats on water. Inspectors examining his ships as they arrived at port to determine their contents confirmed that the first few feet of space was occupied by soybean oil, not realizing that De Angelis had first filled the tanks with seawater, and then topped them off with salad oil. The company would take the inspectors out to a long lunch, then move the same oil in to new tanks in the warehouse, and show those tanks to the sleepy, digesting inspectors. "The Great Salad Oil Swindle,"[3] as it became known after *Wall Street Journal* reporter Norman C. Miller wrote a Pulitzer Prize–winning book of the same name, was one of the worst corporate scandals of its time. It eventually sent De Angelis to jail for seven years for fraud and conspiracy, and tipped a major Wall Street brokerage into bankruptcy. Hunting deep pockets that could pay out a hefty damages award, De Angelis's creditors found a subsidiary of American Express Company had issued De Angelis with $144 million in warehouse receipts verifying the quantum of soybean oil in his tanks. American Express looked dead to rights for the full amount. An award of that magnitude—10 times American Express's 1964 earnings—might have sent it to the wall. American Express's stock price was slashed in half overnight.

His interest piqued, the then-unknown Warren Buffett had his broker, Henry Brandt, stake out banks, restaurants, hotels, and anyone else who dealt in American Express cards to find the "scuttlebutt"—rumors or gossip—on the business.[4] Buffett too visited restaurants in Omaha, and saw that they continued to accept American Express. His assessment of the scuttlebutt was that American Express was temporarily reeling from the effects of a fiscal blow that would not destroy its exceptional underlying economics. It was an "extraordinary business franchise with a localized excisable cancer," and it would survive.[5] He moved quickly, investing 40 percent of the partnerships' capital into the stock. It was the largest investment the partnerships had ever made, and gave Buffett and partners control of over 5 percent of American Express's stock at a cost of $13 million. American Express settled with the Allied Crude creditors in 1965 for $60 million, and the stock, which had plunged below $35, quickly popped to $49 per share.[6] In short order the position would be a more-than-five-bagger for Buffett, at which point he sold out.

While the American Express investment was the largest single investment the Buffett Partnerships had made on both a dollar basis and as a proportion of the partnerships' capital, Buffett had built his track record on large, concentrated positions. In 1959, the partnerships' largest holding at 35 percent of assets had been Sanborn Map, a publisher of extremely detailed maps of power lines, water mains, driveways, building engineering, roof composition, and emergency stairwells for all the cities of the United States. Fire insurance companies purchased the bulk of Sanborn's maps, and used them to underwrite fire insurance. At one stage it was the most successful map company in the United States. As Buffett explained in his 1961 partnership letter, the valuation was extremely compelling: While the business was shrinking as competition materialized and insurance companies merged—profitability was down from $500,000 annually in the 1930s to around $100,000 annually in 1958 on sales of $2.5 million—the company owned an investment portfolio worth more than $7 million or $65 per share.[7] The shares traded for $45. Buffett noted that, in 1938, when Sanborn sold for $110 per share, the investment portfolio was worth $20 per share, implying a business value at that time of $90 per share. By 1958, some 20 years later, the $45 stock price then implied that the same map business was worth *negative* $20 per share, or the investment portfolio worth 69 cents on the dollar with the map business thrown in for free. Such a discount warranted a huge investment position, and Buffett put more than a third of the partnerships' capital into Sanborn. He eventually persuaded the Sanborn board to buy back 72 percent of Sanborn stock—eliminating half of the 1,600 shareholders—through an exchange of portfolio securities at fair value, leaving the remaining shareholders with a slightly improved asset value, substantially higher earnings per share, and an increased dividend rate.

Though it was characteristic of Buffett to invest large portions of his partnerships' capital in single stocks, the significance of Buffett's investment in American Express was that it represented a departure in style from his more *Grahamesque* investments like Sanborn Map. While both were large, concentrated holdings at deep discounts from intrinsic value, the source of value in each was qualitatively different. Sanborn Maps was a purely statistical undervaluation, what Buffett would later characterize as a "cigar butt," a company with a poorly performing or middling business, but a balance sheet value that could be realized in a liquidation. American Express, by contrast, was a great business, but one that held little balance sheet value relative to price he would pay. In his 1989 Chairman's Letter, Buffett would describe the reason for the move away from cigar butts:[7]

> *If you buy a stock at a sufficiently low price, there will usually be some hiccup in the fortunes of the business that gives you a chance to unload at a decent profit, even though the long-term performance of the business may be terrible. I call this the "cigar butt" approach to investing. A cigar butt found on the street that has only one puff left in it may not offer much of a smoke, but the "bargain purchase" will make that puff all profit.*

Unless you are a liquidator, that kind of approach to buying businesses is foolish. First, the original "bargain" price probably will not turn out to be such a steal after all. In a difficult business, no sooner is one problem solved than another surfaces—never is there just one cockroach in the kitchen. Second, any initial advantage you secure will be quickly eroded by the low return that the business earns. For example, if you buy a business for $8 million that can be sold or liquidated for $10 million and promptly take either course, you can realize a high return. But the investment will disappoint if the business is sold for $10 million in ten years and in the interim has annually earned and distributed only a few percent on cost. Time is the friend of the wonderful business, the enemy of the mediocre.

For Sanborn Map the "hiccup" in its fortunes was one that Buffett precipitated himself by insisting that the directors cause the company to buy back stock, and do so in a timely, and tax effective manner. Absent Buffett's intervention, Sanborn Map may have continued to trade as a subliquidation value cigar butt. American Express, on the other hand, had been a high-quality business suffering from a short-term crisis. As the scandal abated, the stock popped, and Buffett was able to realize excellent medium-term returns. But Buffett observed that American Express continued to grow and compound after he sold his position in the Buffett Partnerships. After Buffett got control of Berkshire Hathaway, Inc., he started a new position in American Express, buying in the open market. Berkshire now controls 14.2 percent of the company, worth $13.8 billion, and purchased at a cost of $1.36 billion. Had he held on to the partnerships' initial 5 percent stake, it would now be worth $4.5 billion, equivalent to a compound rate of growth on his original $13 million of 13 percent per year for more than 50 years. In his 1994 Chairman's Letter, Buffett would write about his long association with American Express:[8]

My American Express history includes a couple of episodes: In the mid-1960s, just after the stock was battered by the company's infamous salad-oil scandal, we put about 40 percent of Buffett Partnership Ltd.'s capital into the stock—the largest investment the partnership had ever made. I should add that this commitment gave us over 5 percent ownership in Amex at a cost of $13 million. As I write this, we own just under 10 percent, which has cost us $1.36 billion. (Amex earned $12.5 million in 1964 and $1.4 billion in 1994.)

The more than 100-fold growth in American Express's earnings over the 30 years from 1964 to 1994 bore out Buffett's view that "[t]ime is the friend of the wonderful business, the enemy of the mediocre." Since 1994, American Express has grown its annual earnings to $34 billion, a 25-fold increase in 20 years, and a 280-fold increase since Buffett's first stake in 1964.

In 1967, Buffett wrote in his partnership letter about the difference between quantitative bargains like Sanborn Map and qualitative bargains like American Express:[9]

> *The evaluation of securities and businesses for investment purposes has always involved a mixture of qualitative and quantitative factors. At the one extreme, the analyst exclusively oriented to qualitative factors would say, "Buy the right company (with the right prospects, inherent industry conditions, management, etc.) and the price will take care of itself." On the other hand, the quantitative spokesman would say, "Buy at the right price and the company (and stock) will take care of itself."*
>
> . . .
>
> *Interestingly enough, although I consider myself to be primarily in the quantitative school (and as I write this no one has come back from recess—I may be the only one left in the class), the really sensational ideas I have had over the years have been heavily weighted toward the qualitative side where I have had a "high-probability insight." This is what causes the cash register to sing. However, it is an infrequent occurrence, as insights usually are, and, of course, no insight is required on the quantitative side—the figures should hit you over the head with a baseball bat. So the really big money tends to be made by investors who are right on qualitative decisions, but, at least in my opinion, the more sure money tends to be made on the obvious quantitative decisions.*

Taking concentrated positions like American Express has helped Berkshire to grow at an extraordinary rate. Ed Thorp, on reviewing Buffett's investment record there, observed that when the then-young hedge fund manager had acquired an interest in the small New England textile manufacturer the stock had traded at $20. By 1997, the stock traded at $70,000, representing a multiple of 3,500 and an annualized growth rate of 27 percent. "The Great Compounder," as Thorp called Buffett, had led Berkshire stock price and book value to "follow a growth path quite similar to full Kelly betting."[10] (Berkshire "A"-class stock now trades for more than $200,000 per share, a multiple of 10,000, and an annualized rate of compound growth of 19.4 percent.) The empirical evidence, according to Thorp, is that Buffett has throughout his career consistently concentrated his capital into his best positions in a Kelly-like manner. As we'll see, this is unusual and requires a great deal of skill.

CLOSET INDEXERS

Academics have cast the problem of diversification in terms of seeking to match the return of the market. In constructing portfolios to achieve this end, they look to strike a balance between holding as few positions as necessary to minimize transaction and monitoring costs, and as many positions as required to diversify away from *idiosyncratic risk*, which is the risk that any given holding encounters trouble. In a 1977 paper, Elton and Gruber showed most of the gains from diversification are enjoyed by holding between 20 and 30 securities.[11] They examined an equally weighted universe—*equally weighted* means the same proportion of the portfolio is invested in each stock—of 3,290 securities, and randomly selected from it equally weighted portfolios of varying sizes. Elton and Gruber regarded the lowest risk achievable as the risk of the market, where *risk* here is represented by the market's *variance*. Variance measures the spread of the underlying securities' performance relative to the performance of the market as a whole. A variance of zero means that all the returns are identical. A high variance indicates that the returns are very spread out around the average return. A portfolio containing all 3,290 securities in Elton and Gruber's market would perform exactly in line with the market, and its variance would be zero. (While the market portfolio still has the variance of the market, finance academics treat this as *non-diversifiable* risk, and ignore it for these purposes.) At the other end of the risk scale, Elton and Gruber regarded a portfolio containing a single security as the riskiest because it had the highest variance relative to the market. Table 4.1 is extracted from another paper examining Elton and Gruber's work, and shows the reduction in risk—defined as the standard deviation of annual returns, rather than the variance of weekly returns used by Elton and Gruber—as additional, randomly selected, and equally weighted securities are added to the portfolio.[12]

Table 4.1 shows that with a single security in the portfolio, the risk that the annual return on the portfolio deviates from the annual return of the market has a standard deviation of 49.24 percent. A second security added to the single-security portfolio reduces the now two-security portfolio's risk to 76 percent of the one-security portfolio's risk, a substantial reduction over the single-security portfolio, but still almost twice the market risk at an annual standard deviation of 37.36 percent. A third security reduces the portfolio risk to 60 percent of the risk of a single-security portfolio. Note that as each additional security is added to the portfolio, the reduction in risk relative to the move from a single-security portfolio to a two-security portfolio slows. A 20-security portfolio has eliminated 92 percent of the portfolio's idiosyncratic risk. Adding 10 more securities to create a 30-security portfolio eliminates 95 percent of the portfolio's idiosyncratic

TABLE 4.1 Effect of Diversification

Number of Stocks in Portfolio	Expected Standard Deviation of Annual Portfolio Returns (%)	Ratio of Portfolio Standard Deviation to Standard Deviation of a Single Stock
1	49.24	1.00
2	37.36	0.76
4	29.69	0.60
6	26.64	0.54
8	24.98	0.51
10	23.93	0.49
12	23.20	0.47
14	22.26	0.46
16	21.94	0.45
18	21.20	0.45
20	21.68	0.44
25	21.20	0.43
30	20.87	0.42
40	20.46	0.42
50	20.20	0.41
400	19.29	0.39
500	19.27	0.39
1,000	19.21	0.39
Infinity	19.16	0.39

risk—just 3 percent more. The additional gains beyond 30 securities are minimal, and the costs of acquiring and monitoring those securities likely outweigh the benefits of any further risk reduction.

When Buffett was asked by business students in 2008 about his views on portfolio diversification and position sizing, he responded that he had "two views on diversification:"[13]

> *If you are a professional and have confidence, then I would advocate lots of concentration. For everyone else, if it's not your game, participate in total diversification. If it's your game, diversification doesn't make sense. It's crazy to put money in your twentieth choice rather than your first choice. . . .* [*Berkshire vice-chairman*] *Charlie*

> [Munger] *and I operated mostly with five positions. If I were running $50, $100, $200 million, I would have 80 percent in five positions, with 25 percent for the largest. In 1964 I found a position I was willing to go heavier into, up to 40 percent. I told investors they could pull their money out. None did. The position was American Express after the Salad Oil Scandal.*

Buffett's views on portfolio diversification can be seen as two ends of a spectrum, with the market portfolio at one end, and a concentrated, Kelly-sized portfolio at the other. The efficient market hypothesis holds that, as it's impossible to beat the market, the market portfolio—represented by a low-cost index fund—is the better option. Buffett reaches the same conclusion with a slight nuance, arguing that a low-cost index is best for investors unable to dedicate sufficient time to the markets. For those with the time and ability to identify mispriced securities—those securities for which the market isn't efficient—concentration makes more sense. Do such securities exist? Buffett notes in his 1988 Chairman's Letter:[14]

> *Observing correctly that the market was* frequently *efficient,* [*academics, investment professionals, and corporate managers*] *went on to conclude incorrectly that it was* always *efficient. The difference between these propositions is night and day.*

Buffett's business partner, Berkshire vice-chairman Charles Munger, elucidated further in a 1994 talk to the University of Southern California Business School. Munger compared investing to betting on horse races. Noting that there were some bettors who could consistently beat the house, though horse racing was unpredictable, Munger observed:[15]

> *And the one thing that all those winning bettors in the whole history of people who've beaten the pari-mutuel system have is quite simple. They bet very seldom. It's not given to human beings to have such talent that they can just know everything about everything all the time. But it is given to human beings who work hard at it—who look and sift the world for a mispriced bet—that they can occasionally find one. And the wise ones bet heavily when the world offers them that opportunity. They bet big when they have the odds. And the rest of the time, they don't. It's just that simple.*

A consequence of the market being mostly efficient, and mispricings therefore being rare, is that portfolios contain fewer securities than the market averages. In a later interview, Munger continued that this meant that

"Berkshire-style investors"—long-term value investors—tended to be more concentrated:[16]

> *The Berkshire-style investors tend to be less diversified than other people. The academics have done a terrible disservice to intelligent investors by glorifying the idea of diversification. Because I just think the whole concept is literally almost insane. It emphasizes feeling good about not having your investment results depart very much from average investment results. But why would you get on the bandwagon like that if somebody didn't make you with a whip and a gun?*

Munger observed in a 2013 Daily Journal Company meeting that the Berkshire investors "seem to have done very well with a certain paucity in their portfolios."[17] The more broadly a portfolio is diversified, the more likely it is to match the performance of the averages, and the more concentrated a portfolio becomes, the more likely it is to deviate from those averages, either positively or negatively. Time-poor investors are therefore better served by a low-cost, broad-based index that seeks to match the averages.

The problem with the academic approach is that risk is treated as deviation from the performance of the market. What if our goal is to deviate from the average? How hard is that to achieve? We can use statistical sampling theory to show how likely it is that a given portfolio size will track the average or deviate from it. The S&P 500 is a well-known stock market index that contains 500 of the largest stocks listed in the United States. The equally weighted, total-return version of the S&P 500 (the S&P 500 EW) contains 500 stocks, each of which has the same influence on the index's performance (*total return* also indicates that the index includes dividends). Let's assume that index funds don't exist, and we can't afford to buy 500 stocks. How many stocks do we need to buy to roughly track the performance of the S&P 500 EW? And what are the chances that those randomly selected stocks perform in line with, or underperform, the index? This is a question we can answer statistically. In statistics, if we wish to learn something about a population, for example, the average height of men in California, but for cost or other practical reasons it's not possible to measure the entire population of males in California, we can take a simple random sample by measuring a smaller subset of the population, say 1,000 randomly selected men. We then extrapolate from the sample of 1,000 men the height of the whole population of men in California. Our expectation is that the men we sample are representative of the population, but it's possible that the men we sample are on average taller or shorter than the rest of the population. Statisticians call the extent to which the height of the men sampled differs from the height of the population of men in California "sampling error." All else being equal, the larger the sample size, the smaller the sampling error. This is the same problem we confront with our portfolio. In this example, the population is the entire S&P 500 EW, which contains 500 stocks, the characteristic we are interested in is the index's return, and the sample is our portfolio. We want to know how likely it is that a given portfolio matches or underperforms the return of the S&P 500 EW.

We can test this empirically using a Monte Carlo simulator to construct randomly selected portfolios of different sizes and then compare the performance of each portfolio to the performance of the index. In *The Warren Buffett Portfolio*,[18] author Robert G. Hagstrom examined the impact of portfolio concentration using the Compustat database and 18 years of performance data from 1979 to 1996. He compared the returns of portfolios of 250, 100, 50, and 15 positions to the overall stock market, defined as the S&P 500 for the same time periods. Hagstrom concluded that reducing the number of stocks in a portfolio increased the chance of generating returns that beat the market. He also found that it increases the chances by the same amount that an investor underperforms. We conducted our own version of Hagstrom's study with slight modifications. Where Hagstrom randomly selected companies from a list of 1,200 with the full period of performance data, we randomly select companies from only the S&P 500 so that the statistics of sample portfolios could be compared to our underlying population parameters. We also equally weighted the positions in our portfolios, so we could compare the returns to the equally weighted S&P 500. For each year in the sample, we use a computer to randomly assemble, from 500 companies, data for 8,000 portfolios of the following sizes:

1,000 portfolios containing 250 stocks
1,000 portfolios containing 100 stocks
1,000 portfolios containing 50 stocks
1,000 portfolios containing 30 stocks
1,000 portfolios containing 25 stocks
1,000 portfolios containing 20 stocks
1,000 portfolios containing 15 stocks
1,000 portfolios containing 10 stocks

In all, we created 120,000 portfolios. We calculate the average annual return for each portfolio over the period from January 1999 to October 2014, and then compared the performance to the S&P 500 over the same period. Figure 4.1 shows the results of our Monte Carlo simulations.

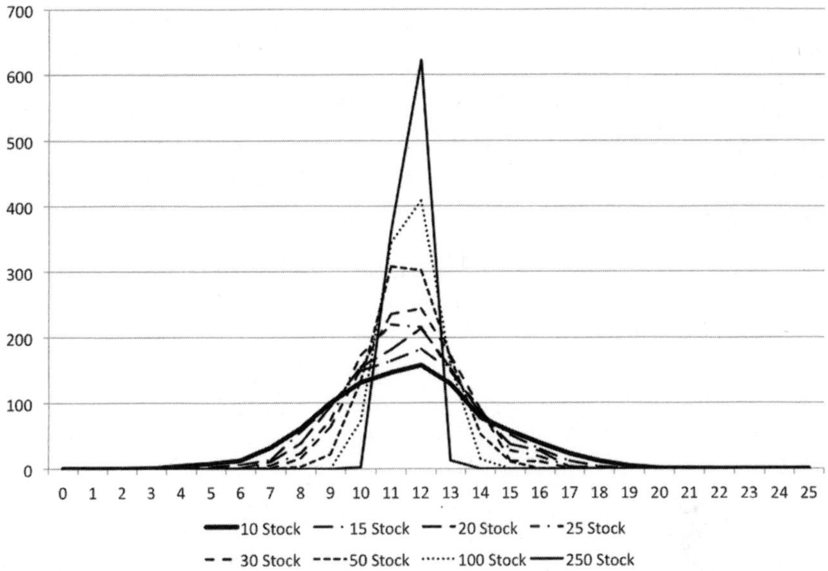

FIGURE 4.1 Chart of Average Arithmetic Annual Returns for Monte Carlo Portfolio Concentration Test in S&P 500 EW (1999 to 2014)
Data source: Carbon Beach Asset Management, LLC.

Table 4.2 sets out the statistics of the 1,000 runs of the portfolios over the 15 years of data.

Figure 4.1 and Table 4.2 show that each portfolio concentration clusters around the mean. Over the 15-year period under consideration, the equally weighted S&P 500 index generated an average annual return of 12.16 percent. The 250-stock portfolio delivered the same average return

TABLE 4.2 Average Arithmetic Annual Return Statistics for Monte Carlo Portfolio Concentration Test in S&P 500 EW (1999 to 2014)

	10 Stocks (%)	15 Stocks (%)	20 Stocks (%)	25 Stocks (%)	30 Stocks (%)	50 Stocks (%)	100 Stocks (%)	250 Stocks (%)	All Stocks (%)
Average	12.01	12.08	12.07	12.09	12.13	12.16	12.19	12.16	12.16
Median	12.05	12.08	12.07	12.09	12.13	12.16	12.19	12.16	12.16
Min	3.71	5.40	5.32	5.90	7.51	8.13	10.12	10.69	12.16
Max	21.32	19.96	18.68	17.23	17.33	15.79	14.78	13.50	12.16
Std. dev.	2.69	2.21	1.93	1.73	1.53	1.18	0.80	0.40	0.00

as did the 50-stock portfolio. The 10-stock portfolio had a slightly lower average return, but still remarkably close to the underlying average. This makes intuitive sense. We would expect that the average annual return of the portfolios tested is approximately the same as the underlying average of the equally weighted S&P 500 EW. The small underperformance of the more concentrated stock portfolios can be ignored. As we increase the number of trials, we would find that all converge on the underlying return of the S&P 500 EW.

The remarkable feature of the chart is the increasing distribution of returns as the portfolios concentrate. The 250-stock portfolios—the thinnest, unbroken, black line on the chart—had the tallest peak and the narrowest distribution. Those portfolios didn't deviate much from the S&P 500 EW. The worst-performed 250-stock portfolio averaged 10.69 percent over the 15 years considered, and the best returned 13.5 percent. Contrast that with the 10-stock portfolios, indicated by the thickest unbroken black line on the chart. Those portfolios had the lowest peak and the widest distribution, indicating that smaller portfolio sizes are much more likely to deviate from the average. The best average annual return from the 10-stock portfolio was an outstanding 21.32 percent, and the worst was a miserable 3.71 percent. In Table 4.3, we take a look at the chance that the performance of a given portfolio deviates from the underlying performance of the S&P 500 EW.

Table 4.3 demonstrates that, as we concentrate the portfolios into fewer positions, the chance that a portfolio outperforms increases. The 250-stock portfolios outperformed by 1 percent or more in just 0.2 percent of cases, and didn't outperform by 2 percent or more at any time. By contrast, the 10-stock portfolios outperformed by 1 percent or more 35.2 percent of the time, meaning that in more than one-third of portfolios, the average return

TABLE 4.3 Chance of Portfolio Outperforming S&P 500 EW (1999 to 2014)

	10 Stocks (%)	15 Stocks (%)	20 Stocks (%)	25 Stocks (%)	30 Stocks (%)	50 Stocks (%)	100 Stocks (%)	250 Stocks (%)	All Stocks (%)
1% or more	35.20	32.40	30.20	27.70	23.40	15.80	7.30	0.20	—
2% or more	22.10	17.50	14.70	10.40	8.20	2.50	—	—	—
3% or more	12.10	7.90	5.20	3.00	1.80	0.30	—	—	—
4% or more	5.90	2.20	1.30	0.60	0.10	—	—	—	—
5% or more	2.60	0.80	0.20	0.10	—	—	—	—	—

was 13.16 percent or more, more than 1 percent greater than the 12.16 percent average annual return of the S&P 500 EW. In 22.1 percent of portfolios sampled, the 10-stock portfolio outperformed by 2 percent or more, which equates to an average return of 14.16 or more. In 2.6 percent of cases, about 1-in-40, the 10-stock portfolios outperformed by 5 percent or more, meaning they generated an average return of 17.16 percent or more. Of course, the corollary here is also true. The 250-stock portfolios only underperformed by 1 percent or more in 0.2 percent of cases, and didn't underperform by 2 percent or more at any time. The 10-stock portfolios, on the other hand, underperformed by 1 percent or more 35.2 percent of the time, and underperformed by 5 percent or more in 2.6 percent of the trials. All that this exercise demonstrates is that concentrating a portfolio improves the chance that the performance of the portfolio deviates from the performance of the underlying index, not that it improves the performance over the underlying index. The expected return of a randomly selected portfolio is still the underlying average. We're not interested in matching the average. There's no point attempting to deviate from the market if we don't intend to outperform it. Let's consider that problem next.

We've long known that undervalued stocks outperform the market. What happens if we rank stocks by undervaluation and then examine the performance of increasingly concentrated portfolios containing increasingly undervalued stocks? While the investors in this book favor free cash flow-based metrics, one very rough proxy for undervaluation is the extent to which a stock's market price is discounted from its book value. The metric for considering this is known as *price-to-book value.* All else being equal, the lower the price-to-book value, the cheaper the stock, and vice versa. Using data collated by Kenneth R. French, the Roth Family Distinguished Professor of Finance at the Tuck School of Business at Dartmouth College, we can examine a universe of stock portfolios ranked on price-to-book value. We divide the universe of 3,443 stocks into five portfolios as of September 2014. The "Market" portfolio contains all of the stocks available for inclusion in the study. We then create four portfolios of increasing concentration. The "Cheapest Half" contains the half of stocks in the Market portfolio with the lowest price-to-book value, or 1,959 stocks as of September 2014. The "Cheapest Third" contains the third with the lowest price-to-book value, or 1,105 stocks; the "Cheapest Fifth" contains the 20 percent of stocks with the lowest price-to-book value, 749 stocks, and the "Cheapest Tenth" contains the 10 percent of stocks with the lowest price-to-book value, or 407 stocks, all as of September 2014. The portfolios are rebalanced annually, and we track the performance from July 1, 1929, through to September 30, 2014. The chart in Figure 4.2 shows the compound performance of each portfolio.

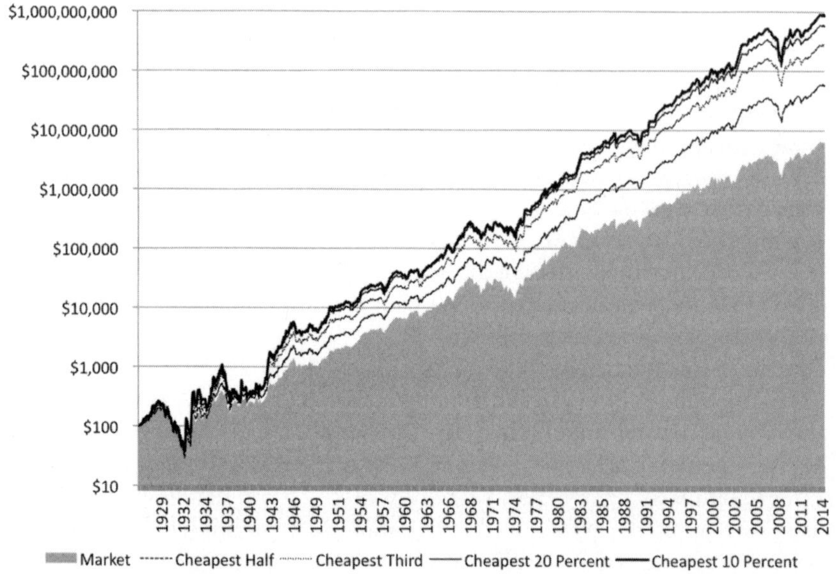

FIGURE 4.2 Logarithmic Performance Chart of Price-to-Book Value Portfolios (1929 to 2014)
Source: Carbon Beach Asset Management, LLC, and Kenneth R. French.

The chart in Figure 4.2 demonstrates that, as we concentrate into increasingly undervalued stocks ranked on price-to-book value, we get increasingly better returns. The Cheapest Tenth winds up ahead of the Cheapest Fifth, which beats the Cheapest Third, and so on. The logarithmic nature of the chart understates how much more capital the Cheapest Tenth accumulates over the other portfolios, so let's look at the performance statistics in Table 4.4.

Table 4.4 contains the return statistics for each of the portfolios. The Market portfolio returned 13.4 percent compound over the full period. Ignoring the impact of taxes and trading costs, $100 on July 1, 1929, became

TABLE 4.4 Performance Statistics for Price-to-Book Value Portfolios (1929 to 2014)

	Market	Cheapest Half	Cheapest Third	Cheapest Fifth	Cheapest Tenth
CAGR (%)	13.4	16.2	18.3	19.4	19.9
Standard deviation (%)	7.4	7.8	8.8	9.4	10.4

$6.2 million by September 30, 2014. The Cheapest Tenth portfolio returned 19.9 percent compounded over the full period, which turned $100 on July 1, 1929, into an extraordinary $863 million by September 30, 2014, 139 times more capital than the market portfolio. The Cheapest Tenth also outperformed the Cheapest Fifth, which returned 19.4 percent compounded over the full period. While that may only seem like a small advantage, it leaves the Cheapest Tenth with 50 percent more capital than the Cheapest Fifth, which accumulated $579 million by the end of the trial. Clearly, concentrating into undervalued stocks led to better performance. But even our "concentrated" portfolio here—the Cheapest 10 percent, which contains 407 stocks—still contains more stocks than we would ordinarily consider to be concentrated. How do *extremely* concentrated portfolios of value stocks perform?

O'Shaughnessy Asset Management's Patrick O'Shaughnessy, CFA, author of *Millennial Money: How Young Investors Can Build a Fortune* (2014, Palgrave Macmillan), considered this question in a November 2014 post on *The Investor's Field Guide* website called "How Concentrated Should You Make Your Value Portfolio?"[19] O'Shaughnessy examined 50 years of market data from 1964 to 2014 to form portfolios of the most undervalued stocks (including American Depositary Receipts) trading in the United States. O'Shaughnessy's value portfolios ranged in size from as many as 100 stocks to as few as 1 stock. To qualify for selection, each stock needed a minimum market cap of $200 million (inflation adjusted to 2014 dollars). He ranked each stock in the universe on the basis of its fundamental value, defined as an equal weighted combination of its price-to-earnings ratio, price-to-sales ratio, enterprise multiple (*earnings before interest, taxes, depreciation, and amortization/enterprise value*), free cash flow-to-enterprise value and total shareholder yield (its dividend yield plus or minus any shares issued or bought back). Each portfolio was rebalanced on a rolling annual basis to remove any seasonal biases and make the test more robust. O'Shaughnessy updated the results to 2015 for this book. Figure 4.3 and Table 4.5 show the updated results.

TABLE 4.5 Performance Statistics for Concentrated Combination Value Portfolios, Rolling Annual Rebalance (1963 to 2015)

Number of Stocks	300	200	100	50	40	30	25	20	15	10	5	1
Return (%)	17.2	17.9	18.6	19.5	19.8	20.1	20.4	20.4	20.7	20.6	21.6	22.8
Sharpe ratio	0.73	0.78	0.81	0.84	0.84	0.84	0.85	0.84	0.83	0.80	0.78	0.63

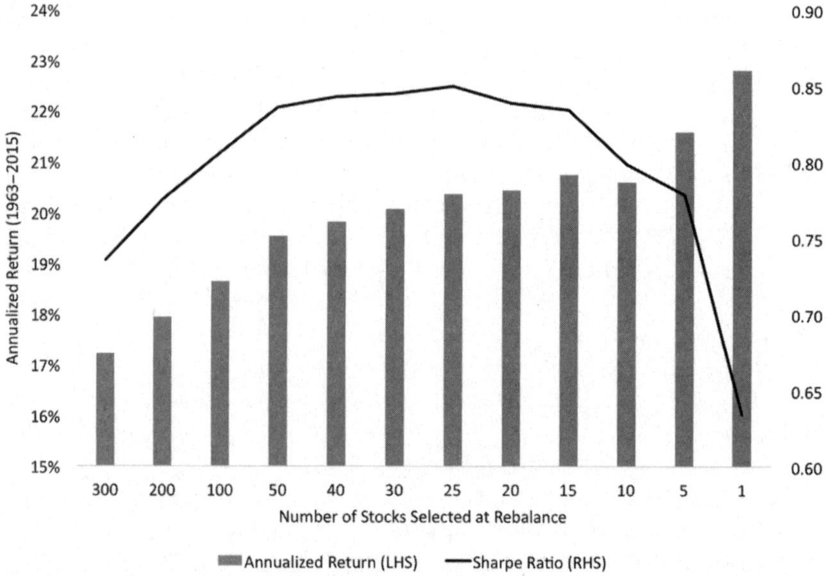

FIGURE 4.3 Concentrated Combination Value Portfolios, Rolling Annual Rebalance (1963 to 2015)
Source: O'Shaughnessy Asset Management, LLC.

O'Shaughnessy found the one-stock portfolios generated the best raw returns at 22.8 percent per year compound. As the number of portfolio holdings swelled from one, the raw returns fell off in rank order. The 25-stock portfolios generated the best Sharpe ratio—a measure of risk-adjusted returns—at 0.85. As the portfolio holdings increased beyond 25 positions, the risk-adjusted returns diminished in rank order. O'Shaughnessy's research shows that portfolios perform better as they become more concentrated on the most undervalued stocks. The findings bear out Buffett's advocacy for concentrated value portfolios. Buffett earlier argued that if he "were running $50, $100, $200 million, [he] would have 80 percent in five positions, with 25 percent for the largest."[20] These analyses assume that we equally weight the positions in each portfolio. Can we do better by increasing the size of our best positions using Kelly theory? If so, what should we consider as we do so?

KELLY BETTIN' VALUE INVESTORS

Though Thorp was a convertible arbitrageur, he closely followed the application of the Kelly Criterion to value investment. His son attended the Value Investors Congress held in Pasadena, California, in May 2007, and reported back to him that "everyone" said they were using the Kelly Criterion.[21] Thorp identified several potential problems with value investors' application of the Kelly Criterion, the first of which is that they may fail to consider the opportunity costs of a position. Thorp offers the following example to illustrate this point. Suppose that a value investor's portfolio has one investment that requires a bet greater than, or equal to, half the portfolio capital, and is offered a second opportunity with the same payoff probabilities. Then the optimal strategy must be to invest in both equally. If the optimal Kelly bet for each is greater than 50 percent of the capital, the total capital committed to the positions cannot be more than the capital. Betting 50 percent of capital or more in both opportunities risks a total loss, which Kelly always avoids. So the optimal bet must be less than 50 percent of capital. Thorp argues that the same reasoning applies for any set of opportunities of two or more, and hence "we need to know the other investments currently in the portfolio, any candidates for new investments, and their (joint) properties, in order to find the Kelly optimal fraction for each new investment, along with possible revisions for existing investments."[22] Thorp notes that Buffett's concentrated bets—35 percent of his fund in Sanborn Map, and 40 percent of his fund in American Express—offer "considerable evidence" that he thinks like a Kelly-betting investor. He notes that, given that bets of that magnitude must be considered in context with other opportunities, and bets must be less than one's capital to avoid total loss, Kelly must have indicated betting much more than 35 percent to 40 percent of capital in those cases, and others like them. He notes that the *opportunity cost principle* suggests that the optimal Kelly bet in isolation must have been "higher, perhaps much higher."[23] Thorp suggests that one of the most common oversights made in the use of the Kelly Criterion is computing the optimal Kelly bet without considering the available alternative investments.[24]

> *It is a dangerous error because it generally overestimates* [*the optimal Kelly size.*]

Thorp also notes that full Kelly betting is characterized by drawdowns that are "too large for the comfort of many investors," and says, "many, perhaps most investors" will find fractional Kelly "much more to their liking."[25] He further observes that errors in estimating the lower bound of possible returns, or the probability of the lower bound occurring in a *Black Swan*–type scenario—an infrequent, unexpected high-impact event—means that the optimal Kelly bet might be overestimated. Properly incorporating these two considerations might lead to a lower Kelly bet than the one calculated. Finally, Thorp noted that "Kelly's superior properties are asymptotic, appearing with increasing probability as time increases," but "an investor or bettor may not choose to make, or be able to make, enough Kelly bets for the probability to be 'high enough' for these asymptotic properties to prevail," by which he means that the long run is simply too long for Kelly's good properties to emerge.

If we concentrate using a simple value investing method, we will deviate from the market over the long run, but in a positive way. And as we concentrate further, we get better and better results. For this reason, value investors have advocated concentration balanced by limited diversification on the basis that even relatively safe investments, purchased at a discount to intrinsic value, have some probability of downside risk. In his book *Margin of Safety*, investor Seth Klarman wrote:[26]

> *The deleterious effects of such improbable events can best be mitigated through prudent diversification. The number of securities that should be owned to reduce portfolio risk to an acceptable lever is not great; as few as ten to fifteen different holdings usually suffice.*

Benjamin Graham too was an advocate of limited diversification. In *The Intelligent Investor* (1949), he advocated a minimum portfolio size of 10 and a maximum of 30 holdings. Graham's recommendations approximately coincide with the academic research, which holds that the optimal number of positions in a portfolio is somewhere between 10 and 30. Klarman, Buffett, and Munger recommend fewer positions—5 for Buffett and Munger, 10 to 15 for Klarman—all of which broadly agree with the research that best returns for value investors can be had at very concentrated portfolios, along with O'Shaughnessy's finding that 25 positions offered the best risk-adjusted return. In the following chapters, we examine the philosophies and returns of several concentrated value investors. Whether they explicitly calculate positions using the Kelly Formula, or simply concentrate into positions intuitively without making an explicit calculation, they all have exceptional long-term track records. First, we examine the track record and philosophy of Buffett's business partner and friend Charlie Munger, vice chairman of Berkshire Hathaway.

NOTES

1. Warren Buffett, "Chairman's Letter," Berkshire Hathaway, Inc. *Annual Report*, 1993.
2. Alice Schroeder, *The Snowball* (New York: Bantam Books, 2008).
3. Norman C. Miller, *The Great Salad Oil Swindle* (New York: Coward McCann, 1965).

4. Alice Schroeder, *The Snowball* (New York: Bantam Books, 2008).
5. Warren Buffett, "Chairman's Letter," Berkshire Hathaway, Inc., 1980.
6. Alice Schroeder, *The Snowball* (New York: Bantam Books, 2008).
7. Warren Buffett, "Chairman's Letter," Berkshire Hathaway, Inc., 1989.
8. Warren Buffett, "Partnership Letter: 1967," Buffett Associates Limited, October 9, 1967.
9. Ibid.
10. Leonard MacLean, Edward O. Thorp, and William T. Ziemba, "Good and Bad Properties of the Kelly Criterion," Unpublished, January 1, 2010.
11. E. J. Elton and M. J. Gruber, "Risk Reduction and Portfolio Size: An Analytic Solution," *Journal of Business* 50 (October 1977): 415–437.
12. Meir Statman, "How Many Stocks Make a Diversified Portfolio?" *Journal of Financial and Quantitative Analysis* 22 (1987): 353–363, doi: 10.2307/2330969.
13. Dang Le, "Notes from Buffett Meeting 2/15/2008," *Underground Value*, February 23, 2008, http://undergroundvalue.blogspot.com/2008/02/notes-from-buffett-meeting-2152008_23.html.
14. Warren Buffett, "Chairman's Letter," Berkshire Hathaway, Inc., 1988.
15. Charles Munger, "A Lesson on Elementary, Worldly Wisdom as It Relates to Investment Management and Business," transcript of talk to University of Southern California Business School, 1994, https://web.archive.org/web/20060208032616/http://ycombinator.com/munger.html.
16. Steven Goldberg, "The World According to 'Poor Charlie,'" *Kiplinger Magazine*, December 2005.
17. Allen's quote from the "Daily Journal Company Annual Meeting 2013."
18. Robert G. Hagstrom, *The Warren Buffett Portfolio* (New York: John Wiley & Sons, 1999).
19. Patrick O'Shaughnessy, "How Concentrated Should You Make Your Value Portfolio?" *The Investor's Field Guide,* November 2014, http://investorfield-guide.com/2014115how-concentrated-should-you-make-your-value-portfolio/.
20. Dang Le, "Notes from Buffett Meeting 2/15/2008," *Underground Value*, February 23, 2008, http://undergroundvalue.blogspot.com/2008/02/notes-from-buffett-meeting-2152008_23.html.
21. Leonard C. MacLean, Edward O. Thorp, and William T. Ziemba, "The Kelly Capital Growth Investment Criterion: Theory and Practice," *World Scientific Publishing Company*, 2011.
22. Ibid.
23. Ibid.
24. Ibid.
25. Ibid.
26. Seth A. Klarman, *Margin of Safety: Risk-Averse Value Investing Strategies for the Thoughtful Investor* (New York: HarperCollins, 1991).

CHAPTER 5

Charlie Munger: Concentration's Muse

Quality without Compromise

That ought to be the general theme of your book because having noticed this subject for a great many decades, I would say practically everybody that I run across that has a very good record for a very long time, he doesn't do it by owning one hundred different securities over twenty different sub-sections of the economy. You get one Bill Miller or something out of people that try to do that and he's fairly concentrated in a sense in little segments but basically the ones that last are people who run fairly concentrated portfolios. How could it be otherwise in a certain sense?

—Charlie Munger, 2014[1]

At the urging of Warren Buffett, Charlie Munger launched his investment firm, Wheeler, Munger & Company in 1962. He partnered with Jack Wheeler, a stock exchange floor trader and co-owner of two specialist posts on the Pacific Coast Stock Exchange.[2] The new firm acquired the specialist posts, rented a tiny mezzanine office at the stock exchange, and set about raising capital for an investment partnership structured along the same lines as the Buffett partnerships. Munger approached family, friends, and former clients to invest, promising the capital would be managed by Munger and his law partner, Roy Tolles, along the same lines as Buffett did. True to his word, Buffett and Munger often invested in the same companies. They talked regularly by telephone. While their portfolios weren't exactly the same—they didn't buy exactly the same securities in the same quantities—their portfolios did overlap.[3] Notably, they shared an investment in Diversified Retailing, which held two chains of retail stores, and bought control of Blue Chip Stamps, in which Buffett was the largest shareholder and Munger the second largest.[4] Munger says that Buffett acted as a mentor to him in money management.[5]

> *Warren's original mentor was Ben Graham. Warren said, "I never outgrew Ben Graham," but he did. You could argue my mentor was Warren. Warren was the one who talked me into going into investment management. But, I had my own way of doing things, too. Warren and I naturally think the same way.*

Like Buffett's, Wheeler, Munger's investment performance was stunning. For the first 11 years of operation, from 1962 to 1972, the partnership grossed 28.3 percent per year compound, beating the market's 6.7 percent compound return by 21.7 percent per year, an enormous margin. While the market experienced three down years in that period (–7.6 percent in 1962, –15.8 percent in 1966, and –11.6 percent in 1969), Wheeler, Munger had just one, a very mild –0.1 percent in 1971. Ignoring the impact of taxes, at the end of 1972, an investor in Wheeler, Munger was almost eight times better off than a similar investor in the S&P 500. The next three years would not be so kind, as Table 5.1 demonstrates.

In 1973, Wheeler, Munger had its first significant down year, –31.9 percent over a period when the market dropped just –13.1 percent. 1974 was almost a replay of 1973, with Wheeler, Munger dropping –31.5 percent while the market dropped just –23.1 percent. Even a monster 73.2 percent return in 1975 couldn't bring the partnership to summit its old peak. When Munger wound it up at the end of 1975, it was still 19.2 percent below the high water mark it achieved in 1972. Still, over the full 14-year period, Wheeler, Munger returned 19.8 percent compound, beating the market's 4.9 percent by almost 15 percent a year. $100,000 invested in Wheeler, Munger at the start of 1962, had by the end of 1975 become $1.26 million before taxes, while $100,000 invested in the S&P 500 became $196,170 before taxes, leaving a Wheeler, Munger investor with 6.4 times the capital.

The sources of Wheeler, Munger's pain in 1973 and 1974 were two positions, one in the Fund of Letters, a registered investment company, and another in Blue Chip Stamps. Munger had bought control of the Fund of Letters in late 1972.[6] It was so called because it was filled with "letter stock," a security issued without the ordinary suite of SEC-mandated disclosure on the proviso that it not be on-sold until a prospectus could be registered with the SEC. During the often-extended period of time in which no prospectus

TABLE 5.1 Returns of Wheeler, Munger

Year End	Return (%)	S&P 500 (%)	Excess (%)
1962	30.1	–7.6	37.7
1963	71.7	20.6	51.1
1964	49.7	18.7	31
1965	8.4	14.2	–5.8
1966	12.4	–15.8	28.2
1967	56.2	19	37.2
1968	40.4	7.7	32.7
1969	28.3	–11.6	39.9
1970	–0.1	8.7	–8.8
1971	25.4	9.8	15.6
1972	8.3	18.2	–9.9
1973	–31.9	–13.1	–18.8
1974	–31.5	–23.1	–8.4
1975	73.2	44.4	28.8
CAGR	**19.8**	**4.9**	**14.9**
AAR	**24.3**	**6.4**	**17.9**
St. Dev	**33.0**	**18.5**	**14.5**

Source: Warren Buffett, "Superinvestors of Graham-and-Doddsville," *Hermes Magazine*, Columbia Business School, Fall 1984.

was registered, the letter stock was unsalable on market and extremely illiquid. As the market surged ahead in the go-go 1960s, letter stock became a popular investment. The slump in the late 1960s saw the closed-end fund trade at a substantial discount to its wilting, mostly letter stock net asset value. Seeing the wide discount to the underlying assets, Munger stepped into the market and eventually got control:[7]

> *In the early days both Warren and I would sometimes buy control of a company in the market. We don't do that anymore by the way. We haven't done that for decades but in the early days we did some of that. Warren bought control of Berkshire Hathaway in the market.*

Munger immediately changed the fund's name to *New America Fund*, and replaced its board of directors. He also changed the investment style to the same approach he was applying in Wheeler, Munger.[8] Where the Fund of Letters had operated like a venture capital fund, the New America Fund became a public company value investor. Munger tipped out the letter stock and redirected the capital to undervalued publishing and broadcast stocks.[9] Preeminent among the holdings were Capital Cities Communications, and the Daily Journal Corporation, 100 percent owned by New America Fund.[10]

Of course, the changes at New America would not bear fruit for some time. In the interim, the stock slumped from Wheeler, Munger's $9.22 average purchase price in late 1972—a substantial discount to its liquidation value—to $3.75 in late 1974, at which time New America had a net asset value per share of $9.28, a testament to how cheaply the stock had been bought.[11] Similarly, Wheeler, Munger's position in Blue Chip Stamps had slumped from its $7.50 average purchase price to $5.25 at the end of 1974.[12] While he didn't mind unrealized losses in his personal account, Munger found the mark-to-market losses in Wheeler, Munger's partnership accounts unbearable.[13] He decided that there were problems with the limited partnership structure that made it suboptimal for managing money. The main problem was that clients could withdraw capital at short notice, and withdrawals tended to coincide with market bottoms. Right when Munger wanted to put the capital to work, he could be forced to pay some out to a partner who wanted to withdraw. Few ever did, but the threat was sufficient for him to decide to liquidate the partnership. In 1976, Wheeler, Munger's limited partners received stock in the New America Fund, which Munger continued to operate until 1986, and the two investments Munger shared with Buffett, Blue Chip Stamps and Diversified Retailing, both of which were later acquired by Berkshire Hathaway in stock swaps. (Wheeler, Munger owned 10 percent of Diversified Retailing, which, like New America Fund, had been acquired at a discount to liquidation value.) When asked if he considered publishing his Wheeler, Munger partnership letters, Munger responds that he'd "never considered it:"[14]

> *Warren worked harder on his than I worked on mine. I would not be ecstatic about—I became gradually a better investor than I started and so did Warren by the way. The secret of [Munger, Buffett, and Simpson's] investment records is not the one people would ordinarily draw. In other words, they would not have been as good as they were except for the continuous learning that made each protagonist better and better as the decades rolled on. The game was getting harder and we were getting better. At the end of course, the records drifted toward mediocrity because there's so much brain power in the investment management field now and so many different little niches and so much diligence that it's a very different field than the one we started*

in. There's way more competition and of course when you have a lot of money that you're managing it's very hard to take positions and get rid of positions. There are smaller companies that you can't really bother looking at because they won't move the needle like most small caps or medium caps in the case of Berkshire. And so as the game got harder, the results got less because we were managing so much more money. That happens to virtually every investment manager who takes in more and more money or keeps all the gains that he's made in the past. Whatever the cause, as they get to managing more and more money it's harder to outperform in relation to the averages.

BLUE CHIP STAMPS AND SEE'S CANDIES

Blue Chip Stamps is an important company in the history of Munger, Buffett, and Berkshire Hathaway. It was the vehicle through which Berkshire Hathaway acquired See's Candies, *Buffalo News*, and Wesco Financial, all of which are also star players in the Berkshire tale. Blue Chip Stamps issued *trading stamps*, which, like a rudimentary predecessor to frequent flyer miles, were distributed by retailers as an incentive to keep customers coming back. Retailers bought the stamps from Blue Chip, and gave them out to customers when they made purchases. Customers collected the stamps and could redeem them from Blue Chip for prizes like toys or toasters.[15] It was created in 1956 by a syndicate of nine retailers—Chevron Oil, Thrifty Drugs, and several large Californian grocery chains—that had been excluded from another trading stamp program, S&H Green Stamps. What attracted Buffett and Munger was the company's *float*. Blue Chip Stamps held cash from the time retailers bought the stamps until customers collected enough to redeem a prize, which ordinarily took time. Many stamps were lost or forgotten, and the float built up until in the early 1970s, when it was worth almost $100 million in a business that generated sales of $120 million a year.[16] Like insurance float, Blue Chip Stamps' float could be invested until it was needed to pay for prizes. Forty-five percent of Blue Chip Stamps' stock was held by the nine retailers who had established it, and the remainder by thousands of little retailers who had received shares after the Department of Justice used the anti-trust legislation to compel the founders to distribute ownership more broadly in 1963.[17] The stock, which was traded over the counter and largely unknown, was "very cheap," according to Buffett.[18] He bought aggressively and became the largest shareholder, with Munger the second-largest. Eventually, Berkshire, Buffett, and Munger controlled 75 percent of Blue Chip Stamps' outstanding stock, with the largest block held by Berkshire at 60 percent.[19] Buffett and Munger quickly gained control of Blue Chip Stamps' investment committee once they were on the board, and as the trading stamp business slowly liquidated, directed the float to more productive uses. The trading stamp business had peaked in 1970 with sales of $124 million, and began a long, slow decline, which saw sales trough in the early 1990s at just $100,000 a year, when trading stamps were issued by a few bowling alleys, about which Munger quipped, "So I presided over a failure of 99.99 percent. I laid an egg."[20] Even so, Blue Chip Stamps did phenomenally well with the capital invested elsewhere. In 1972, Blue Chip Stamps had a net worth of $46 million. By the end of 1981, net worth had increased to $169 million.[21] In 1981, Munger wrote to the shareholders of Blue Chip Stamps about the investment portfolio:[22]

> *We began the 1970s with a single business, trading stamps, which was destined to decline to a small fraction of its former size, and a portfolio of securities, offsetting stamp redemption liabilities, which had been selected by previous owners and would have led to a disastrous result if held through the present time.*

(Coincidentally, one of Blue Chip Stamps' early acquisitions under Buffett and Munger's direction was Source Capital, a troubled closed-end investment company established by the go-go manager Fred Carr—the same Fred Carr who briefly hired Lou Simpson in 1969.[23]) Buffett and Munger quickly found a new target for Blue Chip Stamps' float—See's Candies, the biggest purchase Buffett or Munger had made up to that point.

When Robert Flaherty, an investment adviser to Blue Chip, called Buffett in November 1971 to tell him that See's Candies was for sale, Buffett famously responded, "Gee, Bob. The *candy* business? I don't think we want to be in the candy business," and the line went dead.[24] When they tried to call Buffett back the secretary misdialed the number, and several minutes passed before they could get through. When they did, Buffett spoke before they could get out a word, "I was taking a look at the numbers. Yeah, I'd be willing to buy See's at a price."[25] Buffett and Munger met with Harry See, son of the eponymous founder, See's soon-to-be-retired chief executive, and another See's executive, Chuck Huggins, at a Los Angeles hotel. There were two issues to resolve: (1) the price, and (2) who would run the company.

Knowing the chief executive planned on retiring, Buffett said to See, "If we go through with this, we don't run companies. I need to know who will run the company."[26]

See looked at Huggins, and responded, "Chuck will."[27]

Buffett said, "That's fine,"[28] and Huggins was anointed chief executive-in-waiting. The See family wanted $30 million for the company, but Buffett was unwilling to go above $25 million, which was already more than three times book value. The talks ended without a resolution on the price. Later, Harry See called Buffett and accepted the $25 million, and Blue Chip acquired See's Candies on January 3, 1972, for $25 million.

Until See's Candies, both Buffett and Munger had looked for Benjamin Grahamesque opportunities, those that traded at a discount to book or liquidation value. Indeed, Wheeler, Munger had bought its three main holdings, New America Fund, Diversified Retailing, and Blue Chip Stamps at a wide discount to liquidation value. At three times book value, See's represented a significant departure from Buffett's previous Grahamite investments. It would deliver an important lesson to Munger:[29]

> *It was acquired at a premium over book and it worked. Hochschild, Kohn, the department store chain, was bought at a discount from book and liquidating value. It didn't work. Those two things together helped shift our thinking to the idea of paying higher prices for better businesses.*

See's turned out to be an excellent business, and Buffett and Munger couldn't help but notice how much easier it was to run a business that organically grew at a high rate funded by its own retained earnings. That property allowed it to grow and return cash at the same time, which Buffett and Munger could direct to other purchases. In his 2007 letter to shareholders, Buffett described See's as the "prototype of a dream business."[30] That year it earned for Berkshire Hathaway, Inc., $82 million on just $40 million of capital, generating an extraordinary 195 percent return on capital. The more than sixteen-fold growth in earnings from $5 million to $82 million required only a five-fold growth in invested capital. This allowed See's to return to Berkshire Hathaway all the earnings it generated between 1972 and 2007—$1.35 billion—less the $32 million required for See's organic growth. By way of comparison, Buffett estimated that an average business would have required an additional $400 million invested in working capital and fixed assets to grow earnings in the same magnitude, and would have been worth less than See's after having done so. Instead, Buffett and Munger were able to redirect most of See's excess earnings to purchase other high-quality businesses, and Berkshire Hathaway became a financial powerhouse. It taught Munger that some businesses were "worth paying up a bit to get in with for a long-term advantage."[31]

> [*T*]*he trick is to get more quality than you pay for in price. It's just that simple.*

Through See's, Munger observed that a high-quality business could provide more margin of safety than a purchase price at a discount from liquidation value. They also required less attention and activity from the owners. Stocks trading at a discount to liquidation value typically owned poor businesses. Low-quality businesses took time and energy to right, and often couldn't be helped. Munger had learned how difficult it was to operate a mediocre business as a director of an International Harvester dealership in Bakersfield. The business's problems were baked into its business model. It needed capital to grow because each new machine had to be purchased before it could be sold, tying up capital that just sat on the lot. See's did the opposite. It not only grew without soaking up capital, but threw off cash as it did so. It was a revelation to Buffett and Munger. How could they identify other such businesses?

Philip Fisher, a renowned San Francisco–based growth investor, had written the growth investor's bible with his 1958 book *Common Stocks and Uncommon Profits*.[32] Fisher advocated the use of the "scuttlebutt method" to identify qualitative factors that might give an investor an original insight into a potential investment. Gleaned from competitors, customers, or suppliers, these qualitative considerations might include the quality of management; the utility of the research and development, or technology; the business's service ability or customer orientation; or the effectiveness of marketing. Fisher used information reaped through the scuttlebutt method to determine the business's ability to grow and defend its market against competitors through technological superiority, service excellence, or a consumer "franchise."[33] Buffett readily absorbed the lessons, and blended Phil Fisher's philosophy with Benjamin Graham's. Graham had codified the philosophy of value investment: the concept of intrinsic value as a quantity distinct from price, and the importance of a margin of safety. Fisher showed that the margin of safety could be found in the quality of the business, which would allow it grow organically. In 1989, Buffett would distill the investment lessons he had learned from Graham, Fisher, and See's into a single sentence, "It's far better to buy a wonderful company at a fair price than a fair company at a wonderful price."[34] It would become a familiar refrain. Buffett acknowledged Munger's influence on his "wonderful company at a fair price" investment process. In 1989, he said, "Charlie understood this early; I was a slow learner. But now, when buying companies or common stocks, we look for first-class businesses accompanied by first-class managements."[35] Of course, Munger remained a value investor. In 2013, at the Daily Journal Company meeting, Munger said of the businesses he likes to buy:[36]

> *The desirability of a business with outstanding economic characteristics can be ruined by the price you pay for it. The opposite is not true.*

Still, in 1972, Buffett and Munger weren't done buying at a discount to book value. When a line of stock in the parent company of Pasadena-based Mutual Savings and Loan Association, Wesco Financial, became available in late summer 1972, Buffett and Munger directed $2 million of Blue Chip's capital to purchase the 8 percent stake.[37] In January 1973, Wesco announced plans to merge with another savings and loan, Financial Corporation of Santa Barbara (Financial Corp.), on very unfavorable terms. When they learned about the transaction, Buffett and Munger were incensed.[38] Wesco would be exchanging its undervalued stock for overvalued stock in Financial Corp. Munger wanted to buy enough stock to block the merger. Buffett was reluctant, but Munger prevailed, and Blue Chip Stamps waded into the market, taking its position to 17 percent of Wesco.[39] Buffett and Munger persuaded another large shareholder, Betty Peters, the daughter of Wesco's founder, to vote along with Blue Chip, and the merger was defeated.[40] Allowed to buy just 3 percent more without regulatory approval, Buffett and Munger decided to offer $17 per share—the implied per share value of the merger—even though the stock was likely to decline in the short term. They felt it was the only fair way to behave because it was Blue Chip who had defeated the merger. That decision would draw the attention of the SEC, and become a major impediment to Blue Chip's everyday business.

The SEC alleged that Blue Chip, by making the $17 per share bid, had unlawfully manipulated the stock of Wesco. They suspected that Buffett and Munger had bought shares at a premium to the market to artificially prop up the price of Wesco's shares in the weeks following the defeat of the merger. The SEC also found fault with Blue Chip's acquisition of shares prior to the merger, which they alleged had been undertaken to defeat the merger. On the face of it, the SEC's complaints were true—Blue Chip Stamps had bought more stock prior to the merger in order to defeat it, and had paid above market prices for the Wesco shares to prop up the market—but how those actions amounted to wrongdoing was difficult to fathom. Blue Chip's real problem was that it still had on it the stink of the earlier antitrust action, and though it had occurred under different managers, was still viewed in a dim light by the SEC. Further complicating the issue was the highly complex, crisscrossed shareholdings between Buffett, Munger, Berkshire Hathaway, and Blue Chip, which the SEC thought may be for the purposes of hiding some type of fraud. Buffett and Munger acknowledged the apparent complexity of the shareholdings, which had grown organically over time, but denied that it was constructed with any intent to obscure anything untoward, or that it created a conflict of interest. The SEC filed and concurrently settled a lawsuit against Blue Chip, which did not require Buffett or Munger to admit guilt, but did require them to promise not to do it again.[41] They were also required to provide $115,000 in compensation to

Wesco shareholders whom the SEC identified as being damaged by the trading.[42] In the wake of the settlement, Buffett and Munger decided to restructure the cross-shareholdings in Berkshire, Blue Chip, and Wesco. Wesco was consolidated into Blue Chip, and then Blue Chip and Berkshire merged in 1983. Berkshire acquired the 40 percent it did not own in a scrip-for-scrip transaction that gave Blue Chip shareholders an 8 percent interest in Berkshire. When the dust had settled, Munger ended up with 2 percent of Berkshire and joined the board as vice-chairman. After the merger of the three entities, Berkshire had assets of $1.6 billion. Buffett and Munger had merged their financial relationship, and settled on a single, defining investment philosophy: wonderful companies at fair prices.

THE BUFFALO NEWS

The third piece of the Blue Chip puzzle, and the clearest indication that Buffett and Munger were chasing a new type of target was the 1977 purchase of the nearly 100-year-old *Buffalo Evening News*. Buffett and Munger bid three times for the News, and eventually paid a price that made sense only through the new *wonderful company* lens. Their first offer of $30 million was refused. [43] They raised the bid to $32 million.[44] That bid was also refused. They wrote the final bid on a sheet of yellow legal paper. It was high, considering the *Buffalo News* had earned just $1.7 million pre-tax in 1976. When the amount, $32.5 million, which represented 25 percent of Berkshire Hathaway's net worth, was accepted, Buffett and Munger became the proprietors of an establishment Eastern newspaper. Though it was a marquis acquisition, it was not without its problems. Buffalo was fast becoming a rust-belt city, and the paper had militant unions, and a strong competitor, the *Buffalo Courier-Express*, once edited by Mark Twain. Though the *Buffalo Evening News* sold four times as many issues as the *Courier-Express* through the week, the *Courier-Express*'s Sunday edition kept it alive because the *Buffalo Evening News* didn't publish on Sunday.[45] Buffett and Munger recognized that only one paper could survive in Buffalo, and they were determined that it be the *Buffalo Evening News*. They quickly made two significant changes, dropping the "Evening" from the paper's title, and starting a Sunday edition. The Sunday edition was given away to subscribers, and sold for 30 cents against the *Courier-Express*'s 50 cents. The *Courier-Express* retaliated by suing the News for antitrust violations, obtaining an injunction that prevented the News from publishing on Sunday. The injunction, which persisted for two years, tipped the News into the red, causing it to lose $4.6 million in 1979. At the same time, Buffalo struggled with employment, losing 23 percent of heavy industrial manufacturing jobs. As unemployment in Buffalo surged to 15 percent, retailers failed and advertising revenues dropped. In 1981, Munger wrote to the shareholders of Blue Chip Stamps about his disappointment with the News acquisition:[46]

> *We should now have about $70 million in value of other assets, earnings over $10 million per year, in place of the* Buffalo Evening News *and its current red ink. No matter what happens in the future in Buffalo we are about 100 percent sure to have an economic place lower than we would have occupied if we had not made our purchase.*

Although they couldn't know it then, the *Courier-Express* was suffering even more pain than the News, and would shortly go under. In September 1982, a few months after Munger's note to the shareholders of Blue Chip, the paper folded, and the News saw the first crack of sunshine through the clouds. In his 1983 letter to shareholders, Buffett wrote that the *Buffalo News* had "somewhat exceeded its targeted profit margin of 10 percent after tax," which was "about average for newspapers such as the News:"[47]

> *[T]he paper's performance, nevertheless, was a significant achievement considering the economic and retailing environment in Buffalo. Buffalo has a concentration of heavy industry, a segment of the economy that was hit particularly hard by the recent recession and that has lagged the recovery. As Buffalo consumers have suffered, so also have the paper's retailing customers. Their numbers have shrunk over the past few years and many of those surviving have cut their linage. Within this environment the News has one exceptional strength: its acceptance by the public, a matter measured by the paper's "penetration ratio"—the percentage of households within the community purchasing the paper each day.*

Buffett waxed poetic about the News' penetration ratio, noting that it "stood number one in weekday penetration among the 100 largest papers in the United States . . . far ahead of many of the country's best-known dailies."[48] He tracked the News' penetration ratio because it was "the best measure of the strength of its franchise."[49]

> *Papers with unusually high penetration in the geographical area that is of prime interest to major local retailers, and with relatively little circulation elsewhere, are exceptionally efficient buys for those retailers. Low-penetration papers have a far less compelling message to present to advertisers.*

Buffett held that one important factor contributing to the News's success was the size of its "news hole," which he defined as "editorial material—not ads."[50] At 50 percent of the newspaper's content, the News provided readers with "over 25 percent more news than the typical paper."[51]

> *Properly written and edited, a full serving of news makes our paper more valuable to the reader and contributes to our unusual penetration ratio.*

Buffett noted that the large news hole policy cost the News significant extra money for newsprint, and its "news costs"—"newsprint for the news hole plus payroll and expenses of the newsroom"—as a percentage of revenue ran higher than those of most dominant papers of the same size. He allowed, however, that there was "adequate room . . . to sustain these costs: the difference between 'high' and 'low' news costs at papers of comparable size runs perhaps three percentage points while pre-tax profit margins are often 10 times that amount:"[52]

> *The economics of a dominant newspaper are excellent, among the very best in the business world. Owners, naturally, would like to believe that their wonderful profitability is achieved only because they unfailingly turn out a wonderful product. That comfortable theory wilts before an uncomfortable fact. While first-class newspapers make excellent profits, the profits of third-rate papers are as good or better—as long as either class of paper is dominant within its community. Of course, product quality may have been crucial to the paper in achieving dominance.*

In 1986, 10 years after Buffett and Munger had purchased the Buffalo News, having endured the "dark days of financial reversals and litigation," Buffett could write the "financial rewards it has brought us have far exceeded our expectations and so, too, have the non-financial rewards."[53] The *Buffalo News* had by then become an unusually profitable newspaper. By 2000, almost 25 years after it had been purchased, it would earn $157 million in revenue, $53 million in pretax profit, and return 91.2 percent on assets—making it the most profitable newspaper in the United States.[54]

ON CONCENTRATION

In the book *Damn Right!*, Buffett told Munger's biographer Janet Lowe that Munger initially followed the fundamentals of value investment established by Graham, but was always far more concentrated than other traditional value investors like Walter Schloss:[55]

Charlie's portfolio was concentrated in very few securities and therefore his record was much more volatile but it was based on the same discount-from-value approach. He was willing to accept greater peaks and valleys of performance, and he happens to be a fellow whose whole psyche goes toward concentration, with results shown.

Munger defines "very few securities" as "no more than three:"[56]

My own inquiries on that subject were just to assume that I could find a few things, say three, each which had a substantial statistical expectancy of outperforming averages without creating catastrophe. If I could find three of those, what were the chances my pending record wouldn't be pretty damn good. I just sort of worked that out by iteration. That was my academic study—high school algebra and common sense.

Munger's rationale for holding so few stocks was based on practical considerations—"How could one man know enough [to] own a flowing portfolio of 150 securities and always outperform the averages? That would be a considerable stump."[57] He believes that securities are mostly appropriately valued:[58]

[T]he people that came up with the efficient market theory weren't totally crazy, but they pushed their idea too far. The idea is roughly right with exceptions.

That observation, and his own research, pressed him to seek only the handful of situations where he might have an edge:[59]

It would not be too much to say it was obvious to me that I could not have a big edge over everybody else and all securities. In other words, it was also obvious to me that if I worked at it, I would find a few things in which I had an unusual degree of competence. It was natural for me to think in terms of opportunity costs. So once I owned three securities—A, B, and C—I wasn't going to buy any other security. I had actually studied them. I don't know how much diversification would be necessary over a long period of time. I worked it out with pencil and paper as a matter of probabilities. If you are going to operate for 30 years and only own 3 securities but you had an expectancy of outperforming averages of say 4 points a year or something like that on each of those 3 securities, how much of a chance are you taking when you get a wildly worse result on the average. I'd work that out mathematically and assuming you'd stay for 30 years you'd have a more volatile record but the long-term expectancy was—in terms of disaster prevention—plenty good enough for 3 securities. I had worked that out in my own head using just high school algebra.

In seeking his edge, Munger pursued small, unknown stocks that wouldn't be of interest to the bigger investors:[60]

I tended to operate, as so many successful value investors do, not looking at Exxon and Royal Dutch and Procter & Gamble and Coca-Cola. Most of the value investors, if you analyze who've been successful over a long time, have operated in less followed stocks.

Like Simpson, Munger likes "financial cannibals," companies that buy back a lot of stock:

[W]*hat those* [*successful*] *companies had in common was they bought huge amounts of their own stock and that contributed enormously to the ending record. Lou, Warren, and I would always think the average manager diversifying his company with surplus cash that's been earned more than half the time they'll screw it up. They'll pay too high a price and so on. In many cases they'll buy things where an idiot could see they would have been better to buy their own stock than buy this diversifying investment. And so somebody with that mind-set would be naturally drawn to what Jim Gibson used to call "financial cannibals," people that were eating themselves.*

Munger often refers to the value "mind-set." He considers temperament a crucial element to holding a concentrated portfolio. When Buffett installed Lou Simpson as GEICO's chief investment officer, Munger recognized in him the right temperament, and a kindred spirit:[61]

Warren has this theory that if you've got a lot of extra IQ points in managing money you can throw them away. He's being extreme of course; the IQ points are helpful. He's right in the sense that you can't [*teach*] *temperament. Conscientious employment, and a very good mind will outperform a brilliant mind that doesn't know its own limits and so on and so on. Now Lou happens to be very smart but I would say his basic temperament was a big factor. He has the temperament of the kind of investor we like and we are.*

Like Buffett's and Munger's, Simpson's investment portfolio was characterized by long periods of inaction, and brief periods of intense activity:[62]

> *Lou owned his own style. To some extent, all of us were just taking a style that suited our nature. There are whole fields where it just looked too tough and we all just stayed out of those fields. It didn't matter how hard we worked we didn't end up with any edge. There were long stretches when he did nothing. That was part of his secret. That business of not doing anything, where you think you've got an edge, that is very much the Simpson style, the Munger style, the Buffett style.*

Munger holds that the sit-and-think investment style tends not to work for most money managers. He notes that many "big time" money managers don't do it because there are few sufficiently safe and undervalued positions available at any given time to fill a broadly diversified portfolio:[63]

> [I]*t's not a good way to run an investment management business because if you only own two stocks and you hold them forever and they do well, your client will think, "Why the hell am I paying this guy?" Well, pretty soon he falls in love with the stocks when he's tripled his money and quadrupled his money and so on. It doesn't look like you're doing anything.*

Very concentrated investors' portfolios will suffer from tracking error, which, in simple terms, is the difference between the performance of the portfolio, and the performance of the market or benchmark. Seeking to avoid redemptions from clients for brief periods of underperformance, some managers become "closet indexers"—a manager who holds a portfolio in similar proportions to the benchmark against which she or he is measured. Munger recounts a story about J.P. Morgan Bank, which he says charged a quarter point—0.25 percent—per year to manage a portfolio to invest in the Nifty Fifty "and nothing else, and they bought it regardless of its price to earnings ratio."[64]

> *They were so successful at that that more and more money came in and it was going to be the same 50 stocks. The record was partly creating itself. And of course it eventually puffed up so high that it blew up in a big way. But that kind of success where you have a self-fulfilling prophecy for a while, I don't count that as successful investment. It is successful for a long time. These people were regarded at J.P. Morgan as fabulous investors for a very, very long*

time—at a quarter of a point. And of course that problem is just endemic. That's why we have so many closet indexers. It can't work out very well because you got a zillion guys being paid to manage money who are a very substantial element of the market. There was a little of that at Berkshire nor GEICO.

To achieve very high returns, Munger understood that it was important to ignore the index, and managing outside money removed that ability. It's a common theme among the highly concentrated investors profiled in this book. Permanent capital—capital not subject to withdrawal or redemption—is an essential component for achieving high returns in concentrated portfolios because it offers the luxury of ignoring the short-term fluctuations of the market:[65]

Why would we want those artificial constraints? Lou had considerable periods in the dotcom bubble when the averages were outperforming Lou. It was years and he got well all at once. Nobody was saying to him, "How can you do this to us for three years running?" The money management business is not necessarily a good way to manage money if you are really trying to maximize your returns over 30 years.

In seeking permanent capital, Buffett and Munger were attracted to businesses like insurers and Blue Chip Stamps, both of which generated float:[66]

But the truth of the matter is we drifted into the model by accident. We were naturally attracted to float businesses when we were in a period where we were having investment results year after year that were way the hell better than other people. So it was worth more to us than it was worth to other people and so we got them to float businesses. Once we were in them, we would try to manage them intelligently.

So enamored of float-producing businesses were Buffett and Munger that they broke their ordinary practice of buying businesses to start one:[67]

What's interesting is there's only one business in the history of Berkshire that we created ourselves and that's the reinsurance department under Ajit Jane. That was created out of nothing but Berkshire's surplus cash. It's a huge success in a very fluctuating kind of way. Everything else in Berkshire we just bought and nourished. It's the only thing we created. And that didn't work that well until we had Ajit.

Munger says that Berkshire's reinsurance operation would be "very hard to copy" because it operates in such a unusual way:[68]

How would you copy Berkshire's [reinsurance] operations? It's very idiosyncratic and in a way it's kind of like value investing. We had a tiny workman's compensation company that I bought 40 years ago for Berkshire for $2 or $3 million. We never let it get very big because there's so much fraud in workman's compensation. We were always afraid of the fraud and the politics. Then they passed a law saying that in certain key segments of the workman's compensation business the plaintiff's lawyer couldn't pick the doctor. We instantly saw that would dramatically change underwriting results and we went in the course of a very few months with Ajit guiding the whole process from having nearly 0 percent of the workman's compensation market having 10 percent. And California is a size of a country, so 10 percent of the workman's compensation in California is a lot of business. Counting all things together, the underwriting, and so on, they made several billion dollars. Then when the rates went back we just shrunk way down again. I don't know anybody else that does things like that. That is more like an investment operation than it is a normal insurance operation.

Berkshire operates unusually because Buffett and Munger have maintained a laser-like focus on culture. Buffett credits Berkshire's "hard-to-duplicate culture" as one of its most important competitive advantages:[69]

Cultures self-propagate. Winston Churchill once said, "You shape your houses and then they shape you." That wisdom applies to businesses as well. Bureaucratic procedures beget more bureaucracy, and imperial corporate palaces induce imperious behavior. (As one wag put it, "You know you're no longer CEO when you get in the back seat of your car and it doesn't move.")

As Berkshire has grown, its unusual culture has made it an acquirer of choice. Munger and Buffett have continued to invest as they always have—searching for unknown, or misunderstood businesses—even if acquisitions that move the needle are now too large to fly completely under the radar. They hoover up the private business when the founder wants to retire, or a misunderstood public company that is simply too cheap because it's on the quarterly earnings treadmill. For management remaining with the acquired company, Berkshire offers autonomy. For the shareholders selling to Berkshire, it offers a fair price at which to exit. And Berkshire gets to put its enormous cash holdings to work buying another wonderful business. Berkshire's 2010 acquisition of Burlington Northern Santa Fe Corporation typifies Berkshire's evolution into a preferred home for vendors of even very large businesses, and demonstrates that Buffett and Munger find investments that have a material impact on Berkshire.

Berkshire acquired Burlington in 2010, paying $26 billion for the 77.4 percent of Burlington it didn't already own. Including the assumption of $10 billion in debt, the total acquisition was worth $44 billion and ranks as the largest acquisition in Berkshire's history. Berkshire paid 70 percent of the cost in cash, and, for the remainder, issued shares that increased Berkshire's outstanding share count by 6.1 percent. Buffett noted that Berkshire's $22 billion cash outlay was "quickly replenished."[70] By any measure, Burlington is an enormous enterprise. In describing its heft, Buffett noted in 2012 that it carried about 15 percent of *all* inter-city freight transported by truck, rail, water, air, or pipeline.[71] Its impact on Berkshire was similarly immense. In his 2010 shareholder letter, Buffett noted that Burlington had increased Berkshire's "'normal' earning power by almost 40 percent pre-tax and well over 30 percent after-tax."[72] While the acquisition continued Buffett and Munger's long practice of making big purchases—"fast-moving elephants" as Buffett describes them—it was slightly out of the ordinary for Berkshire. Burlington differs from a typical, cash-generative target like See's Candies in that it requires significant, ongoing capital expenditures. Cash taken from early acquisitions like See's Candies was employed not only to buy Burlington, but will be used to maintain it. Buffett describes as a "key characteristic" of the Burlington acquisition is its "huge investment . . . in very long-lived, regulated assets."[73] Those expenditures are significant, amounting to $6 billion in 2015—"nearly 50 percent more than any other railroad has spent in a single year and is a truly extraordinary amount, whether compared to revenues, earnings, or depreciation charges," according to Buffett.[74] He says it "will have a never-ending need to make major investments in plant and equipment:"[75]

> *Fulfilling our societal obligation, we will regularly spend far more than our depreciation, with this excess amounting to $2 billion in 2011. I'm confident we will earn appropriate returns on our huge incremental investments. Wise regulation and wise investment are two sides of the same coin. Both also need to provide efficient, customer-satisfying service to earn the respect of their communities and regulators. In return, both need to be assured that they will be allowed to earn reasonable earnings on future capital investments.*

Where a See's Candies-type business might throw-off cash, it also offers only limited opportunities for reinvestment. Burlington will absorb cash because it requires enormous ongoing investments, but—provided regulators allowed it—will earn reasonable returns on incremental investments. Munger estimate those returns to be in the order of 10 percent:[76]

> *It was one of the best deals we ever made, particularly considering its size. Not only that, we like having all these capital investments to make now that we're so drowning in money. So the opportunity to invest a lot of money at 10 percent, and it amounts to a mildly regulated use, is not that bad for us.*

As to the risk that regulators don't allow an adequate return on investment, Buffett says:[77]

> *Massive investments of the sort that* [Burlington] *is making would be foolish if it could not earn appropriate returns on the incremental sums it commits. But I am confident it will do so because of the value it delivers. Many years ago Ben Franklin counseled, "Keep thy shop, and thy shop will keep thee." Translating this to our regulated businesses, he might today say, "Take care of your customer, and the regulator—your customer's representative—will take care of you."*

In 2015, Buffett described the acquisition of Burlington "amidst the gloom of the Great Recession . . . the largest purchase in Berkshire's history" as an "all-in wager on the economic future of the United States."[78]

> *That kind of commitment was nothing new for us. We've been making similar wagers ever since Buffett Partnership Ltd. acquired control of Berkshire in 1965. For good reason, too: Charlie and I have always considered a "bet" on ever-rising U.S. prosperity to be very close to a sure thing.*
>
> . . .
>
> *Gains won't come in a smooth or uninterrupted manner; they never have. And we will regularly grumble about our government. But, most assuredly, America's best days lie ahead. With this tailwind working for us, Charlie and I hope to build Berkshire's per-share intrinsic value by (1) constantly improving the basic earning power of our many subsidiaries; (2) further increasing their earnings through bolt-on acquisitions; (3) benefiting from the growth of our investees; (4) repurchasing Berkshire shares when they are available at a meaningful discount from intrinsic value; and (5) making an*

occasional large acquisition. We will also try to maximize results for you by rarely, if ever, issuing Berkshire shares. Those building blocks rest on a rock-solid foundation. . . . Looking ahead, Charlie and I see a world made to order for Berkshire.

Surveying Berkshire post-Burlington, Munger asks with wonder:[79]

How do you start as a scrounge-y value investor and end up so Burlington Northern is willing to sell to you but nobody else?

He puts it down to "gumption" and refers to the Rudyard Kipling poem *If*, which includes the following lines unusually apt for concentrated value investors:

If you can keep your head when all about you,
Are losing theirs and blaming it on you,
If you can trust yourself when all men doubt you,
But make allowance for their doubting too;
If you can wait and not be tired by waiting,
. . .
If you can make one heap of all your winnings
And risk it on one turn of pitch-and-toss,
. . .
Yours is the Earth and everything that's in it,
And—which is more—you'll be a Man, my son!

NOTES

1. Charles Munger, interview, February 23, 2012.
2. Janet Lowe, *Damn Right! Behind the Scenes with Berkshire Hathaway Billionaire Charlie Munger* (Hoboken, NJ: John Wiley & Sons, 2000).
3. Ibid.
4. Ibid.
5. Charles Munger, interview, February 23, 2012.
6. Janet Lowe, *Damn Right! Behind the Scenes with Berkshire Hathaway Billionaire Charlie Munger* (Hoboken, NJ: John Wiley & Sons, 2000).
7. Charles Munger, interview, February 23, 2012.
8. Janet Lowe, *Damn Right! Behind the Scenes with Berkshire Hathaway Billionaire Charlie Munger* (Hoboken, NJ: John Wiley & Sons, 2000).
9. Ibid.
10. Ibid.
11. Ibid.
12. Ibid.

13. Ibid.
14. Charles Munger, interview, February 23, 2012.
15. Janet Lowe, *Damn Right! Behind the Scenes with Berkshire Hathaway Billionaire Charlie Munger* (Hoboken, NJ: John Wiley & Sons, 2000).
16. Ibid.
17. Ibid.
18. Ibid.
19. Ibid.
20. Ibid.
21. Ibid.
22. Ibid.
23. Ibid.
24. Ibid.
25. Ibid.
26. Ibid.
27. Ibid.
28. Ibid.
29. Ibid.
30. Warren Buffett, "Chairman's Letter," Berkshire Hathaway, Inc., 2007.
31. Janet Lowe, *Damn Right! Behind the Scenes with Berkshire Hathaway Billionaire Charlie Munger* (Hoboken, NJ: John Wiley & Sons, 2000).
32. Philip Fisher, *Common Stocks and Uncommon Profits* (New York: John Wiley & Sons, 1996).
33. Ibid.
34. Warren Buffett, "Chairman's Letter," Berkshire Hathaway, Inc., 1989.
35. Ibid.
36. Charlie Munger speaking at the 2013 Daily Journal Company Annual Meeting. Allen Benello's personal archive.
37. Janet Lowe, *Damn Right! Behind the Scenes with Berkshire Hathaway Billionaire Charlie Munger* (Hoboken, NJ: John Wiley & Sons, 2000).
38. Ibid.
39. Ibid.
40. Ibid.
41. Ibid.
42. Ibid.
43. Ibid.
44. Ibid.
45. Ibid.
46. Ibid.
47. Warren Buffett, "Chairman's Letter," Berkshire Hathaway, Inc., 1983.
48. Ibid.
49. Ibid.
50. Ibid.
51. Ibid.
52. Ibid.
53. Ibid.

54. Janet Lowe, *Damn Right! Behind the Scenes with Berkshire Hathaway Billionaire Charlie Munger* (Hoboken, NJ: John Wiley & Sons, 2000).
55. Ibid.
56. Charles Munger, interview, February 23, 2012.
57. Ibid.
58. Ibid.
59. Ibid.
60. Ibid.
61. Ibid.
62. Ibid.
63. Ibid.
64. Ibid.
65. Ibid.
66. Ibid.
67. Ibid.
68. Ibid.
69. Warren Buffett, "Chairman's Letter," Berkshire Hathaway, Inc., 2010.
70. Ibid.
71. Warren Buffett, "Chairman's Letter," Berkshire Hathaway, Inc., 2012.
72. Warren Buffett, "Chairman's Letter," Berkshire Hathaway, Inc., 2010.
73. Ibid.
74. Ibid.
75. Ibid.
76. Charles Munger, interview, February 23, 2012.
77. Warren Buffett, "Chairman's Letter," Berkshire Hathaway, Inc., 2011.
78. Warren Buffett, "Chairman's Letter," Berkshire Hathaway, Inc., 2014.
79. Charles Munger, interview February 23, 2012.

CHAPTER 6

Kristian Siem: The Industrialist

The Importance of Permanent Capital to the Long-Term Investor

> *Industry, by nature, is long term, and the fund management business, by nature, is short term. Financial investors come in and out: They can push a button any day and get out. The principal industrial investors don't have that luxury. They have to think for the long term. I believe indeed the success of industry is that you always think long term, so even if incidents like mergers or takeovers cause you to be out in the shorter term, you take the long-term decision as if you were to be the owner forever. That is healthy for the industry, and therefore also for its shareholders. I think that has been the success of our operation.*
>
> —Kristian Siem, Interview, July 2012[1]

In 1979, at age 29 and just six years out of business school, Norwegian Kristian Siem found an unusual confluence of events had conspired to create a rare opportunity in the offshore drilling industry. The Haakon Magnus, a submersible drilling rig, had been seized by its lender after its owner's default. The rig, which had been built for $37 million, could be had for $22 million. Siem, who described himself as a consultant, didn't have $22 million. He had little more than a business card and an office in the spare room of a small shipping company owned by his godfather. He used the office rent-free in exchange for advice on shipping. Like many businessmen in Norway at the time, his godfather hoped to find an opportunity to get into the new field of offshore drilling. Siem's father and other business associates had advised him that he was too young to start on his own business. "Get more experience under your belt," one of his father's associates advised.[2] Siem ignored them. In 1979, it seemed the whole Norwegian shipping industry wanted to get into "offshore." And Siem was one of the few with expertise in the field.

Though he was only 29, Siem was regarded as an expert in offshore drilling. His business school thesis had been on the transportation of liquid natural gas (LNG), and on graduating, he had been hired by Fred Olsen, a Norwegian shipping industrialist and head of the Olsen Group. (Olsen was once described by *Fortune* magazine as a contender for the title held by the fictional bearded adventurer from the Dos Equis beer commercials, "The Most Interesting Man in the World."[3]) Olsen wanted to have a presence in the oil capital of the world, and he tasked Siem with opening up the Olsen Group's first office in Houston, Texas. Siem had excelled, and in two years had grown the operation from just one employee—Siem—to 600. The Olsen Group had divisions for passenger ships, tankers, and other shipping, but nothing for offshore oil drilling, which was a new field, and one very different from the others. Fred Olsen called Siem back to Norway to start up and lead the Olsen Group's new offshore division. While he had enjoyed working for the Olsen Group when he was based in Houston, thousands of miles away, and in charge of the office, Siem found working in the old establishment culture at the head office in Oslo less than inspiring. After two years as head of one of the biggest Norwegian players in offshore drilling, he decided to strike out on his own.

In 1979, the Norwegian market for offshore drilling was at a low. Semi-submersible rigs that had cost tens of millions of dollars to build were laid up in the Norwegian fjords without work. After Viking Offshore, its owner, defaulted, Chemical Bank foreclosed on the semi-submersible drill rig Haakon Magnus. The bank needed $22 million to clear the debt. Siem could borrow the $22 million, but would also need an additional $4.5 million in working capital to operate the rig. It would have to come from outside investors. He contacted the head of the oil division at Norcem, Jan Tore Odegard, whom he had consulted in the past. On the telephone, Siem said to Odegard:[4]

> *You want to get into offshore drilling? Come into Haakon Magnus. I will give you 15 percent of $4.5 million in equity, which is a very small investment. And I'll give you a chance to buy options to take your equity investment to 50 percent. That means you will control a new semi-submersible with 15 percent of $4.5 million. If you are serious about going into offshore drilling, you won't find a cheaper ticket.*

Odegard got the approval for the investment from Norcem's chief executive—a contemporary of Siem's father, and a man whom Siem describes as a "really self-assured, old school guy"[5]—and Norcem signed the agreement to subscribe for the stock and options. When Siem approached Norcem to pay for its investment, the chief executive refused to complete the sale. The Troll—a huge crane ship—owned by ETPN in France in cooperation with Norwegian ship owners, had just gone bankrupt. The news was in all the papers, and it spooked Norcem's chief executive, who decided that an investment in Siem's rig deal was too risky. He instructed Uldegaard to pull out of the deal. On hearing the news, Siem insisted on a meeting. In the meeting he told him, "You're pulling the rug under my whole project."[6]

Norcem's chief executive responded, "You see, when you get drier behind the ears like me, then you will begin to understand that things are a little bit more complicated, so just accept that we are out of this business."[7]

Siem responded, "So your signature doesn't mean anything?"[8] He didn't receive an answer. Siem's rig deal looked sunk. Then he had an idea.

Most of the Norwegians who had been vendors to Viking Offshore were stuck with a secured claim on the Haakon Magnus. They would not be able to collect if Chemical Bank sold it out of foreclosure for less than $22 million. Siem approached them to argue he was their only chance to collect the full sum they were owed. The catch was that they would have to ante up equity in Siem's syndicate. Though they were reluctant, Siem believes that they were persuaded by his passion:[9]

> *My enthusiasm and drive for this project, and conviction that this was the right thing to do, was contagious on other people around me. They would see that, "Hey, we don't know this as well, but we can see that Kristian is in there and he's absolutely determined. He's putting all his money into it. He's going for it and we want to be a part of it," so that, I think, was a factor also, in raising the capital necessary.*

Most of the secured lenders saw the sense in Siem's proposal, and became investors in his scheme. He knew they would look to exit their investments at the earliest opportunity, and that could become an issue later, but they were his best alternative to secure the rig. Using the secured creditors' cash, Siem was able to fill in the hole Norcem's withdrawal had left. Importantly, he raised the capital without the huge dilution of Norcem's 35 percent option. To Siem, Norcem's response was telling. He saw a large company run by professional managers with lots of experience. They were offered an unbelievable opportunity: An investment in a rig worth $40 million for $675,000 with the option to take the investment up to 50 percent and get control of the rig after the risk had been eliminated. Norcem already had drilling rigs on fixed platforms in Norwegian waters, and organization in place to go for mobile drilling rigs. They didn't follow through on the opportunity because they got scared. Says Siem, "In hindsight they looked very stupid."[10]

The Siem group bid $22 million for the rig, and the secured creditors accepted. A syndicate of Norwegian banks lent the group the purchase price, and Siem and the other investors put in another $4.5 million in working capital. Crucial to the deal, the Norwegian government had set up a guarantee program to preserve the shipping tanker and the drilling industries from being extinguished through sale of all the assets abroad. After assessing the project to ensure it was viable, with sufficient working capital, the government would guarantee up to 100 percent of the purchase price. Bidders would use the guarantee to borrow debt from a bank. Siem obtained a Norwegian government guarantee for the full $22 million in debt, and so eliminated the banks' risk that Siem's syndicate might default. Siem credits that guarantee with saving the Norwegian shipping industry and launching his career. He invested his life savings in the syndicate, giving him a 7 percent personal holding in the Haakon Magnus.

Several months after Siem got control of the Haakon Magnus, he was approached by a shipbroker called Ringdal. They offered $28 million for the rig he had just bought for $22 million. Several shareholders, mostly the formerly secured creditors who had invested to buoy the price, wanted to accept. Though Ringdal's bid was only $6 million more than Siem had paid, that represented a return of $6 million on the $4.5 million in equity invested by the Siem group. They told Siem, "Let's accept it."[11] He responded:[12]

> *I have now attracted you all in here on the theory that the oil price will go up. Exploration activity has been down because the oil price has been down, but the oil price, which was at the rock bottom, has started to come up. With a fast-rising oil price there will be activity. If you believe that activity will come—which I am sure of, and that's why you invested with me in the first place, you should hold on now. The price of rigs will at least reach the cost of building a new rig. That means that this rig will go from $22 million to closer to $40 million. It will almost double before you add any threat of an imbalance in the supply and demand. This is now a no-brainer. Let's stick with it.*

The investors agreed, and the group decided not to sell. Undeterred, Ringdal made a second offer, this time for $29 million. With a $7 million profit on the $4.5 million invested, the shareholders had almost doubled their money in very short order. Siem rejected it again. Several of the shareholders came to him to plead with him to sell. He said to them:[13]

> *Listen, if we make a million in a week, my theory continues to be proven to be right. Let's wait another week and see. What is the hurry right now?*

The Siem group shareholders agreed to wait, but requested a board meeting every two weeks to review any new offers. Several weeks passed. Finally, Ringdal offered $32 million for the Haakon Magnus. Siem's shareholders insisted that the group sell. They said:[14]

> *Kristian, eight months have gone by. We have tripled our money. Some of us didn't want to be invested in the first place. We just wanted our money back. Now we have got three times that money back, so if this goes through, it's a good deal for us. We want out.*

Siem responded:[15]

> *I'll get you another half million by going back to my old employer. I'll sit down with him and I'll explain to him this situation. He will understand it and he will make a lot of money out of this. It's a great opportunity for him.*

Siem visited Fred Olsen and said, "Listen Fred, everything I know I learned from you. Here is a classic example."[16]

He responded, "You don't have to explain much. I understand it. Yes, I'll take it."[17]

Olsen offered $32.5 million, half a million more than Ringdal had offered, and just as Siem had predicted. Siem accepted the offer, and the Siem group sold the Haakon Magnus to Fred Olsen. That rig still exists today, but Olsen has changed its name to the Borgsten Dolphin. Siem notes that it earns around $400,000 a day, up from the $40,000 per day when Siem owned it. He estimates that Fred Olsen has made hundreds of million dollars from it. He also notes that the cost to build a comparable deep-water rig today is $600 million, so the Borgsten Dolphin is worth between $300 million and $400 million. Siem says that when his supply and support vessels work with it from time to time, "I have a little smile to myself; nostalgia."[18]

THE JACK-UP RIG PROJECT

In 1980, Siem saw that the market would shortly need a new supply of *jack-up rigs*—a rig with several movable "legs" that can elevate the hull out of the water. He quickly moved to secure two berths at Davy Shipbuilding in

Canada to have them built. While he was working on the rig specification he received a call from his brother, Ivar, who was running the Olsen Group's operations in Houston, Texas. His brother said:[19]

> *I know you are working on another project for jack-up rigs. I have a jack-up rig that you may want to consider as an alternative at Bethlehem in Beaumont, Texas. We have been negotiating to buy it, and Fred has changed his mind twice already. First he said, "Go," and then he canceled. Then he said, "Go," again and now he has told us to cancel again. You can't do that in the oil industry here. We are about to ruin our reputation. We haven't yet signed the contract, but we have initialed it to indicate that we have agreed [with] the whole text. Bethlehem expected us to sign a few days ago, and Fred has decided that he doesn't want to go for this. The price is $25.2 million. Bethlehem already has five other groups interested in taking the jack-up rig if we don't act on it, so when I tell the yard that we want to cancel, it will be gone very quickly. You have to act fast. And if you want it, you will have to do it through us so that we can preserve our reputation.*

Siem, who was in Oslo, Norway, called Bethlehem in Beaumont, Texas. They told him, "We will sell this rig to you. It's to be delivered in a year, but we need to know where we stand now."[20]

Siem responded, "How much time can you give me?"[21]

The representative from Bethlehem responded, "You have to sign on Monday, and you have to make a non-refundable deposit at the same time."[22]

Wasting no time, Siem got on a plane to the United States that night. He spent the weekend looking at the contract, and found, to his relief, that Ivar and Olsen had done a good job negotiating it: They had obtained exactly what Siem would have negotiated for himself. After heading to First City National Bank on Monday morning to obtain a check for a $25,000 deposit, Siem went into Bethlehem's office in Beaumont after lunch. He said, "Here's my deposit and here is the contract, which I'm prepared to sign now if you agree to one change. I need an additional two weeks to get my finances together."[23] Siem's $25,000 deposit bought him the two weeks to line up his financing.

To finance the purchase of the rig, Siem knew that he needed a multi-year operating contract with a customer. He found one in Malaysia called IIAPCO. He also needed $7 million in equity. Siem put all of his own money into the equity portion, and scraped together the rest from all over the world. When Fred Olsen heard that he was close to finalizing a deal, he got his appetite for risk back. He asked Siem if he could participate. To Siem's surprise, Fred Olsen offered to become the biggest shareholder on the condition that Olsen's subsidiary, Dolphin, got the management rights to the rig. Siem told him, "Fine. No problem with that at all."[24] Olsen came on board, but had to pay Siem a finder's fee for the project: A project that Olsen had himself found. All the other investors paid 1 percent for the work Siem had put in getting the deal together.

Olsen said to Siem, "Isn't it fair that I get a little discount on my one percent?"[25]

Siem responded, "Absolutely. You get 0.7 percent."[26]

A year later in December 1980, the jack-up rig was built on time, and slightly below budget at $24.8 million. Siem delivered it to the IIAPCO with Dolphin in place as the manager. In 1981, it became clear to Siem that the drilling market was about to collapse, and would stay depressed for a long time. He saw lots of new rigs were being built on pure speculation, without a customer, and without any concern for the balance of the supply and demand for rigs in the market. As the industry started to pull back, one operator, Global Marine, actually increased its pace of rig construction. Siem says that one theory for increasing production was that, in bankruptcy, partially completed rigs are more valuable than scrap iron:[27]

> *You'd better have some new rigs and heavy debt because banks have more reason to be interested in rescuing you. That was the theory. It's a really shrewd move if it indeed was right.*

Siem told his team, "We need to sell this rig with a customer contract and manager in place."[28] He called Zapata Corporation, a company that was started by former U.S. President George Bush Sr., in 1952. It was engaged in exploration and also undertook contract drilling. Zapata had a joint venture with a Norwegian group in the North Sea, and Siem thought they might be interested in another operating jack-up rig. Siem invited Zapata's chief executive to London to negotiate. He wanted to test how keen he was to buy the rig. When Zapata's chief executive, Ron Lassiter, arrived, he had the firm's chief financial officer in tow, so Siem knew that he was very interested. Siem thought to himself, "This guy is in the mood to buy."[29]

In the negotiation, Siem played coy, and the meeting broke up without a deal. As Zapata's chief executive was on the way back to the airport, he called Siem and said, "It's a pity that we couldn't do a deal. You know, I've come all this way."[30]

Siem responded, "Then let's split the difference and do a deal."[31] Zapata's chief executive leapt at the opportunity, and the deal was done. Siem says that he would have done a deal at any price: "I knew we had to sell because we were in front of a precipice. That was reality."[32] He had sensed in Zapata's chief executive how ardently the Zapata man wanted to do a deal, and knew that he was going to buy. Siem sold the rig, which had cost $24.8 million just two years earlier, for $34.5 million. In the two years Siem's syndicate had owned it, it had remained operating the whole time and generating income for the group. The almost $10 million capital gain represented a fantastic return on the $7 million that Siem's group invested. Siem, who received a carried interest on the rig, and had also invested, made several million dollars personally. As he had predicted, the drilling market soon collapsed completely, and remained depressed for 10 years, but not before Siem got one more deal done.

DIAMOND M DRAGON AND COMMON BROTHERS

In 1981, Siem found the deal that would be key to his foray into the shipping world. The Diamond M Dragon, a drill ship, was up for sale. The partners wanted to be rid of it because it was plagued with problems. Though it was a near-new drill ship, the crew employed by Diamond M had done a terrible job managing it, and it was in disrepair. The owners only wanted $34 million, about what it had cost to construct, because it had such a bad reputation. Siem knew the specifications of the drill ship were not industry best practice, which meant that it would not be attractive to many customers. He also believed the drilling market was about to collapse, but he saw an opportunity. He knew that Phillips Petroleum needed a drill ship for the Ivory Coast. He contacted them, and offered the Diamond M Dragon on a three-year contract that would earn him enough to completely pay off the $34 million purchase price.

Phillips Petroleum called Siem and said, "We cannot do three years. We can only do two years, but we are very keen to do two years."[33]

Siem responded, "Fine, we will take the same amount of revenue and divide it over two years."[34] Phillips needed the ship, and accepted Siem's offer. Even with a contract in place that would pay out the cost of the ship over two years, Siem still needed to finance the purchase. He approached Den Norske Bank (DnB), the largest merchant bank in Norway. The head of Norske sat down with Siem and said, "Well, it's an interesting project. We are happy to finance it."[35] Norske agreed to finance the entire purchase price, and crucially, required no equity from Siem. The Phillips contract made DnB look at the loan not as a bet on Siem, but a bet on Phillips Petroleum, limiting DnB's risk. They would have the first mortgage on the drill ship, and Phillips Petroleum would pay out the debt. The mobilization fee alone was $7 million, so before the bank took any risk, Siem started with a $7 million cash infusion. The deal, however, was not without drama.

The Diamond M Dragon lived up to its reputation as a mishap-prone ship. Shortly after it reported for duty with Philips, the *blowout preventer*, a valve that sits on top of the wellhead at the sea floor and an essential part of a drill ship, broke. Worse, the blowout preventer was an unusual size, which meant there were no spares available. Worst, it couldn't be repaired in the Ivory Coast. The only way to fix it was to take it to a workshop in Aberdeen, England. Siem left his honeymoon to fly to Abidjan, where he arranged for an Air Afrique Boeing 747 cargo plane that opened in the front to pick up the blowout preventer and transport it from the Ivory Coast to England. Next he needed an oven hot enough to repair the part, which was essentially a metal-on-metal seal that operated under tremendous pressure. It needed a perfect seal. Any imperfection in the surface would mean that it would not seal fully, and wouldn't function. The only way to get such a perfect seal was to melt the part by heating it to 900 degrees Celsius. Siem found an oven that could do the job in Aberdeen, but he had a new problem: The cargo plane was too big to land at Aberdeen Airport. It could only land in Manchester Airport, which didn't have an elevator large enough to handle the huge blowout preventer. Siem had to build a new elevator in Manchester Airport just to take the part from the plane's nose into a truck. It was then carried to Aberdeen, where repairs were started.

While repairs were under way, Siem sat down with Phillips Petroleum to explain what had occurred. Under the drilling contract he was to be paid while undertaking repairs, but at a lower repair rate, which was 80 percent below the operating rate. Phillips was very upset when Siem explained to them how long the repair would take. Under the agreement, if the repair took too long, then Phillips could terminate the contract. Siem suggested to Phillips that they be "off-hire" completely—pay him nothing while the blowout preventer was repaired—and simply add to the length of the contract every day that the ship was off hire. For Siem, it was more important that he keep the contract intact than get paid while the ship was being repaired because the contract paid for the whole rig. Once it was fully repaired, the drill ship would have a useful life of 30 years. Fortunately for Siem, Phillips readily agreed. It was a huge undertaking, but the drill ship was repaired, and the Diamond M Dragon continued under contract for Phillips.

Though the Diamond M Dragon was a deal too good to pass up, Siem still believed that the offshore drilling market was about to crash. In 1982, while the drill ship was under contract to Phillips, he started to consider his options. He says that, in hindsight, he should have sold it, and believes that he could have sold it for as much as $70 million in cash. Instead, he merged the Diamond M Dragon into Common Brothers Plc., a British shipping company founded in Newcastle, England in 1892, and listed on the London Stock Exchange. Common Brothers had a storied history. It had been one of the original shipping companies in India during the time of the British Raj, when British shipping was at its peak. Siem says that he was mesmerized by such a fantastic, old-line British shipping company. He saw that he could get control by merging the drill ship into Common Brothers for stock. In so doing, he would become the largest shareholder by far. When Siem merged the Diamond M Dragon into Common Brothers, he received through his Bermudian company Norex Corporation Limited $70 million in Common Brothers' stock. He believes that he got a good price for the drill ship, but the currency he received—Common Brothers' stock—was inflated. "Everybody felt very good about the deal:"[36]

> *We felt we got a good price for the drill ship and they felt they got a good price for the shares. I don't remember what the share price was now, but it was certainly not worth it.*

On paper Siem had received $70 million in stock—a 55 percent controlling interest—but he quickly discovered that Common Brothers was in trouble. He had bought into a workout situation. Common Brothers owned a fleet of vessels that were all being mismanaged. Not one single asset, except the pension fund, which was overfunded, had a pleasant surprise. Emblematic of the company's problems, the company's main asset—its tanker ships—was poorly run, and losing money. When Siem went onboard a tanker to inspect it, he found that only the officer's bar had been maintained:[37]

> *In those days the officers onboard the Common Brothers vessels met for drinks every evening in a bar. It was really shiny. The rest of the ship was falling apart. I think that was very symptomatic of all the assets and the care.*

The liabilities were equally ugly. Common Brothers had several hundred employees spread throughout the world. Siem was aghast when he found out the head office in Newcastle was situated over three floors in a brand new office building that Common Brothers had leased for 40 years at a very high rent. He moved immediately to end the lease and the huge liability it represented.

Common Brothers was a mess that would take Siem four years to clean up. The problem, he says, was that the two members of the founding family who ran it were not interested in the detail of shipping. Both were "gentleman who were a pleasure to deal with"[38] but the company had no controls, and they had lost grip of the financial details. For example, Common Brothers had an arrangement with a Greek who was their representative in ship broking. Under the terms of the arrangement he was allowed to do deals on the side. He kept all of the good deals for himself, and off-loaded the bad ones onto Common Brothers. Common Brothers also had a poorly run insurance broking business. Siem didn't know the insurance business at all, and realized that he needed to get involved. He found the whole industry to be run by people whom he describes as "not very high caliber:"[39]

> *It was more important to them what kind of car they were driving, and having their yacht and claret for lunch and so forth. I tried to get them to renounce some of these benefits in return for a participation in something much bigger. There was no interest at all.*

Siem decided that he needed to move urgently to make the insurance business profitable, and then merge it with somebody else who could run it. Over a series of transactions, it eventually became Lowns Lambert, then Heath and Willis, now owned by the buyout shop Kohlberg Kravis Roberts of New York.

Common Brothers' newest asset was the Bahamas Cruise Line, owned by a Cayman Island subsidiary called Bahamas Cruise Line, Inc. They had bought its only vessel just eight months before Siem bought into Common Brothers. The vessel operated in the U.S. market and was called the Veracruz, which was an old ship from the 1930s—so old that it had been used to resettle Jewish people in Israel after World War II. Common Brothers bought the cruise line after a meeting with management who would lose their jobs if the owner sold out. They were losing money and the owner wanted out. The main problem was that it had no marketing organization, critical for a cruise line. They had a single marketing agent in Canada who, within weeks of Siem taking over, went bankrupt. Siem was now confronted with the challenge of building up a cruise marketing organization from scratch. Worse trouble lay ahead. One morning Siem woke up to discover that the floor of the dock housing the Veracruz had given in, causing the Veracruz to topple over onto one of the walls. The press got a dramatic photo of the fallen Veracruz that appeared in all the newspapers in the United States where Siem was attempting to sell tickets. The accident set back ticket sales. Though Siem got a small insurance settlement to cover the repairs, it didn't cover the damage to the ship's reputation and consequent loss of income.

Siem knew that economies of scale were fundamental to success in the cruise business. One cruise ship would not be enough to compete. He discovered two old, yet beautiful, cruise ships for sale. The Tung Group from Hong Kong, much bigger than Common Brothers, bought the ships. Fortunately, they needed only one, and agreed to rent out, on a bare basis, one of the vessels to Siem. Siem renamed the ship the Bermuda Star. He negotiated permits to dock in Bermuda and changed the name of the company from Bahamas Cruise Line, Inc., to Bermuda Star Line, Inc. Siem says that the Bermuda Star was a popular ship for the passengers because it was so spacious. The cabins and the common parts were beautiful, with mahogany panels and polished brass. The problem was that the ship had a steam turbine, which burned a huge amount of fuel. Siem's solution was to put the ship on routes that didn't need high speed and so would burn less fuel. The ship was a success, and the Bermuda Star Line stopped hemorrhaging money. With the company in the black, Siem contacted C. C. Tung, the owner of the Tung Group, to buy the second vessel. C. C. Tung was a very tough negotiator. Little did Siem know that the Tung Group was in dire financial straits. While C. C. Tung was negotiating with Siem, the Tung family had given $2.7 billion in personal guarantees to the Tung Group's bankers. He couldn't get a deal done with C. C. Fortunately for Siem, the Tung Group shortly tipped into bankruptcy, and he was able to buy the second vessel out of the bankrupt estate. To fund the acquisition the company issued 960,000 new common shares at $6 each—increasing its share count to 4,060,000 million shares—and listed on the American Stock Exchange in February 1987.[40] (At the end of its fiscal year on June 30, 1987, the net shareholders' equity was just $5.3 million.)[41] Siem called the new ship the Canada Star because it was a sister ship to the Bermuda Star and would be used in St. Lawrence, Canada, in the summer. With three ships, Siem began to see the benefits of economies of scale. Recognizing that the nature of the cruise industry was changing, he told the board, "Now, our strategy must be to continue to increase economies of scale and get much bigger."[42] The company would either have to significantly increase its size and capacity through mergers or acquisitions or it would have to commence a new building program. Siem's instinct was to grow through acquisition. He approached Effjohn, a Finish and Swedish partnership that operated two cruise ships in Miami, Florida. Siem proposed that Effjohn and the Bermuda Star Line merge. Effjohn understood Siem's rationale, and initially entered into discussions with him, but soon cooled on the idea. There were already two independent partners and the partners found that complicated enough. Instead, they offered to buy out Siem. Siem went back to the board and said, "It's much better to be out than to be small."[43] So the Bermuda Star Line, Inc., sold out of the Bermuda Star Line.

In 1982, Siem had bought a drill ship for $35 million, and put up no equity. Over four years he had turned it into a 55 percent share of a publicly listed company in London with a controlling share in a company listed on the American Stock Exchange with $35 million in cash, but little in the way of operating assets. Now he needed a new challenge.

BACK TO THE DRILLING BUSINESS

By 1989, Bermuda Star Line, Inc., had sold out of the cruise business, its main asset. Though he had been attracted to the storied name of its parent, Siem decided that Common Brothers had been so poorly run that the goodwill in the name was gone. He changed it to Norex Plc., and changed the name of the American Stock Exchange–listed Bermuda Star Line, Inc., to Norex America, Inc. Norex still owned the Diamond M Dragon drill ship. Though it had paid down its debt, the vessel had no residual value. The offshore drilling market had collapsed, just as Siem had feared, rendering the cursed Diamond M Dragon worthless. He'd turned around and sold the hodgepodge of struggling assets in Common Brothers, but only the cruise business, which he'd built up from scratch, delivered full value for the time spent on it. The company's main asset now was the cash proceeds from the sale of the cruise business. Siem was looking for a place to invest.

In 1990, he saw that, though the offshore drilling industry had suffered through 10 tough years, offshore drilling would survive. It would also need to go into deeper and deeper water, meaning that drilling revenues would be pushed up. He told the board of Norex America:[44]

> *Offshore drilling is an exciting place to be and we know the industry. We've had a long period of time now without any new building and therefore the possibility of balance in supply and demand is there. Let's go back into the industry, but, rather than build more supply, let's go into existing companies.*

The board agreed, and so Siem set about figuring out Norex America's strategy. Most drilling contracts were either in Norway or America, but Siem wasn't sure if Norex should buy into a Norwegian group or an American one. He decided that the most important element for offshore drilling was a close relationship with the oil companies. As most of the oil companies were American, and the American contractors were much closer to the oil companies than the Norwegians were, Norex America would look at the American drillers. Siem analyzed several companies before discovering that Global Marine—which had sped up its rig-building activities to survive bankruptcy—had recently come out of its Chapter 11 bankruptcy proceedings. Siem held Global Marine in high regard, not only for its marketing ability, but also for its technical operations. Importantly, he felt the fit was right with Norex America. As part of the reorganization, the governments of Canada, France, and the United States had taken stock and debt. The debt traded at a discount of as much as 40 percent to face value of the debt. The Global Marine notes, which carried an annual 9 percent interest rate, paid an effective yield of approximately 16 percent annually.[45] Siem engaged investment bank Drexel Burnham Lambert to buy the debt in the market. He planned to convert it into stock, and become one of Global Marine's largest shareholders. Drexel got to work, and in short order had bought two-thirds of Global Marine's outstanding debt for Norex America and various unaffiliated associates for $220 million.

Siem got the attention of Global Marine's management when he moved to convert the debt. They met his proposal with fierce resistance, arguing that, if there was a change in control, Global Marine would no longer be able to carry forward the tax loss from the reorganization. The company had incurred huge losses that, carried forward, could be used to shield future income from tax. Siem found it to be a plausible argument, but believed that management used it only to avoid getting a controlling shareholder:[46]

> *I think management was very keen to control the company and would prefer to have a spread of institutional shareholders who don't want to sit on the board and control the board.*

Siem told the board of Norex America that he didn't have a problem holding the debt to term. If and when Global Marine repaid the debt, Norex America would receive face value for securities it had purchased at 65 percent of par, and would be paid interest in the interim. He told the board:[47]

> *We are in the drilling business, but in the financial way for a change rather than an operating way. So be it. We'll just see what happens.*

By 1992, the offshore drilling industry was recovering and, in December 1992, Global Marine refinanced and redeemed the notes. Norex America received approximately $100 million for a portion of the notes and recorded a gain of $33.7 million, a 50 percent return. At the end of its fiscal year on June 30, 1993, the net shareholders' equity had grown to more than $80 million, up from just $5.3 million at the 1987 year-end. Flush with cash from its holding in Global Marine's debt, Siem dabbled in a few other positions, buying a small, 10 percent holding in Transocean Norway, but nothing significant. He was hunting for a new big deal.

In late 1993, just after he turned 43, Siem was approached with an opportunity to invest in *Wilrig*, the Willhelmsen Group Drilling Company. Julian Robertson of Tiger had a substantial shareholding, along with the founding Willhelmsen family. The family wanted to exit the company, and weren't giving it their full attention. A Willhelmsen sat on the board and set the strategy, but Tiger disagreed with the direction. In the end they could only agree on one thing: That they needed to appoint a new chairman and it needed to be Siem. Wilrig was in a precarious situation with Citibank, its main banker, because it was having difficulty meeting interest payments. Before Siem invested and took the job as chairman, he visited Citibank in London. He told them:[48]

> *Wilrig is close to default on the loans. There's no point me taking this job if you don't endorse the rescue plan because you are the main creditor, so here's the plan for rescuing the company. I need to make sure that we can work together.*

Citibank was unwilling to give him a formal endorsement, but they gave him an informal commitment to work with him and buy into the plan. The first step was an injection of capital. Wilrig would need to issue $110 million in debt, but before it could complete a bond issue, it would need to raise more equity. Siem offered to have Norex America underwrite the equity, and Salomon Brothers would undertake the bond issue. Even with the equity underwritten, Salomon Brothers had difficulty getting the bond financing off the ground. Norex America underwrote more than half—$60 million—of the bond issue as well. The bond issue went ahead, and with Siem Industries taking the largest portion of it, it was sold very quickly. After buying in the open market, and taking stock in the underwriting, Norex America ended up holding 40 percent of Wilrig's equity for less than the construction cost of Wilrig's rigs. Siem notes, at that time, the market for drilling was depressed, and nobody paid attention to construction costs. Within a year, Siem had sold some idle rigs to free up capital, and Wilrig was back in the black. Norex America benefited, too. By year-end 1994, it had grown shareholders' equity to $93 million.

In June 1995, Transocean Norway, in which Norex America still had its 10 percent holding, approached him about merging with the healthier Wilrig. Siem, as the chairman of Wilrig, saw the sense in the transaction, and the two groups entered into merger discussions. The combined entity took the name Transocean because it was the largest and almost the only drilling contractor in Norway. Siem found the two companies to be compatible, delivering genuine synergies after the merger. He felt that they had achieved scale, and were large enough to compete on the world market, but came under pressure from U.S. institutional investors who had seen the synergies that Siem had wrung out of the merger. They were keen for Siem to continue making further mergers and told him, "If you don't find other merger partners then we will take charge."[49] Siem saw that his only option was to take control of the process, and entered into negotiations with Sonat Offshore Drilling, Inc. In April 1996, Sonat agreed to acquire all of the outstanding shares in Transocean. The merged entity took the name Transocean Offshore, Inc. Siem stepped down as chairman though he continued to serve on the board as a nonexecutive director for 16 years. While Siem was very focused as a director, loved the business, and felt pride in having been part of building the world's largest drilling contractor, he no longer felt it was his sole responsibility. Without what Siem describes as the "owner's responsibility,"[50] he elected to sell out. In 2007, Siem Industries, Inc., as Norex America was then known, finally sold its stake in Transocean for $300 million. Reflecting on the Transocean sale, Siem says that it bore out his decision to re-enter the drilling business again in the early 1990s:[51]

> *I'm quite proud of that because we actually sat down and thought it through. If you get the principles right, then it's likely to be a lower risk going forward.*

In June 1995, in a series of transactions Siem Industries acquired its London Stock Exchange–listed parent, Norex Plc., and Siem's family-controlled Bermudian company Norex Corporation Limited. Norex Corporation had in 1994 bid for and acquired all of the outstanding shares in Norex, Plc. Siem Industries had then acquired Norex Corporation in exchange for 3 million shares in Siem Industries. Norex Plc.'s interest in Siem Industries stock was extinguished at the same time and Norex Plc. liquidated, leaving Siem's family trust with control of Siem Industries. By year-end 1996, Siem Industries shareholder equity had exploded to $193 million.[52]

NORWEGIAN CRUISE LINE

In 1995, the Norwegian Cruise Line had run into financial difficulties. It had borrowed a huge amount of debt, and was in default. To survive, it needed an immediate $20 million infusion. The lead lender, DnB, who was responsible for this engagement, had syndicated the debt to many, many other lenders, including the French Government, and a host of international banks. They were afraid that a competitor, Carnival Corporation, would move in and buy the debt very cheaply, leaving many of the syndicate banks high and dry. They approached Siem about making the $20 million investment. Siem called up the board of Siem Industries, and explained the situation. One of the directors said:[53]

> *This is too complex for us to get our arms around it. If you want to go ahead with $20 million we will support you. We're not going to stop you doing it, but we cannot help you by taking this decision.*

Siem told DnB that he was unable to make a decision, but DnB refused to take no for an answer. Siem had gone to the same business school as the of head of DnB's shipping division, Anne Oian, and they knew each other well. She had struggled with Norwegian Cruise as a client for a long time. The credit committee and the board of DnB were rapidly losing faith. She finally persuaded Siem to support a plan to prevent bankruptcy and Siem Industries committed $20 million. The money bought Norwegian Cruise a little breathing room, but not much. With $870 million in debt outstanding, its income wasn't sufficient to meet even its interest repayments, and it was close to bankruptcy.

Siem saw that the incumbent board was tired, and worried about the impending bankruptcy. Siem understood that he had to get involved to rescue Siem Industries' $20 million investment. They were more than willing to give up the chair to Siem. Within a month he was nominated to take over as chairman of the board, and he was elected two months later at the shareholders meeting. The company's main problem was that the cash drained away by the 13 percent interest payments on its bonds was killing it. Previous management had tried to solve its short-term liquidity problems by issuing bonds with a 13 percent coupon, a high cost of funds in any industry. Now distressed, those bonds sold in the market at a wide discount, but the company didn't have the financial wherewithal to buy them back. To tackle the debt issue, Siem traveled across the United States to meet with bondholders. He needed to persuade them to agree to lower the coupon and reduce the debt. He told them that the wide discount in the bonds was justified by the financial weakness of Norwegian Cruise. Says Siem:[54]

> *I showed them the reality of the company. The market is right when they are trading these bonds at the discount. I now need to refinance these bonds at the same discounted level, maybe higher than the market but not at full price. And then that refinancing needs to be done urgently.*

Siem proposed that the bondholders accept a 4 percent coupon instead of the 13 percent coupon they were receiving. He traveled twice around the United States talking to the bondholders trying to sell his plan. The more Siem talked, the more convinced the bondholders became that they should be fully repaid. They knew that Siem had been successful in previous turnarounds and also that he had capital available. They didn't believe that he would let Norwegian Cruise go under, and refused to allow him to refinance the bonds at a lower rate.

Siem looked to raise equity at the same time. One investment came from Prince Alwaleed bin Talal in Riyadh, Saudi Arabia. Siem flew to Riyadh on a Sunday to get an audience with the prince at 8 P.M. Alwaleed opened up the meeting by saying, "I'm sorry you came all this way because we have decided not to invest. But since you are here, let me hear about the company."[55] Siem sat for two hours telling Alwaleed about Norwegian Cruise. By the end of his presentation, Alwaleed was excited about the prospect of an investment in Norwegian Cruise. He said, "We'll let you know tomorrow if we are going to take it."[56] Siem returned on the night flight back to London. He was very tense because of the debt load. By the time he got to the office in the morning on Monday, Alwaleed had decided to proceed, and by Tuesday, Alwaleed's organization had paid, which was an extraordinarily short time to undertake a private placement.

Just as the banks had feared, Carnival pounced on Norwegian Cruise's distressed bonds, attempting to do with the company what Siem had tried to do to Global Marine. Over several weeks, Carnival bought a controlling position in Norwegian Cruise's bonds, forcing Siem to the negotiating table. In one marathon session, Micky Arison, Carnival's chief executive, and son of the founder, turned to Siem and said:[57]

> *You're sitting there negotiating. You don't have any cards in your hands and you're negotiating. We got you by the balls, so what are we negotiating about?*

Siem responded:[58]

> *Micky, be sensible. You wouldn't be here if it wasn't for Koster Cruise Lines. Let's find a constructive way forward that is easier for everyone.*

Arison's father had worked for Koster Cruise Lines, as Norwegian Cruise was then known, as its agent in Miami, Florida. He collected all the advance deposits from the passengers, and used that cash to buy his own vessel, which became Carnival. This was a breach of his agreement with Koster: Arison Sr. should have been working in Koster's interests, not setting up in competition. He was later forced to settle a claim from Koster Cruise. Siem recalls the history between the two companies:[59]

> *If Koster had a more litigious mentality, which is not typical for Norwegians, but had he been bred in America, perhaps Koster would have squeezed that lemon dry.*

Arison eventually relented, and agreed to sell the bonds to Siem at a discount, a victory for Norwegian Cruise. Siem believes that Arison saw that the process would be messy because Siem was at the very beginning of the turnaround. No important measures had been taken. Once Siem had persuaded Carnival to accept the bond offer, the other bondholders followed suit, and accepted Siem's terms. Norwegian Cruise was able to buy back the bonds at 80 percent of par, and replace them with bonds with a 4 percent coupon, further reducing its obligations. The turnaround of Norwegian Cruise had begun.

Siem's first step was to terminate the chief executive. He learned that he had been working behind the scenes to tip the company into Chapter 11 bankruptcy protection so that he could buy it out of bankruptcy with assistance from a private equity firm. Instead, Norwegian Cruise paid the chief executive $1 million to walk away.[60]

Though the cash drain had been removed, the situation was still very precarious. Siem looked to the company's fleet of vessels. Norwegian Cruise owned the SS Norway, previously the SS France, which was a beautiful, historic ship, but an expensive vessel to run. Siem wanted to slow its speed as much as possible to conserve fuel and reduce operating costs. He believes that its acquisition was "strategically a wrong decision by the Kosters:"[61]

> *Norwegian Cruise got a lot of publicity out of the SS Norway, and it was [a] significant part of Norwegian Cruise Line's image. It's hard to measure what that is worth, but all told, I think that the simple approach of punching out sister vessels—similar vessels—out of the ship yard at the lowest possible capital cost, which was Carnival's approach, was much better. If you look at all the money that Norwegian Cruise Line spent over the years on upgrading and changing the SS Norway, and if you look at the operating cost of those turbines, huge fuel consumption, the economics don't stack up at all. They should have built the largest, most brilliant new cruise ship in the world for the money. What all the cruise lines have learned over time is that, though they have built bigger and bigger ships, they need only one captain, one engine, one radar and one each of the other expensive equipment. So if you can share the cost over 2,000 passengers instead of 1,000, you get economies of scale.*

More vessels and an overall larger capacity also allow a cruise line to spread its marketing cost, which is substantial, over a much higher number of passengers. Its purchasing power goes up on supplies, food, and airline tickets, so the price per passenger comes down. For cruise lines, synergies from economies of scale are "very, very important," he says.[62]

Siem's solution was to take Norwegian Cruise's modern vessels and "stretch" them: cut them in half, and insert between the two halves a prefabricated midsection. The prefabricated midsections would be about 40 meters long, and add 500 passengers each to the vessels. Additional passengers would give Siem the economies of scale he needed to survive. The problem was that the vessels represented collateral for bank debt lent to Norwegian Cruise, and Siem proposed to cut it in half. He needed the bank's permission to do so. Société Générale S.A., the lending bank, refused. What if Norwegian Cruise went into bankruptcy and at that time the boat was in two pieces? How could they sell it? Siem said, "We can't take a no for a no."[63] Société Générale suggested Siem meet with Coface, the French government scheme that guaranteed ships built in France. So Siem met with Coface in Paris and explained the importance of stretching the ships. Coface was very nervous because Norwegian Cruise was close to default, and the collateral in the ships was the only security that Coface held. Here was Siem suggesting that they cut that collateral in half. He received a second "no," but Siem contacted the French Ministry of Finance and insisted that he meet with the director. The director was persuaded to intervene on Siem's behalf, and Norwegian Cruise was allowed to stretch the ships.

Siem slowly improved Norwegian Cruise's marketing, and the company started gaining momentum. When he had bought in, the stock price was 7 kroner. The price had dropped as low as 5 kroner, but had traded up to 30 kroner by 1999, when Carnival's Arison called Siem from Miami. Arison said to Siem:[64]

> *Kristian, we have a very friendly proposal here to buy your company for 30 kroner a share. We will never go a penny above 30 kroner because it is too much. We want to do this in a most friendly way, but we'd like to have acceptance from you before the end of the day today, and if you don't accept, then we will go live with that offer.*

Siem responded, "Micky, thank you for your *friendly* offer, but that sounds quite hostile to me. I will talk to my board and call you back."[65] Siem gathered the board together by telephone. They agreed with Siem that Norwegian Cruise should decline the offer. When Siem relayed the message to Arison, Carnival took the offer public, as he said he would. Siem contacted Star Cruises in Malaysia, which was owned by the Genting family, who had indicated they were interested in Norwegian Cruise Line. They agreed to buy some stock at 35 kroner. In the meantime, Arison and his team went to Norway, where Norwegian Cruise Line was listed, and where many of the institutions that were holding shares in the company were based, and met with all of them. They also went on national television, and criticized Norwegian Cruise management, including Siem and his team. At the same time, it became clear that the Genting's Star Cruises also had hostile intentions as they continued to buy shares in the market. Siem saw Star Cruises rapidly creeping up on a controlling position in the equity. Arison asked for a meeting with Siem in London.

When Siem arrived, the atmosphere in the meeting room was tense because Carnival had gone hostile, and Arison had criticized Siem in the media. Arison opened by saying to Siem, "If I said something that was hurtful when I was in Norway, I apologize."[66] Siem saw that as a good start. He continued, "I can assure you, I didn't say anything negative about you on the television."[67]

Siem replied, "Micky, I didn't watch the television, but my mother did, and she had a very different impression of it."[68] Siem told Arison that most of the financial institutions in Norway knew that he had engineered the turnaround at Norwegian Cruise, so he and his team had credibility. Arison agreed. While he had assured Siem that he would never go "a penny above 30 kroner," he now said to Siem that he would match the 35 kroner being paid by Star Cruises. The bidding between Carnival and Star Cruises continued.

At the end of January 2000, Siem received a phone call at 4 A.M. from Arison who said, "Kristian, you won't believe it but we have agreed to join forces with Star and do a joint bid for the whole company. With our combined shareholding, we have control."[69]

Siem responded, "You have the company. And you have my full corporation. I have a big stake in the company."[70] Siem had been diluted from 40 percent to 14 percent as a result of all the equity issues needed to undertake the various projects, but it represented a substantial sum to him. The end of the six-week takeover saga was almost at hand. He hadn't relished the publicity, including almost daily appearances on television in Norway, and other media in London and the United States. The shareholders' meeting to elect the new board and hand over to the new owners and to the new management was televised. Siem read out a letter he had written to all 6,000 Norwegian Cruise employees. In the letter, Siem said, "What a fantastic journey it's been together. We have avoided bankruptcy. You have built this to be a viable company. I am now leaving due to the circumstances, and I thank you for the good work together. The company is now on its right track. I wish the company all the best, and I'm available to all of you at any time."[71] Siem had controlled Norwegian Cruise Line for five years, from 1995 to 2000, and had increased the share price five times, from 7 kroner to 35 kroner.

DSND SUBSEA

While Siem was preoccupied with Norwegian Cruise Line, he made another investment that would draw unwanted attention. DSND Subsea, formerly known as *Det Sondensfjelds-Norske Dampskibsselskab*, or South of the

Mountain Norwegian Steamship Company, was founded in 1854, and was the oldest shipping company listed on the Norwegian stock exchange. DSND had a mishmash of marine investments, including a jack-up rig, and various shipping interests, including some timber carriers and vessels that were rented out to the offshore service industry. Importantly, it was profitable. Siem found a large, strategic shareholding in it for sale and Siem Industries bought it. All was well until DSND ran into financial trouble attempting to expand internationally. It lacked international control systems. The chief financial officer was inexperienced and incapable of building the control systems needed. Siem was forced to personally lend 200 million kroner to the company to keep it afloat. He didn't go through Siem Industries because he didn't have time to go to the board and felt it was too difficult to justify:[72]

> *I was just putting myself in the position of a board member of Siem Industries. If I got this kind of request, and the only reason for approving it is that DSND needs it, I'd ask, 'Is it Siem Industries' role to take this kind of risk? Shouldn't it rather be a share issue?' Of course it should have been. I had to take some blame for being distracted by Norwegian Cruise Line, so I made a quick decision to take the risk personally.*

Siem knew the decision would be criticized as not serving the interests of Siem Industries' shareholders. To compound his problems, a few months later the board received from Cal Dive in Houston an indicative interest—not enough to amount to a formal offer—of 14 kroner per share for DSND.

Cal Dive's 2003 informal offer came at a time when Siem Industries' share price was suppressed at or near an all-time low. Siem didn't believe that it was the time for any shareholder to sell. He was also concerned that the offer wasn't concrete. He regarded it as a "fishing trip."[73] The board looked at it and decided not to pursue it. Siem told Cal Dive that he had better ideas for the shareholders. Cal Dive responded by increasing its offer 1 kroner to 15 kroner per share. Siem Industries again rebuffed the offer, and, says Siem, "all hell broke loose."[74] He was criticized in the media for not disclosing the "offer" to the investors. A full, two-page spread article appeared in one newspaper saying that Siem was set on controlling DSND, rather than looking after shareholders' overall interests, and that he should be jailed. Siem responded by saying, "If anybody wants out I'm happy to give them an offer,"[75] and offered to buy any shares at 17 kroner per share. To Siem's surprise, the newspaper article had an impact on the financial community in Norway, and lots of shareholders accepted. Siem got a lot more shares than he expected, and had to borrow money from the bank to be able to pay for it. He now regards it as one of the best deals he's ever done, even though it was totally unintentional. Ten years later the share price was up more than 10 times, not including dividends and various companies spun off, like Siem Offshore and Veripos. Siem invested tens of millions that, in 2015, became worth $1.5 billion.[76] He says:[77]

> *We have put in some more money along the way but it has been a good example of how, if you have a long-term goal of building a solid industry that provides a product or service you believe the market needs, then you are bound to win. You're building value over time. Sometimes it takes a bit longer, and there will always be some setbacks, but over time you build value that way. This is a good example. Maybe I've proven that.*

Siem Industries made numerous successful investments since it became a publicly traded company in 1987, growing its shareholders' equity from $5.3 million in June 1987 to over $2.01 billion at the end of 2014, growing at a compound rate of 25 percent. Siem has been instrumental to the success for many of the company's investments, being named as chairman of the investee company in almost every instance for the purpose of enacting the strategies he outlined. It is a testament to his hands on, industrial investment philosophy.

SIEM ON VALUATION

Siem's success in the oil and gas drilling and shipping industries points to an unconventional facility for identifying and valuing investment opportunities there. How does he find those opportunities, and what does he look for when presented with an investment? He has worked his entire career in oil and gas drilling and shipping, with a particular focus on offshore drilling and other services. His first investments were made in individual assets, and he was fully concentrated in each of those deals, investing all of his capital into a single asset. Siem argues that such a huge concentration of capital was warranted because he had done his homework. The downside risk, from his perspective, was relatively small because he knew the industry so well. He also notes that he was young and "didn't have the experience to see all the potential pitfalls that come with age, and the problem when you have old people deciding is that you get the benefit of their experience, but also they may lack the courage at times."[78] He says that, though he didn't have a lot of experience at the time that he acquired the Haakon Magnus, his first investment, he had spent all of his working life in the oil and gas offshore drilling industry, and knew it well:[79]

> *I knew all 118 submersible rigs in the world by name, where they were, and their contracts. I came young into a young industry, so I had a very good grip and understanding of all the dynamics in this industry, and therefore the quality of my judgment was high. I saw it as a fantastic opportunity to put all my wealth and energy into it.*

His view is that the best way to get the valuation right is to have industry knowledge that can only come from experience. This knowledge gives him context to understand how each asset develops, its earning capability, and the state of the market for the asset's services. This leads to an instinctive valuation. He knows the market value and cost to replace all the vessels, rigs, and other hardware that he depends on as operating assets. He also knows the earning capability as a yield on each of those assets. Siem's favorite metric for calculating that yield is the earnings before interest, taxes, amortization, and depreciation (EBITDA) in proportion to the investment or capital expenditures (CapEx):[80]

> *It's a simple calculation. It's basically EBITDA in relation to the CapEx. And it's amazing what that simple calculation can do. I always do it myself when I sit in boards, whether it's Transocean or Subsea or smaller companies. Management often present reams of calculations, internal rates of return, and so forth. And I have been surprised at some fellow directors who say, "Yeah, the internal rate of return looks fine, and it's better than our weighted average cost of capital, so let's go for it." But you need to examine the model's assumptions. How is the internal rate of return defined? What is the residual value that you put into that calculation, for instance? That makes all the difference.*

With an idea of the cost to replace each asset, its market value, and its likely EBITDA yield after backing out operating CapEx, Siem calculates the asset's earnings power. He looks at what it is currently yielding, and what he thinks it is likely to earn in the future based on how he, and management, see the market for its services developing. He says that some of the best asset plays he has done have been based on no income at all. If he can find an asset that has been *laid off*—not operating—it will have negative EBITDA because the owners have to pay the layoff costs. Those assets can often be acquired very cheaply. His first, the Haakon Magnus, was such a deal.

Siem says that having a permanent source of capital provided by the public company has allowed him the requisite time to complete many projects. A problem for many investors in terms of expressing their own investment philosophy is that they don't have this access to permanent capital.

A source of permanent capital, whether his own money or that of Siem Industries, is dedicated for the long term and allows him to invest for the long term. He can think differently about an investment than another investor, like the more typical fund manager, who has two tasks: (1) to produce returns and (2) keep the investor base happy. Siem believes that his long time horizon has been central to his success:[81]

> *Industry, by nature, is long term, and the fund management business, by nature, is short term. Financial investors come in and out: They can push a button any day and get out. The principal industrial investors don't have that luxury. They have to think for the long term. I believe indeed the success of industry is that you always think long term, so even if incidents like mergers or takeovers cause you to be out in the shorter term, you take the long-term decision as if you were to be the owner forever, that is healthy for the industry, and therefore also for its shareholders. I think that has been the success of our operation.*

Table 6.1 shows the remarkable growth in Siem Industries' book value per share since 1990.

TABLE 6.1 Growth in Siem Industries Book Value Per Share (1990 to 2014)

Year	Shareholder's Equity	Shares Outstanding*	Book Value/Share
Jun 30, 1987	$5,274	16,240,000	$0.32
Jun 30, 1988	$2,975	17,573,332	$0.17
Jun 30, 1989	$17,214	17,573,332	$0.98
Jun 30, 1990	$36,271	23,301,788	$1.56
Jun 30, 1991	$50,542	25,751,788	$1.96
Jun 30, 1992	$49,778	24,647,312	$2.02
Jun 30, 1993	$80,375	24,464,112	$3.29
Jun 30, 1994	$93,513	24,424,112	$3.83
Dec 31, 1995	$125,236	25,185,424	$4.97
Dec 31, 1996	$193,447	19,524,624	$9.91
Dec 31, 1997	$291,016	19,524,624	$14.91
Dec 31, 1998	$189,463	19,066,907	$9.94
Dec 31, 1999	$308,207	17,354,657	$17.76
Dec 31, 2000	$306,561	17,002,244	$18.03
Dec 31, 2001	$259,875	16,996,644	$15.29
Dec 31, 2002	$289,834	16,796,644	$17.26
Dec 31, 2003	$307,850	16,794,144	$18.33
Dec 31, 2004	$426,490	16,793,744	$25.40
Dec 31, 2005	$451,042	15,052,492	$29.96
Dec 31, 2006	$560,935	15,052,492	$37.27
Dec 31, 2007	$883,623	15,529,927	$56.90
Dec 31, 2008	$1,028,467	15,379,927	$66.87
Dec 31, 2009	$1,158,613	15,379,927	$75.33
Dec 31, 2010	$1,304,984	15,359,927	$84.96
Dec 31, 2011	$1,823,855	15,289,927	$119.28
Dec 31, 2012	$2,086,610	15,289,927	$136.47
Dec 31, 2013	$2,227,606	15,139,681	$147.14
Dec 31, 2014	$2,053,537	15,139,681	$135.64
Compounded Annual Gain in Book Value/Share—1987–2014			25.6%

*Adjusted for 4-1 split

NOTES

1. Interview with Kristian Siem, July 2012.
2. Ibid.
3. Shawn Tully, "The Crazy, True-Life Adventures of Norway's Most Radical Billionaire," *Fortune* magazine, March 7, 2015, http://fortune.com/2015/03/07/fred-olsen/.
4. Interview with Kristian Siem, July 2012.
5. Ibid.
6. Ibid.
7. Ibid.
8. Ibid.
9. Ibid.
10. Ibid.
11. Ibid.
12. Ibid.
13. Ibid.
14. Ibid.
15. Ibid.
16. Ibid.
17. Ibid.
18. Ibid.
19. Ibid.
20. Ibid.
21. Ibid.
22. Ibid.
23. Ibid.
24. Ibid.
25. Ibid.
26. Ibid.
27. Ibid.
28. Ibid.
29. Ibid.
30. Ibid.
31. Ibid.
32. Ibid.
33. Ibid.
34. Ibid.
35. Ibid.
36. Ibid.
37. Ibid.
38. Ibid.
39. Ibid.
40. Financial Summary of Siem Industries; Siem Industries internal papers.
41. Ibid.

42. Interview with Kristian Siem, July 2012.
43. Ibid.
44. Ibid.
45. Financial Summary of Siem Industries; Siem Industries internal papers.
46. Interview with Kristian Siem, July 2012.
47. Ibid.
48. Ibid.
49. Ibid.
50. Ibid.
51. Ibid.
52. Financial Summary of Siem Industries; Siem Industries internal papers.
53. Interview with Kristian Siem, July 2012.
54. Ibid.
55. Ibid.
56. Ibid.
57. Ibid.
58. Ibid.
59. Ibid.
60. Ibid.
61. Ibid.
62. Ibid.
63. Ibid.
64. Ibid.
65. Ibid.
66. Ibid.
67. Ibid.
68. Ibid.
69. Ibid.
70. Ibid.
71. Ibid.
72. Ibid.
73. Ibid.
74. Ibid.
75. Ibid.
76. Ibid.
77. Ibid.
78. Ibid.
79. Ibid.
80. Ibid.
81. Ibid.

CHAPTER 7

Grinnell College: The School of Concentration

Concentration and Long-Term Investing for Endowment

Put it in the safety deposit box and forget you have it.

—Joe Rosenfield[1]

Grinnell is a private liberal arts college notable for its academic excellence and being among the wealthiest educational institutions of any size in North America. With total endowment funds of $1.83 billion in 2014, and just 1,734 full-time students in 2014, little Grinnell College in Grinnell, Iowa, can lay claim to having the largest endowment per student in the United States.[2] It is a testament to unconventional investing, and having Warren Buffett sit on an investment committee for 43 years.[3] Buffett, who served from 1968 to 2011, thought Grinnell to be "kind of a strange place."[4] His first college loyalty was to the University of Nebraska.

"He bleeds 'big red,'" said George Drake, former Grinnell president and professor of history, noting Buffett's support for the University of Nebraska ("big red" is an unofficial nickname). Said Drake:[5]

> *He once told me, "I don't particularly care about Grinnell College. Joe Rosenfield asked me to do this, and I'll do anything for Joe Rosenfield."*

While Buffett has been described as the "architect of the endowment,"[6] it was little-known Joe Rosenfield who played the most important role in

Grinnell's success. Rosenfield, whom *Wall Street Journal* personal finance columnist Jason Zweig once described as "the best investor you've never heard of,"[7] was a 1925 graduate of Grinnell College. After practicing law for 20 years, in 1948, Rosenfield became chairman of Younkers, a retail chain that had bought out his family's department store in Des Moines, Iowa.[8] Though he joined the board of Grinnell College in 1941, he would not take on responsibility for the endowment until 1968, when he stepped down as chairman of Younkers because he had reached the mandatory retirement age of 65.[9] The endowment held just $11 million in assets when he took it on.[10] When he stepped down in 1999, the Grinnell endowment held an astonishing $1 billion, a compound growth rate of 15.1 percent per year, not counting the 4.75 percent of assets the endowment sent to the college every year for operating expenses. One trustee, Gardiner Dutton, says that the day he joined the board in 1970, Rosenfield told him, "Our job is to make this institution financially impregnable."[11] He exceeded even that lofty measure. When Rosenfield stepped down in the late 1990s, Grinnell College's endowment was already the largest per student of any private liberal arts college in the country.[12]

The key to the endowment's rare investment performance was its unusual investment strategy. Under the stewardship of Buffett and Rosenfield, the endowment bought a handful of positions and then held on to them for decades. Notes Zweig in his *Wall Street Journal* article on Rosenfield, "In 30 years, [he] made fewer than a half-dozen major investments and has sold even more rarely."[13] Said Rosenfield:[14]

> *If you like a stock you've got to be prepared to hold it and do nothing.*

Rosenfield hadn't always been a long-term investor. Zweig reports that he started out in the aftermath of the 1929 crash as a trader:[15]

> *In the early days I was doing too much short-term investing. I'd buy and sell stocks in 30, 60, 90 days: Studebaker, Dodge, Nash Motors. I thought I could make real money doing that, but I was wrong. I didn't go broke, but I got badly bent. Buying for short periods of time is always going to hurt you in the end.*

The endowment would also largely avoid U.S. treasuries, which was very unusual:[16]

> *I figured government bonds wouldn't get the college anyplace. So I started looking for good common stocks we could own for the long term.*

The endowment would follow Rosenfield's simple template for more than 30 years: It would own just a handful of stocks at a time and hold them for the very long term. Buffett said of Rosenfield that he was "a triumph of rationality over convention,"[17] and his plan for Grinnell demonstrated so.

Rosenfield met Buffett in 1967 at the insistence of mutual friends. Buffett, who was then unknown outside Omaha, was still managing his private partnerships, which held just $75 million in assets. Rosenfield said that he "could see what a fine mind he had, and I was immediately attracted to him."[18] Buffett reciprocated the feeling:[19]

> *We hit it off immediately. Joe is an extraordinarily generous and smart man. I'd never have wanted to replace my real father—but if after my dad's death I could adopted Joe as my father, I would have.*

Shortly after meeting Buffett in 1967, Rosenfield bought $5,252 worth of Berkshire Hathaway—300 shares—for the endowment, and persuaded Buffett to join Grinnell's board, which he did in 1968.[20] Grinnell held the Berkshire position for more than 20 years, finally selling between 1989 and 1993 for $3.7 million for reasons that neither Buffett nor Rosenfield could remember.[21]

The endowment would make a second serendipitous investment when Robert Noyce, a Grinnell trustee and alumnus, offered Grinnell stock in his then-private start-up, NM Electronics.[22] Noyce had almost been expelled from Grinnell for stealing a pig and roasting it at a campus *luau.*[23] He would have been expelled but for the intervention of his physics professor who felt that Noyce was the best student he'd ever taught. [24] The professor managed to persuade the school to reduce the expulsion to a one-semester suspension.[25] Noyce never forgot the favor, and made the stock available to the school if it wanted it.[26] Rosenfield told Noyce that the endowment would take all the stock he'd let it have.[27] Grinnell's endowment took 10 percent of the $3 million private placement (Grinnell put up $100,000, and Rosenfield and another trustee put up $100,000 each).[28] Shortly thereafter the company, then renamed *Intel*, went public in 1971. Grinnell started selling the stake in 1974, at which time it was worth $14 million, more than half the value of the $27 million endowment. Noyce was concerned that Grinnell should have so much exposure to a single name associated with him, and cajoled Rosenfield to sell. He recalls, "Bob [Noyce] was trembling about it. He'd say, 'I don't want the college to lose any money on account of me.' But I'd say, "We'll worry about that, Bob. We'll take the risk."[29] Noyce eventually wore Rosenfield down, however, and Grinnell fully exited the stake by 1980. On its sale, the Intel investment had generated a profit of 4,583 percent. Rosenfield told Zweig, "I wish we'd kept it. That was the biggest mistake we ever made. Selling must have cost us $50 million, maybe more."[30] Zweig didn't have the heart to tell the then 96-year-old Rosenfield that the shares he sold would have been worth several billion dollars in 2000. Perhaps this is why Rosenfield "considers selling to be indistinguishable from error."[31]

The third investment that set Grinnell apart was its 1976 acquisition of a TV station, *WDTN* in Dayton, Ohio. A direct, private investment in an operating business was unprecedented at that time for a college endowment.[32] Indeed, college endowments still rarely control private companies. Grinnell bought WDTN for $13 million—just 2.5 times revenues when comparable TV stations were selling for 3 to 4 times revenues.[33] Grinnell would sell the station to Hearst Corporation five years later in 1981 for $49 million—a 280 percent profit.[34] The endowment sold only because the station had swollen to a disproportionate size relative to the endowment's other assets. Rosenfield felt he couldn't justify maintaining so much of the endowment in an illiquid, private investment.[35]

The final holding critical to Grinnell's incredible performance was its investment in the Sequoia Fund. In 1977, Warren Buffett had proposed to Rosenfield that the endowment invest with a new firm called Sequoia.[36] Between 1978 and 1981, Rosenfield directed a third of the endowment—$10 million—into the Sequoia Fund.[37] It would prove to be a prescient bet. Between 1977 and 1997, Sequoia would outperform 94 percent of all mutual funds.[38] That holding would grow to $600 million by 2000—then one of the largest investments ever amassed in a mutual fund by a single shareholder. Ten thousand dollars invested in Sequoia at the beginning of 1977 would be worth $1.7 million at the end of 2015—a compound annual growth rate of 14 percent, after fees. That $600 million holding in Sequoia represented almost two-thirds of Grinnell's endowment in 2000.

GRINNELL UNDER GORDON

Rosenfield stepped down from Grinnell's investment committee in the mid-1990s, but Grinnell continued to implement the principles of his simple investment plan after he left. That was largely because 10 years before Rosenfield left Grinnell, he had tapped Jim Gordon to head the investment committee. Gordon started helping Rosenfield with investments informally in 1990, and was formally made the head of the investment committee in 1992. Buffett would continue to serve as a Grinnell trustee until 2011, when he stepped down from all boards not relating to Berkshire Hathaway, but he hadn't attended any Grinnell board meetings from at least the mid-1990s.

Rosenfield passed away in 2000, shortly after stepping down from Grinnell. Gordon was another investor from the same mold as Rosenfield. They had known each other for years before Rosenfield asked Gordon to join the board. The Rosenfields and the Gordons had a long family history together, and the families were close. Rosenfield was one of Gordon's father's very best friends. They ate lunch and played *gin* together at least five days a week, Monday to Friday, at the Des Moines Club. In his twenties, Gordon would occasionally accompany his father to the Des Moines Club for lunch with Rosenfield, who over time became a mentor to Gordon.

Gordon had started out working in his family's small trucking business in Des Moines, where he was born. He attended Northwestern University, and when he returned he took over the family business, becoming president of Gordon Foods, Inc., a firm started by his then 23-year-old grandfather in 1897. At the time he took it over, Gordon describes it as a local Des Moines and Central Iowa business. He expanded it from food and frozen food into petroleum and petroleum byproducts. Eventually the company expanded into anything that needed moving, including Gordon's own brands of motor oil and antifreeze and food. It expanded geographically, too, from Central Iowa into every state in the United States. In 1982, Gordon formed a Chicago-based private equity firm called *Edgewater Funds*. He used Edgewater Funds to engineer a leveraged buy-out of his own and his family's interests in the Gordon companies:[39]

> *We called them* bootstraps *back then, we didn't call them leveraged buy-outs. I was a minority seller and a majority buyer.*

In 1986, Gordon sold the company to a European multinational corporation, but retained a piece of it, reversing the earlier transaction: Gordon was now the majority seller and a minority buyer. In 1992, the company was sold for a third time, and Gordon became a full-time private equity investor. In the time that he operated Gordon Foods, he completed 19 leveraged buy-outs, including Fender Guitar, Chuckles candy, and Pine Brothers Cough Drops. In 2015, he has gone on to complete over 200 private equity transactions, and Edgewater now has $1.4 billion under management.

Gordon would occasionally throw investment ideas at Rosenfield. In 1990, he suggested one to Rosenfield that he particularly liked. During the junk bond crisis, Gordon had seen RJ Reynolds bonds trading at $53. Gordon told Rosenfield he had done some research on the company and found it "very financially sound:"[40]

> *I told him that he should buy some because people weren't about to stop smoking. And the bond subsequently went from $53 to $105.*

Rosenfield was starting to get older, and needed some help on the Grinnell investment committee because it was still run as a one-man committee. Though he was not a Grinnell graduate, Rosenfield asked Gordon, "Would you do it?"[41] Honored and pleased to work with his mentor, Gordon readily agreed. He joined the board in 1992, and started helping manage the endowment. Gordon observed that Rosenfield was "good at picking people, in particular, more than companies:"[42]

> *If I talked to him about a company, Joe would say, "I don't want to read the book." He would say, "Just tell me about the guy who runs the company. Is he honest"—because you can't do a good deal with a bad person, no matter how smart they are—"Is he smart? Is he hungry?"*

If Rosenfield got an affirmative answer to those three questions, says Gordon, then he would invest.[43] Gordon says that Rosenfield was an "amazing, just an amazing person. He could pick people:"[44]

> *It's a gut instinct that you're born with. It's pretty hard to pass it along. It's just a talent that most people don't have. I don't think you can learn it. Yeah, and he had it. He was obviously an extremely generous man. He had one child who was killed in an automobile accident, but he probably would've left all his money to charity anyway. He lived very modestly. Lived extremely modestly. And basically, he always found a way. Amazing man, learned a lot from him, that's for sure.*

Gordon had "a ton of fun" working with Rosenfield.[45] They were very close, spending a great deal of time together on the board of Grinnell. Gordon would always drive Rosenfield to the meetings, where they would sit together during the meetings and at the breaks, and then Gordon would drive Rosenfield home:[46]

> *He used to love it because it was about an hour-and-a-half drive, and I could make it in an hour.*

Gordon estimates that the endowment stood at $150 million when he took it over in 1992. From the moment he took it on, Rosenfield gave Gordon a free hand to manage it as he saw fit. Gordon could bounce ideas off him, but Rosenfield wanted Gordon to make the investment decision. Gordon managed the endowment from the get-go, with Rosenfield serving as cover for his investments. Rosenfield had been like another father figure to Gordon, and he wanted him to be proud of his performance. One of his first trades was Wells Fargo. Gordon bought it in the early 1990s before Buffett and Berkshire did, when it traded around $50. Just two months later it traded over $90, and Gordon sold it. He called Rosenfield:[47]

> *I was very proud of myself, because it was one of my first deals, and I wanted Joe to be happy. I hadn't conferred with him about buying it. I hadn't conferred with him about selling it. And so I said to him, "I just bought this stock Wells Fargo a few months ago at $50. It was very depressed. And I just sold it at $90." I thought I was going to get a bunch of praise. He said, "That's pretty good, I guess." And I said, "Joe, my grandfather taught me that no one ever went broke making a profit." And Joe said to me, "Let me correct that—no one ever went broke making a big profit." That's something I'll never forget.*

As Buffett had stopped attending board meetings in the mid-1990s, and Rosenfield was getting older and about to step down from the board, he wanted another sounding board for Gordon on the endowment committee. Buffett remained available to Gordon by telephone, and he did call Buffett every once in a while, but he says they mostly discussed Rosenfield. Gordon didn't use it as an opportunity to run an investment idea by him, or go over endowment issues with him at all.[48]

> *I spent time every day on it. I was picking stocks. I was basically a one-man committee with no office. Northern Trust gave us monthly reports [on our holdings], and that's where I got my reports. I didn't even get them from the office.*

Gordon also had access to Sequoia's William J. Ruane and Robert D. Goldfarb:[49]

> *I would talk to originally Bill Ruane, and then I would talk to Bob Goldfarb. We would take some time and spend it together once a month. We would go through the portfolio and what they were thinking of buying and what they were thinking of selling and what they had currently held, et cetera. They were very useful. They're smart people. You always learn something when you talk to other smart people.*

Even so, Rosenfield felt that Gordon should have someone else on the investment committee:[50]

You should have someone else on the committee that you can bounce things off of, who gives you a little cover, so that it's not a complete one-man committee.

Gordon responded, "What about Larry Pidgeon? He would be great for this."[51] Rosenfield readily agreed to Gordon's suggestion. Thirty-two-year-old Pidgeon wasn't a Grinnell alum, but Gordon knew him because he had grown up in Des Moines with Pidgeon's parents, who were family friends. He had attended Yale, and Gordon thought he was "very bright":[52]

I liked him a lot, and he seemed to have the same philosophies as Joe and me.

Gordon asked Pidgeon to join the board of trustees to help run the investment committee, which he did in 1995. Pidgeon had started his career in 1986, at Goldman Sachs, and remained there until 1989, when he moved on to work with Lou Simpson.[53] Simpson was then running the money management arm of GEICO. In 1995, Pidgeon founded New York–based CBM Capital: the initials "CBM" were said to stand for "Coke Big Mistake," intended to serve as a constant reminder to him of his failure to buy shares of Coca-Cola, Co. in the 1980s, after he analyzed the stock when it traded below $6. CBM Capital made long-term investments in undervalued businesses and managed almost $500 million in 2012.[54] In 2005, *Forbes* magazine said he was one of nine "hard-to-access investment wizards."[55] Pidgeon helped Gordon run the endowment for a few years, and then became the head of budget committee. He served as an influential member of Grinnell College's Board of Trustees and its investment committee from 1995 to 1999.[56] He passed away at 49 years of age in 2012, after a struggle with cancer.[57] Says Gordon:[58]

He wasn't an alum. He came on because I asked him to, just the reason I came on because Joe asked me to, and Warren came on because Joe asked him to.

In his investment career, Gordon has bought and sold over 300 companies, and says he regrets only one sale. It was one of the 19 companies Gordon bought while running Gordon Foods. He made 20 times his money when he eventually sold into a public offering, which is a great return, but he wasn't satisfied. After he sold, it went up another 2 or 3 times in the public markets:[59]

The last 2 to 3 times turns 20 times into 40 or 60 times your money. You think you've gotten 20 times and you could've gotten another

2 times, but that 2 times is a big deal because it's on such a bigger base.

It was a valuable lesson. And it made Rosenfield's admonition about "big profits" hit home. Gordon would go on to be a dyed-in-the-wool, buy-and-hold investor like Rosenfield. Even so, Gordon wasn't completely disappointed. He used the proceeds from the sale to buy a stock that did very well—one that Rosenfield also bought for Grinnell: Freddie Mac.[60] In 1989, Rosenfield had put $25 million into Freddie Mac, the Federal Home Loan Mortgage Corporation:[61]

We bought a ton of that when it was one issue in about 1990. Joe said, "Buy this Freddie Mac." That was one that he did right before I got on the board, or contemporaneously with it. And he said, "We should buy it for Grinnell."

One of Rosenfield's investment principles was to treat buying a stock as a very long-term commitment:[62]

Joe would say, "Put it in the safety deposit box and forget you have it." He was a long-term value investor.

Rosenfield and Gordon held on to Freddie Mac through its boom in the 1990s, selling it all just before Rosenfield left the board in 1999. Gordon recalls that he started selling around the same time Buffett and Berkshire sold out of it in the late 1990s:[63]

Luckily, I didn't [*hold it forever*]. *Grinnell ended up with literally hundreds of millions of dollars' worth that would be worth zero now. We didn't sell ours all at one time because I didn't want to miss a lot of upside. We sold it over time, different tranches of it, to reduce the risk of the concentration in the portfolio.*

All told, Grinnell made $130 million in profits from its $25 million stake in Freddie Mac, exiting before it ran into trouble in the mid-2000s.

Gordon's specialty was private equity investing, and he undertook several private equity investments on behalf of Grinnell. Grinnell had already broken the endowment mold by buying the TV station, and Gordon looked to make other direct private equity investments over the years. Grinnell bought a rendering business in Des Moines called the Flemings Company from the family who had founded it.[64] In a departure from the typical private equity deals, which are financed with a lot of debt, Grinnell used minimal debt in its direct private equity investments. He also looked at other unusual investments for Grinnell:

> *I would even do some IPOs, which I would flip the next day. And so, it was just, we did a number of IPOs that also, through my connections with the underwriting houses, including the spin-off of Kansas City Southern, the financial spin-off, DSL, Downey Savings and Loan. So, we did everything from that to Wells Fargo, and Morgan Stanley. We bought Morgan Stanley at $15 and sold it at $100. Anything we thought was a value play, if it got down to a very low multiple.*
>
> *We used to have a thing that any time Goldman recommended a stock, I would sell it, and every time they recommended a sell, I would buy it. I knew if they put out a sell, they wanted it to go down so they could buy it, and I knew if they recommended a buy, it was going to go down because they wanted to sell. And it practically always worked. And people paid them fees for that kind of service.*

During Rosenfield and Gordon's tenure, Grinnell had only one permanent outside manager, Sequoia. Grinnell considered other money managers under Gordon's tenure, and even invested with a few of them, but never to the extent that the endowment invested with Sequoia. One was a technology investor.[65] Says Gordon:[66]

> *His claim to fame was that he was the original guy to discover Microsoft. He had leverage in his main fund, and we had a specially managed account that had no leverage. We restricted it to less than 20 names, where his main fund might have 40 names. It was much more of a concentrated portfolio than his main fund, and obviously less leverage. He was a real go-go fund. And he did very well for us, although he ended up bombing out. We actually got out before then.*

Outside its holding in Sequoia, and its brief flirtation with a technology investor, Grinnell also directly held between 8 to 10 other stocks, but little in the way of cash and fixed income. Rosenfield and Gordon purposely minimized Grinnell's exposure to fixed income:[67]

> *We didn't really like having fixed income. We always had the philosophy that cash was the inverse relationship of having enough good ideas. We didn't have asset allocation, no consultant. If we had enough good ideas, we had zero cash.*

The board, however, wanted Gordon to hold more in fixed income so that the endowment didn't need to sell stocks to pay the college's operating expenses. The board would say, "You're encroaching upon endowment:"[68]

The board would say, "You've had to sell stocks to give us our 5 percent," if we'd be fully invested. And I would say, "You're making 3 percent on your bond portfolio, we're making 10 percent on our stocks. You're much better off being in the stocks and just selling some shares instead of taking the 3 percent coupon." That was hard for the board to understand. The board was about 90 percent attorneys when I was there. It was really amazing.

Gordon says they often had trouble finding ideas anyway, and tended to hold more cash than they thought was ideal:[69]

Cash and good ideas were an inverse relationship. So, if we had cash, it means we had a shortage of good ideas. It wasn't because of asset allocation. And there were times we didn't have any cash when we would need to spend capital gains [*to meet the college's 4.75 percent annual draw*].

Rosenfield and Gordon kept Grinnell's investment expenses cut to the bone. Grinnell had no investment staff, no consultants, and no chief investment officer. Says Gordon:[70]

I was picking stocks, and we had no staff, zero staff, so zero expense. And when I retired, we were number one in the 1, 3, 5, and 10-year records, which was pretty good. But as a net, nobody else, taking their expenses, compared to us. Their office is the Harvard Endowment Office or the Duke Endowment.

The rapid growth in the endowment created its own problems. As the investment capital swelled from $150 million to $1.1 billion, the college's 4.75 percent annual draw for operating expenses leapt up proportionately, too. The college started to rely on the gains. Says Gordon:[71]

Basically, people get lazy. The development office doesn't bring in any gifts, food service doesn't put out competitive bids, and so on. They just get lazy from A to Z.

For example, they were going to build this new building. They didn't get competitive bids and then didn't raise enough money in the fund drive to build it. They had a bid that I thought was terribly high. And I said, "You need to get competitive bids." And the president of the university said, "I don't have time to get competitive bids. The building won't be done by next fall. All the science professors will go on strike." I used to say, the inmates are running the prison.

Gordon wanted the school to try to remain efficient. He was concerned that if the stock market wilted, the operating budget would fall commensurately, and it might impact the operation of the school:[72]

We showed them a projection where, if the market goes down like it did in the 1970s, then eventually the school will go broke. It's like drugs. They're so used to being on not only all this money, but having it increase every year. We had to have some discipline and save some money for a rainy day.

Gordon's solution was to change the college's draw for operating expenses from the average of 4.75 percent over 12 quarters to what each department got the previous year plus the education consumer price index (CPI). Gordon recalls that the education CPI was the CPI plus 1 at the time:[73]

If you got $20 million last year, and inflation is 1 percent, you're going to get $20 million plus 2 percent. The rest of it is going to go in a fund for special projects to make Grinnell one of the best schools in the country.

Gordon describes his final investment in 2000 in AutoZone and ESL Investments as "a parting gift" to Grinnell because it occurred just before he left the endowment.[74] He categorizes AutoZone as a private equity investment because, though it was public, it was a single-stock, special-purpose vehicle and therefore private equity-like. Gordon was alerted to the opportunity when his friend, hedge fund manager Eddie Lampert, who runs ESL Investments, began buying into the stock in the low $20s. Lampert and Gordon often discussed stocks they were buying, and Gordon liked Lampert's plans for AutoZone. When Lampert offered to let Grinnell invest in a *sidecar*—one investor controls where and how another investor's capital is invested—for AutoZone and cut his fee in half, Gordon leapt at the chance. I said, "That's a great idea. We should definitely do that. So, we bought a fair amount of AutoZone in the $20s. Subsequently, it ran up to $400 or $500."[75] The investment wasn't without drama. Lampert's funds typically have a five-year lockup period, during which capital cannot be withdrawn. When Gordon retired from the board and the endowment committee, the new head of the investment committee approached Lampert about exiting before the lockup period had expired, when the stock was trading at $200. Lampert refused.[76]

I understand they even got some attorneys, and Eddie said, "No, you're not breaking the lock." It wasn't long thereafter the stock was up another $200. It was by far the most money Grinnell had ever made on anything, multiples on what they had made on the television station with Warren.

In an illustration of the adage *no good deed goes unpunished*, Gordon says that he was criticized for locking money up with a friend, even though the lockup "saved them from themselves:"[77]

Everybody complains about lockups, but the lockup saved them from themselves. And then they continued to make money. But I think Eddie may have eventually let them out of the lock and let them take their money in the fund. I was gone at that point, so I don't know, but nevertheless that was a great deal.

The story has a happy ending. When Grinnell exited AutoZone, the college reinvested in Lampert's fund, which still continues to hold AutoZone.

In 2000, Gordon decided to move from Des Moines to Chicago, and took the opportunity to step down from the board and the investment committee.[78]

It was a good time to move on since we had a lot of big-cap stocks in year 2000. It turned out to be a good time. To start in the early 1990s and get out in 2000 of the big-cap stocks was good timing.

He formally resigned from running Grinnell's investment commitment in 2000. When Gordon left, he had grown the Grinnell endowment from $150 million to $1.1 billion in nine years, which is an accomplishment, but even more impressive when the college's annual 4.75 percent in operating expenses is accounted for. Every year, the endowment paid to the school 4.75 percent of the 12-quarter moving average of the endowment's assets to help in running the school:[79]

They had no gifts during my tenure. And when I gave it back to them it was around $1.1 billion. So, if you replace expenses for the amount that was withdrawn to run the school, that's like a 5 percent expense ratio.

Though he has not kept track of Grinnell's investments since, Gordon says he still has a few good friends on the board, and he stays in touch with them. Gordon clearly misses Rosenfield:[80]

When Joe was around, it was much better because I got to be with Joe. It was kind of crazy after that.

Jason Zweig distilled Rosenfield's investment principles down to three:[81]

> *Do a few things well: Rosenfield built a billion-dollar portfolio not by putting a little bit of money into everything that looked good but by putting lots of money into a few things that looked great. Likewise, if you find a few investments that you understand truly well, buy them by the bucketful.*
>
> . . .
>
> *Sit still: Patience—measured not just in years but in decades—is an investor's single most powerful weapon. Witness Rosenfield's fortitude: In 1990, right after he bought Freddie Mac, the stock dropped 27%—and Grinnell's total endowment shriveled by a third. And although Sequoia crushed the S&P 500 cumulatively from 1979 to 1998, the fund underperformed the index in eight of those years, or 40% of the time. . . . Rosenfield never panicked.*
>
> . . .
>
> *Invest for a reason: Rosenfield is a living reminder that wealth is a means to an end, not an end in itself. His only child died in 1962, and his wife died in 1977. He has given much of his life and all of his fortune to Grinnell College.*

THE MODERN ENDOWMENT

While Gordon resigned from running Grinnell's investment commitment in 2000, severing the last direct link to Rosenfield, Grinnell continues to be managed according to Rosenfield's precepts. Grinnell's current investment manager is Scott Wilson, a 38-year-old Grinnell alumnus who arrived in 2010 as director of investments and now serves as chief investment officer. Wilson's philosophy sounds remarkably similar to Rosenfield in its "high-conviction . . . hands-on approach that focuses on a handful of investments."[82] Wilson's small team looks to find "one or two great investment ideas a year:"[83]

> *That's a very doable strategy. If they're trying to find 100 great investments a year, that's impossible.*

Grinnell's investment team continued the practice of employing outside investment managers, who now manage 80 percent of the capital, up from 60 percent under Gordon.[84] Grinnell's capital is allocated 45 percent to stocks, 45 percent to alternative investments, and 10 percent to cash and fixed-income instruments. The biggest change is that Grinnell focuses on the cash and fixed-income portion of the college's investment holdings, while outside managers handle the stock portfolio. Grinnell continues to have some private investments directly managed by the endowment. Wilson eschews "macro" money managers who bet on big-picture theses, preferring managers whose performance is repeatable.[85] He favors managers who rely on analysis, rather than instinct or "gut feelings," as Wilson describes it.[86]

Another significant shift is the focus on international investments. Grinnell has private equity investments in Africa because, Wilson says, the region has strong growth, attractive valuation, and fairly stable governments, particularly in sub-Saharan Africa:[87]

> *Most of our Africa investments are too soon to tell, though we think they are very compelling.*

Wilson's approach seems to be working. The endowment has increased to $1.8 billion from $1.3 billion under his tenure. He says:[88]

> *We have very good 1-, 3-, 5- and 15-year returns. Our 10-year return is relatively poor, but we have a strategy that tends to deviate from our peers because we run a more concentrated portfolio.*

In 2014, the school's $1.8 billion endowment posted a 20.4 percent return—tying it for the best one-year performance among the largest 100 U.S. colleges.[89] That puts tiny Grinnell ahead of Ivy League endowment powerhouses like Harvard and Yale.[90]

NOTES

1. Jim Gordon, interview, October 2015.
2. "U.S. and Canadian Institutions Listed by Fiscal Year (FY) 2014 Endowment Market Value and Change in Endowment Market Value from FY2013 to FY2014 (Revised February 2015)," National Association of College and University Business Officers and Commonfund Institute, 2015, www.nacubo.org/Documents/EndowmentFiles/2014_Endowment_Market_Values_Revised.pdf.
3. Joe Engleman, "Buffett Ends Term as College Trustee," *The Scarlet and Black*, Grinnell College Newspaper, November 4, 2011, www.thesandb.com/news/buffett-ends-term-as-college-trustee.html.
4. Ibid.
5. Ibid.
6. Ibid.
7. Jason Zweig, "The Best Investor You've Never Heard Of," *Money magazine*, June 2000, http://money.cnn.com/2000/06/01/zweig_on_funds/zweig_on_funds/a.htm.
8. Ibid.

9. Ibid.
10. Ibid.
11. Ibid.
12. Ibid.
13. Ibid.
14. Ibid.
15. Ibid.
16. Ibid.
17. Ibid.
18. Ibid.
19. Ibid.
20. Ibid.
21. Ibid.
22. Ibid.
23. Ibid.
24. Ibid.
25. Ibid.
26. Ibid.
27. Ibid.
28. Ibid.
29. Ibid.
30. Ibid.
31. Ibid.
32. Ibid.
33. Ibid.
34. Ibid.
35. Ibid.
36. Ibid.
37. Ibid.
38. Ibid.
39. Jim Gordon, interview, October 2015.
40. Ibid.
41. Ibid.
42. Ibid.
43. Ibid.
44. Ibid.
45. Ibid.
46. Ibid.
47. Ibid.
48. Ibid.
49. Ibid.
50. Ibid.
51. Ibid.
52. Ibid.
53. Saijel Kishan, "Lawrence Pidgeon, Investor Taught by Buffett Protege, Dies at 49," *Bloomberg*, November 15, 2012, www.bloomberg.com/news/articles/2012-11-16/lawrence-pidgeon-investor-taught-by-buffett-protege-dies-at-49.

54. Ibid.
55. Ibid.
56. Grinnell College, "Careers in Education Program," https://www.grinnell.edu/academics/offices/careers-in-education/about.
57. Ibid.
58. Jim Gordon, interview, October 2015.
59. Ibid.
60. Ibid.
61. Ibid.
62. Ibid.
63. Ibid.
64. Jason Zweig, "The Best Investor You've Never Heard Of," *Money* magazine, June 2000, http://money.cnn.com/2000/06/01/zweig_on_funds/zweig_on_funds/a.htm.
65. Jim Gordon, interview, October 2015.
66. Ibid.
67. Ibid.
68. Ibid.
69. Ibid.
70. Ibid.
71. Ibid.
72. Ibid.
73. Ibid.
74. Jason Zweig, "The Best Investor You've Never Heard Of," *Money* magazine, June 2000, http://money.cnn.com/2000/06/01/zweig_on_funds/zweig_on_funds/a.htm.
75. Ibid.
76. Jim Gordon, interview, October 2015.
77. Ibid.
78. Ibid.
79. Ibid.
80. Ibid.
81. Jason Zweig, "The Best Investor You've Never Heard Of," *Money magazine*, June 2000, http://money.cnn.com/2000/06/01/zweig_on_funds/zweig_on_funds/a.htm.
82. Silvia Ascarelli, "How Tiny Grinnell College's Endowment Outperformed the Ivy League," *MarketWatch*, May 20, 2015, www.marketwatch.com/story/how-tiny-grinnell-colleges-endowment-outperformed-the-ivy-league-2015–05–20.
83. Ibid.
84. Ibid.
85. Ibid.
86. Ibid.
87. Ibid.
88. Ibid.
89. Ibid.
90. Ibid.

CHAPTER 8

Glenn Greenberg: The Iconoclast

Simple, Common Sense Research, and Tennis Shoes

As a concentrated investor, you had "better really know what you're talking about."

—Glenn Greenberg, 2015[1]

On January 14, 2008, fed up with a series of acquisitions that had resulted in "zero return" for shareholders, Glenn Greenberg and his colleagues at New York–based Chieftain Capital Management sent a letter to J. Michael Cook, the presiding director on Comcast's board.[2] Styling the 45 percent slide in the share price as a "Comcastrophe," Chieftain called on the board to oust incumbent chief executive officer Brian Roberts and replace him with a "highly qualified CEO" who would "focus on maximizing the value of Comcast for its shareholders."[3]

We want and deserve the best CEO Comcast's board of directors can find, and, based on his record, Brian Roberts is not it.

In the letter, cosigned by managing directors John Shapiro and Thomas Stern, Chieftain pointed to a laundry list of complaints.[4]

Returns on invested capital have been anemic, high-priced acquisitions have proven a waste of capital, [capital expenditure] has ballooned and free cash flow has consistently disappointed. While management has boosted Comcast's operating cash flow by 10-fold in the past decade (mostly through acquisitions), it has created zero return for shareholders.

The solution, according to Chieftain, was for the company to institute stricter financial discipline on management, and more closely manage the firm's capital expenditures. In practice, this meant restraining Roberts's spending on acquisitions and other "low-return investments."[5] Chieftain said that Comcast had spent "$80 billion on acquisitions in the past decade, regularly paying in excess of 20 times operating cash flow for cable and media properties."[6]

> *The result has been a significant dilution of free cash flow per share and returns on capital, and with Comcast's assets now valued by the market at only 5.5 times projected operating cash flow, a staggering destruction of value.*

Chieftain demanded that the company initiate a "meaningful dividend" and boost its debt to "an appropriate level."[7] Comcast's board had just authorized a $7 billion increase in its share buyback program. Chieftain described the move as inadequate as the buyback was to take place over several years.

The letter was an unusually public step for Chieftain, which was not known as an activist. Its chances of prevailing in a proxy fight with the board seemed slim. The company was founded by chief executive Brian Roberts's father, Ralph, in 1963,[8] and the Roberts family retained control of Comcast through a dual share-class voting structure.[9] The family's super-voting stock gave Roberts a third of the vote despite holding an economic interest equivalent to just 1 percent of Comcast's 3 billion outstanding shares. Chieftain had urged the company to eliminate the dual-class voting structure, arguing that the Roberts family's voting position was "inconsistent with 21st-century corporate governance."[10]

> [*T*]*he maximization of shareholder value has been an after-thought for this management team. Protected by super-voting stock, management has been free to ignore shareholders entirely.*

The Roberts family seemed unlikely to surrender control of the company by scrapping the dual-class stock. Chieftain's only hope was that public embarrassment and Comcast's poor stock performance might lead the family to start caring about its public shareholders. One anonymous source suggested in the *New York Post* that Chieftain's letter had more to do with its fund's performance than with Comcast's, saying that its huge holding in Comcast, " . . . might be considered too heavily weighted towards one company."[11]

Chieftain's holding in Comcast was the largest single position Greenberg and company had ever put into the portfolio. The fund held 60.2 million shares in Comcast, representing just 2 percent of its outstanding stock, and roughly 30 percent of Chieftain's $5 billion in capital. The firm had started investing in Comcast six years earlier in 2002, following the late 1990s melt-up and crash of the technology, media, and telecommunications industry. Greenberg had previously invested successfully in several cable companies, and felt confident that Comcast could be a similar experience. The Comcast stock price had a stellar run in 2006, ending the year up almost 66 percent, most of which Greenberg attributed to the market recognizing the company's undervaluation, rather than strong underlying business performance. Chieftain took the opportunity to start selling stock. Then, based on faulty new modeling of the outlook, the partners reversed course and convinced themselves that Comcast was "a better buy up 66 percent."[12] It was, says Greenberg, "just a grave mistake to place so much confidence in a financial model."[13]

2007 was a bad year for the company. A lot of the assumptions that were in the model didn't turn out. The stock got crunched and we had a bad 2007. And it wasn't like we built the position up on new information.

Comcast would amply demonstrate for Chieftain the hazards of a highly concentrated portfolio. Comcast's slump continued into 2008, contributing to a 34 percent loss for clients that year. This no doubt contributed to tensions, and the eventual split between Greenberg and the other partners a year later in 2009. After his campaign went public, Comcast quietly began to make a lot of changes. A new chief financial officer, Michael Angelakis, joined the company and brought discipline to capital spending, operating budgets, and acquisitions. Compensation, which was entirely based on EBITDA size, was broadened to include more appropriate performance metrics. Share retirement and dividend increases became regular and predictable, while remaining somewhat anemic. Free cash flow became, for the first time, the company's mantra.

Although Comcast generates a lot of free cash flow they don't return a significant amount of it. They just move up the dividend and buy back gently over time. They're massively under-levered relative to where the rest of the cable industry is, and where they were historically. They want to save firepower to buy things. They have a predilection for empire building.

Greenberg exited his position in early 2014, after Comcast's proposal to acquire Time Warner Cable. He thought the deal was strategically wrong-headed because of the increased regulatory scrutiny it would attract. Greenberg says that the announcement of the acquisition spurred the Obama administration's renewed interest in regulating cable under the "net neutrality" banner:[14]

> *Comcast already has 20 percent of the cable homes. There aren't going to be any greater efficiencies [from the acquisition], and they already pass 50 percent of the homes in the U.S. where they can offer their broadband service. Instead of just quietly going about their business implementing usage-based pricing, they've now made a huge issue by trying to get much bigger and drawing focus on the fact they'll be going past 70 or 80 percent of cable homes. And suddenly they put a target on their back and they're going to be re-regulated because everybody now realizes they control too many broadband homes and they could stick it to people in pricing. I think they brought this on themselves.*

THE FAMILY BUSINESS

Greenberg hadn't set out to be an investor. After leaving high school at Andover, he studied English at Yale. He took one math class, but dropped it at the end of the first semester because he did so poorly. He says Yale had a great English department. After graduating during the Vietnam War, he became a teacher in New York City for three years. He didn't know what he wanted to do with his life, but he didn't think he'd be a teacher forever. By chance, the headmaster of a school where he worked suggested that he go to business school. Greenberg's family through his mother was a controlling shareholder in Gimbel Brothers, a U.S. department store company started in 1887, and publicly listed in 1922. Gimbels bought Saks & Co. in 1923, and launched the iconic Saks Fifth Avenue. It started the tradition of a Thanksgiving Day parade in 1920, which was copied by Macy's in 1924. In the 1930s, Gimbels was the largest department store chain in the world by revenue, and the family controlled around 20 percent of the company. Gimbels's stock performed woefully between 1971 and 1973, dropping from $50 per share to less than $10 per share. The family hoped that Greenberg, now at business school, would work in the family business after graduation. Unfortunately for the family, Greenberg had "less than zero interest in retail."[15]

During the course of business school, Greenberg was asked to write a paper on the planning process of a business. He approached his uncle, who ran Gimbels, and asked if he could write the paper on the family firm. His uncle readily agreed. Greenberg met with the company's heads of marketing, merchandising, and finance. He was deeply unimpressed with the company, and wrote a "scathing indictment of it."[16] Greenberg felt Gimbels was "very poorly managed."[17]

> *They missed the whole move to the suburbs. Then when they went to the suburbs they went to places like Bridgeport, Connecticut, which didn't have a lot of discretionary income. They built a store on 86th Street in Manhattan, which turned out to be a disaster.*
>
> *They couldn't get their accounts receivable system to work so they had to write off a massive amount of receivables. And basically the stock collapsed during the bear market.*

His uncle read the paper, and "thanked" Greenberg "by calling me every name he could think of."[18] That ended any notion of him going to work in the family business.

Soon after, investor Laurence "Larry" Tisch—the self-made billionaire known for buying into failing companies when their share prices were at a low ebb and then turning them into profitable enterprises with much higher stock valuations—emerged with a large holding in the company.[19] Tisch, who would later play the role of white knight for broadcaster CBS, Inc., sought the role of corporate raider and liquidator of the department store chain. He wanted to take over the company and liquidate it for its undervalued New York real estate. Greenberg says that Tisch's approach put his family "in a dither."[20] They hired investment bankers to advise them on strategic options, and an improbable white knight was located in the form of Brown & Williamson Tobacco. Brown & Williamson bought the company in 1973, paying $23 per share, and buying out the family in the process. Greenberg felt fortunate not to have acceded to his family's pressure for him to become a merchant. He would have been out of a job in six months.

Brown & Williamson's takeover of Gimbels turned out to be a disastrous investment for them. They were eventually forced to close all the Gimbel-branded stores because they couldn't find a buyer. The Saks-branded stores continue to exist, though they've passed from owner to owner since then.

BECOMING A MONEY MIS-MANAGER

The takeover of Gimbels freed Greenberg to consider what he wanted to do with his life.[21] At business school he had taken an introductory finance class taught by Samuel Stewart, PhD, who started Wasatch Advisors, a successful

Utah-based mutual fund firm, and with whom Greenberg became close friends. In the class, Stewart asked the students to undertake some securities analysis for a few weeks. Greenberg analyzed the stock of Trans World Airlines, which was then one of the "big four" domestic airlines in the United States. Stewart had the class write a paper on why they would invest in it or not, and Greenberg found it to be "a lot of fun."[22]

> *Basically, just to look at a business and decide whether you'd want to own the stock. It felt very comfortable. It felt very obvious to me.*

Based on this experience, he decided to try to get a job in a bank investment department. He applied to Citi and Morgan Guaranty. Both offered him a position. He accepted Morgan Guaranty and went to work in their investment research department in 1973, starting as a media analyst just after the media companies went public in the late 1960s. Greenberg covered ad agencies; television operators like ABC, CBS, and Capital Cities; information companies like Dun & Bradstreet, Nielsen, and Commerce Clearing House; and newspaper chains like Gannett. He says that though they were "pretty great businesses," they were all new to the public, and misunderstood as a result.[23] Greenberg was one of the few who could see that they enjoyed high barriers to entry.

At his first presentation to the trust committee, his group head approached him just minutes before he was supposed to present and asked him what he planned to say. Greenberg responded, "Well, I'm going to say that this is a fabulous business and that the future's very bright for these monopoly newspapers."[24]

His supervisor said, "You can't say that. You've got to couch it. You've got to be more conservative."[25]

Greenberg responded, "Well, it's great that you're telling me this now, two minutes before I go into the trust committee."[26] The 26-year-old was already nervous about presenting at the meeting, and it was too late to change the content, so he presented what he had planned to say. The committee must have been impressed because within a year of him joining the firm, they moved him to forest products, paper, and building materials, which he says was a big industry at that time. The stock prices of the companies in the industry had been killed in the 1973 to 1974 recession, and Greenberg was very enthusiastic about their prospects. When the economy snapped back vigorously, the stocks that he had recommended "did incredibly well."[27]

Impressed with Greenberg's performance, Morgan Guaranty made him what he jokingly describes as a "money mis-manager."[28] He joined the pension investment department, and was put to work on a commingled fund, one that consisted of assets from many accounts blended together. The fund invested in medium-sized companies, which Greenberg found interesting because he got to know a lot of different businesses.[29] He also was assigned responsibility for looking after a flock of large pension accounts. His first task was to accompany the head of the department as he explained to the pension fund investors how Morgan Guaranty had lost half of their capital by owning the *Nifty Fifty*. And by the way, here is the "junior ensign" now managing your account. The Nifty Fifty were the 50 most popular large capitalization stocks held by institutional investors in the 1960s and 1970s. They were characterized by extremely high prices relative to their earnings, and the common conceit was that they were "one decision" stocks, those that could be bought and held forever because the businesses were destined to grow for a long time. They were especially hard hit in the 1974 stock market crash. Greenberg flew with his boss to visit with each client. Ordinarily, the money managers would have met with each company's pension administrator, but the crash had so impacted the pension assets of the firms that the issue was elevated to the board of directors. Greenberg recalls that each company was very concerned because they were going to have to pony up a great deal of money to meet their pension obligations. Such a move would hit their financial statements at a time when the market for their stocks was already devastated. Flying all over the country meeting with these boards of directors, listening to the head of the department attempt to explain why the Nifty Fifty stocks were still worth holding, and why they lost so much money, made a huge impression on Greenberg. Being forced to face people for whom he'd lost a lot of money was a formative experience for him.

Greenberg also found there was tension between the research department analysts and the money managers at Morgan. The research analysts visited companies, held meetings with management, and built financial models. They thought the fund managers should listen to them. The money managers could get research from many brokers, and had those banks' salespeople calling on them. As a result, they often didn't follow the advice of the internal research staff. The research analysts felt disrespected by the investment managers, and it created tension in the meetings between the two groups.

Someone thought it would be a good idea if the money managers met without the research analysts present to discuss their top holdings. They met. IBM, the biggest holding, was the first to be discussed. No one had anything to say about it. In that moment Greenberg realized that the money managers, who had been running funds for 10 to 15 years, didn't know anything of substance about their holdings. They didn't really follow the companies closely enough or at all. They didn't know the businesses. There wasn't anything to discuss. He reflected that if he had been asked about any paper company, an industry that he'd just been following as a research analyst, he'd have been able to give them chapter and verse on why they should or shouldn't own it. It made a huge impression on him that an investor should be both an analyst and a money manager. Both roles are important facets of the investment process. Without all the facts that a research analyst has, and without the impressions that analysts get from meeting with managements, and studying them closely, fund managers can't make good investment decisions. The experience showed Greenberg the type of fund manager he wanted to be.

ARTHUR ROSS'S TENNIS SHOES

After five years at Morgan Guaranty, Greenberg saw that he was not going to learn how to manage money by remaining at the firm. He wanted to work for someone he could learn from. He joined the family office of Central National-Gottesman, which was based in New York and run by a little-known money manager named Arthur Ross. Greenberg thought he was a "brilliant, brilliant investor."[30]

> *Nobody's ever heard of him because he handled private money and he didn't get written up in books or get quoted in the newspapers, but he was a really phenomenal investor. The story was that one of the Gottesman family members came into his office one day and said, "Arthur, what's the secret to your success?" Ross said, "Tennis shoes. Now get out of my office." And the guy went out of the office and said, "Tennis shoes? I don't get it."* [So] *he went down the hall to the office of one of Ross's analysts and said, "Arthur told me the secret to his success is tennis shoes." He meant, 10 issues. He owns 10 issues. Just 10 stocks.*

Where previously Greenberg had specialized in a single industry—media or paper—he was now expected to be a generalist. Even so, Ross was incredibly demanding about understanding what he called the *blood and guts* of a business. Ross's analysts were welcome to find their own investment opportunities, but Ross handed out assignments based on things that he was interested in. He liked to call an analyst into his office and start peppering him with questions about a business the analyst covered. The analysts weren't allowed to bring in any notes. He'd keep asking questions until the analyst couldn't answer one. When that happened, Ross would get furious. He asked good questions and insisted on an unbelievable level of detail. Ross taught Greenberg to be a "very, very careful and thoughtful analyst."[31] He would think about everything that Ross might want to know, and he believes it made him a better investor as a result. Most of all, he learned to identify the key factors that would make or break an investment concept. Greenberg spent five years with Ross. He invested for himself while he was there, but Ross did all the investing for the family. Nobody but Ross traded a stock for the family. Ross's portfolios had very low turnover. "He didn't trade at all," says Greenberg. "He was a true investor."[32]

> *And his record, which I still keep as an inspiration, was just phenomenal. There were no shorts or hedges or anything like that. He was just an unbelievably astute investor.*

After 10 years in the business—five years with Ross and five years with Morgan Guaranty—Greenberg felt ready to strike out on his own.

Greenberg founded Chieftain Capital Management with John Shapiro in 1984. The firm launched with $43 million under management, $30 million of which was Gimbel family money that he had already been managing while he was with Ross, and another $13 million from a father and two sons introduced to Greenberg by his brother. The father and sons had just sold a meat-grinding business that vended meat to California school lunch programs and suddenly had more than $4 million each. They invested with Greenberg at the beginning of 1984. The market immediately fell sharply. Chieftain fell much less, but was down. Every month the father would call Greenberg wanting to know what his budget was for the next month. Greenberg tried to explain to him that wasn't how investing worked. Three or four months later, the father withdrew his capital, and then two weeks later the older brother did the same. Chieftain had lost 20 percent of its capital, and two-thirds of its outside capital, in its first five months. The younger brother contacted Greenberg and told him that he'd give him until year-end because it wasn't fair to judge him after only a few months.

After starting the year down, Chieftain's first year turned out to be strong. (The younger brother who told Greenberg that he'd see out the year has been a client ever since, and "has a very large account."[33]) Money started pouring into the firm as clients started telling their friends about the firm. Even so, for the first eight years, Chieftain only managed money for high net worth individuals. In 1990, Greenberg was invited along with other young alumni for a "back-to-class" weekend at Yale. David Swensen, who administered Yale's endowment, gave a talk about the endowment's investment strategy. Swensen had been in charge of the endowment for several years, and had placed a quarter of its capital in stock market index funds. Greenberg thought it was preposterous. He thought, "I could beat the market with my hands tied behind me."[34] Greenberg raised his hand and said,

"Yale has always stood for excellence. I can't believe that you're willing to take the market return. You can do so much better than that."[35] After the talk, Swensen approached Greenberg and arranged to meet with him for lunch. After a series of lunches over a year and a half, Swensen finally asked if Greenberg would take on some money from Yale. Greenberg says that it ended up being a "really great relationship. I was honored to be part of the management of the Yale endowment."[36] Chieftain's record and the endorsement from Yale made it easy to raise capital, but the focus was always on investment performance—not asset gathering.

After putting together a 26-year track record with annual returns of 18 percent before fees, Greenberg and the other partners separated in 2009.[37] Shapiro left to start a new firm, and named it Chieftain Capital, while Greenberg remained with the existing firm, and renamed it Brave Warrior Advisors. Greenberg says the holdings of the two firms are "very different."[38] Brave Warrior seeks out advantaged businesses with above-average growth. He reasons that the rationale for investing in equities is to grow the capital, "and I don't think you grow your capital faster than the market by buying a business that's barely piddling along."[39]

After splitting with Shapiro and Chieftain, Greenberg's portfolio has been open to a greater variety of businesses, including those classified as technology. He says that the difference is not due to a change in philosophy, but a change in work environment.[40]

> *I'm working with guys who are in their late twenties and thirties and they are at a stage of life when they enjoy working very hard. They're trying to build a career and they're hungry. They cover a lot of ground. We have a very rigorous vetting process. They also understand technology and have helped me understand rapidly growing businesses like Google, Vistaprint, MasterCard, and Valeant.*
>
> *I have found it easier not to have to negotiate decisions with partners. We had 20 percent cash from 1992 until 2008, which hurt our performance and reflected the clash of male egos as well as differences of judgment.*

GREENBERG'S THEORY OF VALUE

Asked to describe himself as an investor, Greenberg says that he is not a "pure" value investor if "pure" value investing means a mechanical focus on arbitrary relationships like market value to book value or sales. He does not seek out cigar butts or look at liquidation value or breakup value. The few times that he's deviated and bought something because it seemed really cheap on a breakup basis, he hasn't done well. He prefers to buy a growing business where earnings are likely to rise over time and where a positive change in perception of that growth will lead to a higher multiple.[41]

> *If a business is growing one to two percent, how do you know it's not going to start to shrink one to two percent? There's not much of a margin of error there. When you talk about a crappy business that's barely moving forward, ask, "*Is *it moving forward?" How do you know it's not going to start shrinking?*
>
> *The optimist says, "What if instead of growing two percent, it grows four, and that 1 percent pretax margin then becomes two?" But it can go the other way. It's a much riskier bet. I look for situations where there is little downside risk if things continue as they are and a lot of money to be made if a few things go right. In other words, a highly favorable risk/reward balance.*

One example he provides of his preferred kind of investment is one of his big positions in the early 1980s: Gotaas-Larsen Shipping. Greenberg says it was perceived as a tanker company, but it was actually a liquid natural gas ship-leasing company. It leased out vessels for 20 years on *take-or-pay contracts*—whereby the customer uses the ship or pays a penalty to the lessor—to AAA-rated oil companies to transport natural gas from Indonesia to Japan. Greenberg says the value of the business could be determined by taking the present value of its charters because that was the source of most of the firm's cash flow, and it was guaranteed. (The company also owned a third of Royal Caribbean cruise lines, which turned out to be very valuable, but was an unproven industry at the time.) Greenberg says he saw the leases were giving shareholders a 15 percent rate of return, and asked, "What else do I need to know?"[42] He says it worked out extremely well.

Greenberg provides another example: Freddie Mac went public in 1989. (Fannie Mae was already public.) The basic model of the industry was that the two competitors, Fannie Mae and Freddie Mac, bought mortgages and issued mortgage-backed securities. They were paid guarantee fees of 0.23 percent of the face value of the mortgages to insure their creditworthiness. Greenberg recalls Freddie Mac's overhead was "about five basis points"—0.05 percent—and their losses on the mortgages were anywhere between one and five basis points depending upon where they were in the business cycle.[43] The business got 23 points in revenues and costs ran 6 to 10 points, leaving the rest as profit. With only two competitors and a growing market, it seemed like a no-lose proposition. Then Freddie Mac developed the capacity to sell callable debt and leverage its own balance sheet by owning mortgages. That gave it the opportunity to reinvest its cash flows at about a 20 percent return, and "there aren't many businesses where you can reinvest at 20 percent," he says.[44]

> *It was an unbelievable situation. They took all their cash flow and invested at 20 percent by buying mortgages and selling callable debt.*

Greenberg says that Freddie Mac was perceived to be an interest rate sensitive stock, "It never sold at a high multiple, and it traded up and down with interest rates. If interest rates went up, the stock multiple went down."[45] He made a chart of the earnings of Freddie Mac over 10 years plotted against the earnings of Coca-Cola over the same 10 years, from 1989 to 1998. He would show the chart to people and ask, "Which is Coke and which is Freddie?"[46] He says that no one could tell the difference, but Coca-Cola sold at a very high multiple of earnings, and Freddie sold at a modest multiple. "Freddie Mac was a badly misunderstood business," he says.[47] Greenberg says that Chieftain owned Freddie Mac for about nine years before it got "really screwed up."[48]

He says Gotaas-Larsen Shipping and Freddie Mac typify his idea of the kind of situation he prefers: a business that's likely to grow and where little can go wrong.[49]

> *And of course, you've got to watch it carefully, but that's my idea of being a value investor as opposed to the traditional Graham and Dodd thing, which was written in the 1930s. It's totally different. It's almost irrelevant. I never read Graham and Dodd's* Security Analysis *until I was asked to write the foreword to one of the chapters on equity investing. There were a few general thoughts that you could say, "This makes sense. This is good philosophy." But it was really not relevant to me.*

Greenberg employs an eclectic search strategy to find the businesses he likes to buy. He reads the newspapers and follows 13F filings—the quarterly filing of holdings by investment managers—of a handful of like-minded investors. He also looks at industries that are down and out. When oil and gas prices collapsed in late 2014, he started hunting in oil- and gas-related companies. (He notes that it's not his favorite industry because it's capital intensive, cyclical, and price dependent.) He also maintains a watch list of diverse companies that he's examined in the past, that he thinks are first-rate businesses with competent management, but are simply too expensive at prevailing prices.

When he finds a company he likes, Greenberg begins the process of analyzing its business. He has his team start with the construction of a financial model. An analyst takes the historical numbers and "scrubs them as clean as possible, not to project the future, but to help us understand the business better." He prefers to write down numbers by hand on a yellow legal pad, rather than into a computer spreadsheet.[50]

> *John [Shapiro] and I, we're the yellow pad people. We always did our analysis just on the yellow pad. It makes you much more sensitive to getting something generally right, as opposed to a multivariate, 600-line model that can get everything precisely wrong. The younger guys from the model generation figure that if it's in the model with all the assumptions then it must be right. I believe that model building sometimes distracts from time spent figuring out the key strategic questions that should be addressed to management.*

He also reads the annual report and a great many transcripts of quarterly earnings calls and presentations.

> *I like to read transcripts. I get a good feel for the management and trends in the business by reading a year's worth of transcripts.*

Greenberg tries to simplify the financials, reports, and presentations down to a thesis.[51]

> *Is this an advantaged business? How much competition does it have? Can it raise prices? And is it priced at a level where you could see making a very attractive rate of return without much risk of loss? The first thing we decide is whether it's a good business. And if it's not, we just drop it.*

He will review the team's model, and it will lead to questions that help him understand the business better. For example, he might ask, "Why did margins hold up so well in 2008?" or, "Why has this business slowed down so much?" or, "Why do they get such great returns on capital in this particular business?" He wants his team to think about the core issues of the business, and not get hung up on the detail of the model. He wants them to understand what factors allow the business to earn high returns and whether these are sustainable in the long term.

> *It's thinking about the issues and then kind of coming to the right conclusion. A lot of times it comes down to judgment about people. Do I believe the people who run this business to be honest and*

credible? Or do I think they're promotional? Or do I think they're delusional? Or do I think they're trying to raise more money and therefore they want to pump things up?

Like his old mentor Arthur Ross, he doesn't like his team to speculate when answering questions. He places a great deal of weight on getting the details right.[52]

Even though I think getting it approximately right is what you want to do, I'm really a stickler on them knowing the details and being very careful about how they do numbers. I never want them to answer a question with "I think . . ." "I feel . . ." or, "My guess is . . ." No. We don't invest large sums of money based on your guess. I'd like you to really know, and to work off the latest public figures. Don't use stale numbers.

If Greenberg and the team are still excited about the opportunity, one of his analysts sets up calls with former employees, directors, competitors, private companies, regulators, and industry experts.[53]

We do this ourselves. We talk with a lot of people who we hope have no ax to grind and who will just tell us what the business is really like. "What are the competitive dynamics? Does the CEO care about shareholders?" Whatever the key questions are, we try to get a lot of information from people who are out of the picture but are knowledgeable. Usually they're retired and they're really happy to talk. We've studied the industry and ask a lot of good basic questions, so they seem to enjoy educating us. We have a lot of those conversations and that tends to be an important factor in our process.

He then talks to the company. If he's feeling enthusiastic about the business, he wants to meet management as quickly as possible. He may buy stock before he has a chance to meet, but usually he will wait. The meeting leads to a complete financial analysis, and a model incorporating the conversation with management.

Greenberg has no use for large, complicated models. He provides his assumptions, and the team then builds the model. He wants to make sure that when he looks at the output, he understands what has been included and what's been excluded.[54]

How much of the free cash flow is from stock comp versus something else? And what do we assume about that new drug? Did we assume it's in the numbers or not in the numbers? So I don't make the model, but I make sure that all the inputs are ones that I feel comfortable with.

After checking out the business, and the people, and calling unbiased sources, in the end it becomes about judgment.[55]

There are positives. There are negatives. How do I weigh them? Do I think the negatives hold me back from making the investment? Do I think it's priced so attractively that even if one or two of those negatives come to pass, we'll still do okay? That's where the rubber meets the road. It is the hardest thing. You can't put it down in a how-to book or on a checklist for someone any more than I could learn to paint like Picasso by attending his lectures or buying a paint-by-numbers instruction book.

Greenberg doesn't limit himself to one kind of valuation metric, but he always looks at free cash flow yield.[56]

The absolute best thing would be a business like Freddie Mac where all the money they generate every year was free cash flow but they have an investment opportunity that is very high and certain.

The next best is a fine business that is under a cloud that can use its cash flow or borrowings to retire its stock inexpensively. When business recovers, the stock can really shine with materially lower shares outstanding.

Greenberg believes that the use to which a company puts its free cash flow is a crucial consideration. He notes that a fabulous business that sells at a high multiple of earnings, say 40 times, and buys back stock like crazy is burning money. On the other hand, another company with a fabulous business that takes the money and piles it up on the balance sheet or overpays for acquisitions is also not doing any favors to its owners.

There's no real formula to it. Part of it is understanding what the business is, part of it is understanding what its opportunities are, and part of it is understanding what the management's likely to do.

He isn't rigid about requiring a certain rate of return over time. "It depends on where the market is," says Greenberg.[57] One method he uses to value a business is to seek ones that generate a free cash-flow yield of, say, 10 percent in the next year or so, with modest underlying growth of, say, 5 percent. He found MasterCard as such an opportunity, albeit with a higher growth rate. MasterCard stock was crushed in 2010, when the *Durbin Amendment*—part of the *Dodd-Frank* financial reform legislation—passed. The Durbin Amendment required banks to limit *swipe fees*, the little tolls charged to retailers, for processing debit cards. Greenberg's interest was piqued by the tanking stock. He instantly recognized MasterCard as a phenomenal business. He also knew that 85 percent of worldwide transactions still took place in cash, and felt that the world was inexorably moving toward "plastic," creating a very long runway for potential growth. The thesis boiled down to how much the Durbin Amendment would impact MasterCard's business. Specifically, how much money was MasterCard making from debit interchange, and by how much would the Durbin Amendment reduce earnings?

Greenberg realized that the market had misperceived the impact of the reduction in debit interchange rates. The retailers paid to MasterCard and the banks approximately 1 percent of the face value of each debit transaction. MasterCard processed the transaction and then remitted most of this charge to the banks. There was no easy way to know how much of their cut they were going to have to give up. The market's perception was that a reduction in the interchange rate from 1 percent to 0.2 to 0.3 percent would mean that MasterCard got "creamed."[58] Greenberg took a lot of telephone calls from industry participants who told him, "This is the end of the world for MasterCard."[59] It wasn't obvious, but MasterCard only received a tiny portion of a transaction's economics; most went to the banks. Greenberg believed that the banks had no leverage to make the networks share the pain of the fee reduction.

After diving into the business, Greenberg also saw that MasterCard might actually benefit from the change in regulation. Debit made up only a small part of its business, while it was a larger part of Visa's business. What was bad for its main competitor might be good for MasterCard. He knew it was a phenomenal business. Though it had much lower margins than Visa, it would grow those margins as the business grew. Greenberg calculated that the Durbin change could knock off six months of earnings growth. Instead of growing 15 percent, MasterCard would grow 7 percent for a year before reaccelerating to 15 percent. It was the rare opportunity Greenberg sought: a "really great growth business for a 10 percent free cash flow yield two years out."[60]

Greenberg found another such opportunity in 2010. It seemed an unusual departure for him—a technology stock with an advertising-based, Internet business—but he couldn't ignore how cheap it looked. It was trading at $500 with $100 per share in cash and $30 per share in earnings, which were growing at 20 percent year-over-year. The stock was Google, the web search company. Greenberg knew that the Internet got one-third of people's leisure time but garnered only 15 percent of advertising spend. He reasoned that advertising dollars would follow the eyeballs, and Google, with most of search revenues and half of all digital advertising revenues, would be a major beneficiary. "It was pretty obvious that they were going to grow really fast,"[61] he says. He acknowledges that industries like Google's, which are enjoying fast growth and high profitability, generally attract competition, but he believed that Google had insuperable competitive advantages.[62]

> *You have to look at the search business and say, "Do I believe that Google's search business is a business that's a great franchise and one that's likely to be around for a long, long time? Does it have advantages that Bing doesn't have or Yahoo! doesn't have?" Well, now Yahoo! doesn't even do their own search.*
>
> *It's a duopoly like Freddie Mac and Fannie Mae. Who doesn't like businesses where there are few competitors and where the business has done brilliantly well, and there's a strong reason to think that it's going to be able to attract more revenues, and where it seems to have an incomparable advantage?*

Greenberg valued the opportunity as a $500 share price less the $100 per share in cash, which left a purchaser paying an effective $400 for $30 per share in earnings growing at 20 percent per year. The implication: Google could be had for about 10 times its earnings in two years time.

After Greenberg initiated his position the stock went up very quickly, and he sold down a large portion of it. The stock price then proceeded to fall, and the firm bought anew, just ahead of another ramp, at which point Greenberg sold out completely. In the years since, the share price has struggled, and he sees new opportunity in Google in early 2015. Greenberg says the company has doubled in size since 2010, but a two-for-one stock split means that the numbers on a per share basis are almost exactly the same as they were in 2010. The stock trades at $500, which is approximately where he bought it in 2010. The earnings per share are back to $30, and it holds $75 per share in cash. The reason Google has struggled, according to Greenberg, is that it didn't do anything with its cash, and, while its revenues have grown very quickly, its margins have contracted. He notes that, though its prospect looks superficially similar on a per share basis, there are qualitative differences that reduce Google's growth opportunities.[63]

> *We're further along in terms of growth in online advertising revenue—we've doubled revenues—so digital revenues as a percentage of total*

advertising are much higher. The opportunity for that to grow fast for much longer is diminishing. And there's no other significant business in there, despite all the talk, that really contributes a whole lot.

Greenberg says the key question for Google is one of management.[64]

I've never seen a company where you grow your revenues 18 percent or 20 percent and you grow your expenses 25 to 30 percent in a business that you'd think would have huge leverage. And yet five years later, they still get all their earnings from the search business. I can't even imagine what they would earn if it was run by a business guy. Just so many things they don't monetize.

His primary concern about Google's management is its stance on capital allocation.[65]

They re-priced all the options at the very bottom. They split the stock so they can keep control even after they sell their stock. They spend all this money without telling shareholders why they're spending it or what their strategy is. They dilute their margins when their revenues are growing really fast instead of having operating leverage. They have negative leverage on their balance sheet, which is really punitive to equity returns. To have 20 percent of the value of the investment in cash earning nothing is really punitive to your returns.

He says of the current opportunity in Google, "How much would you pay for a locked box that's got a fire hose pouring money into it but that you can't get into? That's kind of Google."[66]

CONCENTRATION AND BREAKFAST WITH BUFFETT

Greenberg's friend Lou Simpson arranged for Greenberg to meet Warren Buffett for breakfast to celebrate Greenberg's 50th birthday in 1997. He had just initiated a huge investment in three cable companies, and wanted to discuss the industry with Buffett. Greenberg had found the first cable company, TCA Cable, in rural Texas. He thought it was well situated and took a position. When a client heard about the holding, he contacted Greenberg and told him about another cable company, US West Media Group, where he was once a director. Greenberg and his team studied it and then eventually bought a big position in it, too. Finally, Greenberg turned his sights to Canada and found Shaw Communications, a well-run cable operator there. Together, the three cable companies represented 40 percent of the firm's capital. The cover story of *BusinessWeek* magazine at the time was, "The Death of Cable," accompanied by a picture of a satellite dish sitting on a cable box. Greenberg says the cable stocks were "incredibly cheap" because of the new competition in video distribution by the satellite operators. His team thought cable had many distinct advantages over satellite. They saw the future in high-speed Internet services.[67]

> *The satellite dish at that time had some serious problems. Every TV in the house had to be tuned to the same channel, and they couldn't get the over-the-air stations. There were a lot of issues that were going to limit satellite's penetration for a while. But mainly it was the opportunity in broadband that excited us.*
>
> *Everyone who used the Internet at home used dial-up, and it was obvious that every single person would one day use high-speed data service. Cable was a much better platform for delivering this service than DSL provided by the telcos. Broadband was a phenomenal tidal wave of opportunity. That's what underpinned our belief in the industry.*

This insight led Greenberg and his team to build a very large position in the three cable companies. He knew that Buffett owned shares in and sat on the board of the *Washington Post*, which was in the cable business through Cable One. Over breakfast, he took the opportunity to ask Buffett what he thought of the outlook.

Buffett dismissed the opportunity out of hand. He was concerned that the cable companies didn't generate any free cash flow. He told a story about See's Candies and how he paid $27 million for it in 1972, and it threw off over a billion in cash flow over the next 25 years, saying, "I always follow the money."

Greenberg was stunned. He calmed himself as he came away from that breakfast with the thought, "Okay. That's his view. That's his view. Our view is that they are very well positioned."[68] Greenberg knew that the cable companies would need to invest a lot of money to upgrade their systems to compete with satellite and deliver broadband, but after a few years it would be "an incredible business that generated a massive amount of free cash flow."[69] Despite Buffett's concerns, Greenberg kept his firm's positions in the cable companies.

Greenberg's view turned out to be right. During that period of heavy investment the cable companies had no free cash flow, but they eventually turned the corner. He didn't have to wait that long, however, because two of his positions were quickly bought out at huge premiums. TCA Cable was taken over by Cox three years later at four times Greenberg's cost, as was US West Media Group by AT&T at four times Greenberg's cost. He says that

Shaw Communications was at one point "a six- or eight-bagger but ended up being a four-bagger," as well. It was helpful that cable stocks were caught up in the telecommunications, media, and technology bubble in the late 1990s. Eventually, the few remaining public cable companies, like Comcast, came crashing back down to Earth.

Greenberg says it's an amusing anecdote that demonstrates that a concentrated investor "better really know what you're talking about."[70]

> *You better really have studied things in depth because sometimes you're going to hear people say, "Oh my gosh! How could you do that? It's a terrible idea." And if you don't have confidence in your analysis, or if you haven't done your analysis right, either you can get shaken out of your position or you can get an expensive demonstration that your understanding of the business was inadequate.*

The corollary to knowing a great deal about the positions in the portfolio is ignoring a lot of noise.[71]

> *That's the beauty of being a concentrated investor. You can look at everything, but you don't have to have an opinion on everything. Until you really say, "Wow. I believe this is a great opportunity," you don't have to come to a conclusion. You don't have to guess the ones where you feel unsure.*

Greenberg prefers to own a highly concentrated portfolio. For Chieftain, that meant the firm maintained no more than 10 positions, with several sized to between 15 to 20 percent of the portfolio's capital. He notes that it's difficult to narrow down to the 10 best ideas.[72]

> *It's adding up all the plusses and minuses, uncertainties and so forth, and ultimately deciding which 10 of all the ones you're looking at are the ones that deserve to be in there and not changing your mind all the time.*

He employs a rough rule of thumb to favor the safer positions.[73]

> *The trick with a very concentrated position is to buy a business where you can't lose a lot but where you have some idea about why you might make a lot.*

He says that very concentrated investors must focus on stable businesses and avoid those in rapidly changing industries. He keeps a watch list of companies that check the boxes on the following criteria: a strong franchise, some sustainable competitive advantage, not too much competition, and outstanding management that's shareholder return oriented. He generally won't invest in cyclical businesses, but will make exceptions.[74]

> *Making a huge bet on a cyclical business, which turns on the price of a commodity, to me is a less secure way to invest money. There are a few on our watch list that happen to be cyclical like Halliburton and John Deere, but most of the things that we are interested in owning are non-cyclical like MasterCard or Google. Successful investors are the ones who have this figured out.*

Unlike Buffett, who looks to hold companies forever, Greenberg emphasizes a long *enough* time horizon.[75]

> *There are quite a few companies we might own. At a certain price, though. It's just a question of finding the right one, at the right price, at the right time. We're not holding them forever. Our time horizon is two or three years. If it turns out the business continues to progress and the valuation never gets high, we may hold it for 10 years. But our thought process as we enter an investment is, "We think over the next two to three years, we can make a very attractive rate of return." And we get to know the business better and we see what happens.*

One of the consequences of running a concentrated portfolio is the occasional mark-to-market or unrealized loss. There's nothing to stop a fine business selling at a reasonable price from falling sharply after a position is started. Greenberg views these as opportunities. An example was his holding in Laboratory Corporation of America Holdings, commonly known as LabCorp. LabCorp is one of the two national clinical laboratory networks in the United States, and provides testing for a variety of diseases. Greenberg initiated his position in August 2002 at $34. Almost immediately, LabCorp announced a disappointing third quarter, and by October 2002, the stock had almost halved to $18. Chieftain had initiated a 5 percent position, so the slide to $18 reduced the size of the position to 3 percent of the portfolio.

> *If you buy and it goes down because you misanalysed the value of the business, left out some detail or a new regulation has come into effect that dramatically lowers the value, that's a problem.*
>
> *But if it's because the market gets in a tizzy, and if you confirm that your analysis is right, then it gives you the opportunity to really get a bargain.*

The work on LabCorp was reviewed. They saw it was just the market overreacting to the fact that a regional competitor had begun to outcompete them in a few local markets. Greenberg says the market just assumed LabCorp couldn't respond, so they panicked and bailed out. His team concluded it was still a great business.[76]

That year it had $2.30 or $2.40 [per share] of free cash flow, so at $34 it was okay. It was like 13 times earnings or something like that, which was higher than we ever paid before. It got down to where it was trading at a 12 to 14 percent free cash flow yield. This was a crazy price.

Greenberg bought a very large position at the much lower prices. On the quarterly conference call a year later, he quietly noted that the name of this competitor, which had been the main reason for the precipitous slide, didn't even come up.[77]

Nobody even asked a question about, "What happened to Spectrum Labs? Are they still around?" They took care of it. And the cash flow just kept growing. It was just unaffected.

The stock now trades for $116, a huge winner for his team.[78]

It ended up being a good investment. The drop gave us a chance to make a lot more money than if we had just bought a 5 percent position at $34.

Greenberg views volatility in a portfolio as an opportunity to trade around core positions from time to time when they get cheap or expensive. He doesn't believe that concentration has caused his portfolio to be more volatile. He pays such close attention to large holdings that he feels he knows what's happening in the business, and how they should trade over time.[79]

Let's take the case of Freddie Mac. We found it traded with interest rates even though its earnings weren't affected. That means in a rising rate environment the stock will get cheap, and in a falling rate environment the stock will get relatively more expensive.

That gives you the opportunity to trim your position when it's gone up and the only reason it's done well is because interest rates have fallen. And then it gives you a chance to buy back your position when interest rates rise. And so we do that opportunistically with our portfolio.

He notes that, though many of the most successful stock market investors are concentrated, most people won't be temperamentally suited to investing in a very concentrated way. Doing so requires confidence in the investment process and the judgment following it. Then one must have patience, as an investment may not pay off in months but rather over many years. Along the way, every position will have "experts telling you why you're completely wrong."[80]

As I listened on the MasterCard calls, all sorts of payments experts predicted the end of Visa and MasterCard. "This is a really big negative and they're not going to be able to get out of the hole." And these are industry experts. And what do I know? I never worked in the industry. Most people are plagued by doubts. And if something you buy goes down, suddenly the negative arguments against it [sound] a lot stronger. The further down it goes, the more those negative arguments, the worries and concerns start to get front of mind and they begin to prey on you. You begin to feel like, "Well, this is a sign. Somebody knows more than I do and is selling."

He says that when this happens, few investors have the constitutional makeup to stay with their bets and see them through.

Even if you've done a lot of homework, you know things that can go wrong. You know some trends that you're not too happy about. And you do know that there's some risk involved. And in the end you're making a bet with a lot of money that you're going to be right, but you know that you may be wrong.

Greenberg is firmly in the stay-the-course camp. Few people would have the confidence to ignore Warren Buffett's advice on cable stocks, or the advice of the payment experts on credit card interchange fees. From where does his confidence emanate?[81]

You feel a lot more confident when you go through a lot of companies and you say, "Boy, this situation really stands out. It is special. I really understand why it's well priced. I understand what's good about it. I really have a good feeling about the management. So instead of having a 2 percent position in it, I'm going to have 10 percent of my money in it and I only have to find nine others like that."

NOTES

1. Glenn Greenberg, interview, January 2015.
2. Yinka Adegoke, "Comcast CEO Under Fire from Investor," *Reuters*, January 17, 2008, www.reuters.com/article/2008/01/18/idUSN1723901820080118.

3. Ibid.
4. Andrew Bary, "Institutional Shareholder Seeks Ouster of Comcast CEO," *Barron's*, January 17, 2008.
5. Ibid.
6. Ibid.
7. Yinka Adegoke, "Comcast CEO Under Fire from Investor," *Reuters*, January 17, 2008, www.reuters.com/article/2008/01/18/idUSN1723901820080118.
8. Todd Shields, "Comcast Investors Seek Buyback, Payout as Shares Drop," *Bloomberg*, February 13, 2008, www.bloomberg.com/apps/news?pid=newsarchive&sid=a7p4TnwwxTBU.
9. Andrew Bary, "Institutional Shareholder Seeks Ouster of Comcast CEO," *Barron's*, January 17, 2008.
10. Ibid.
11. Peter Lauria, "Investor Rips Comcast CEO," *New York Post*, January 18, 2008, http://nypost.com/2008/01/18/investor-rips-comcast-ceo/.
12. Glenn Greenberg, interview, January 2015.
13. Ibid.
14. Ibid.
15. Ibid.
16. Ibid.
17. Ibid.
18. Ibid.
19. Jonathan Kandell, "Laurence A. Tisch, Investor Known for Saving CBS Inc. from Takeover, Dies at 80," *New York Times*, November 16, 2013, www.nytimes.com/2003/11/16/business/laurence-a-tisch-investor-known-for-saving-cbs-inc-from-takeover-dies-at-80.html.
20. Ibid.
21. Glenn Greenberg, interview, January 2015.
22. Ibid.
23. Ibid.
24. Ibid.
25. Ibid.
26. Ibid.
27. Ibid.
28. Ibid.
29. Ibid.
30. Ibid.
31. Ibid.
32. Ibid.
33. Ibid.
34. Ibid.
35. Ibid.
36. Ibid.
37. Shira Ovide and Gregory Zuckerman, "Investment Firm Splits in Two Over Internal Rifts," *Wall Street Journal*, November 23, 2009, www.wsj.com/articles/SB10001424052748703819904574552223436111980.

38. Glenn Greenberg, interview, January 2015.
39. Ibid.
40. Ibid.
41. Ibid.
42. Ibid.
43. Ibid.
44. Ibid.
45. Ibid.
46. Ibid.
47. Ibid.
48. Ibid.
49. Ibid.
50. Ibid.
51. Ibid.
52. Ibid.
53. Ibid.
54. Ibid.
55. Ibid.
56. Ibid.
57. Ibid.
58. Ibid.
59. Ibid.
60. Ibid.
61. Ibid.
62. Ibid.
63. Ibid.
64. Ibid.
65. Ibid.
66. Ibid.
67. Ibid.
68. Ibid.
69. Ibid.
70. Ibid.
71. Ibid.
72. Ibid.
73. Ibid.
74. Ibid.
75. Ibid.
76. Ibid.
77. Ibid.
78. Ibid.
79. Ibid.
80. Ibid.
81. Ibid.

CHAPTER 9

Conclusion

The Concentrated Investor's Temperament

[T]he trick is to get more quality than you pay for in price. It's just that simple.

—Charlie Munger[1]

The concentrated value investors profiled in this book are a rare breed. The singular trait that separates this group from the herd of investors who try their luck on the stock market is temperament. Asked in 2011 whether intelligence or discipline was more important for successful investors, Buffett responded that temperament is key:[2]

The good news I can tell you is that to be a great investor you don't have to have a terrific IQ. If you've got 160 IQ, sell 30 points to somebody else because you won't need it in investing. What you do need is the right temperament. You need to be able to detach yourself from the views of others or the opinions of others.

You need to be able to look at the facts about a business, about an industry, and evaluate a business unaffected by what other people think. That is very difficult for most people. Most people have, sometimes, a herd mentality, which can, under certain circumstances, develop into delusional behavior. You saw that in the Internet craze and so on.

. . .

The ones that have the edge are the ones who really have the temperament to look at a business, look at an industry and not care what the person next to them thinks about it, not care what they read about it in the newspaper, not care what they hear about it on the television, not listen to people who say, "This is going to happen," or, "That's going to happen." You have to come to your own conclusions, and you have to do it based on facts that are available. If you don't have enough facts to reach a conclusion, you forget it. You go on to the next one. You have to also have the willingness to walk away from things that other people think are very simple. A lot of people don't have that. I don't know why it is. I've been asked a lot of times whether that was something that you're born with or something you learn. I'm not sure I know the answer. Temperament's important.

Munger says of Buffett's theory:[3]

He's being extreme of course; the IQ points are helpful. He's right in the sense that you can't [teach] temperament. Conscientious employment, and a very good mind, will outperform a brilliant mind that doesn't know its own limits.

Temperament

Buffett and Munger have famously similar temperaments. They met in 1957, after an early investor in the Buffett Partnerships, Dr. Edward "Eddie" Davis, told Buffett that he was investing with him because Buffett reminded Davis of Munger.[4] Sitting in the Davis's living room, Buffett had laid out the rules for investing with him for over an hour while Davis sat in the corner, doing nothing, and not, so it seemed to Buffett, listening. When Buffett finished, Eddie said to his wife, Dorothy, "Let's give him a $100,000."

Buffett responded, "Doctor Davis, you know, I'm delighted to get this money. But you weren't really paying a lot of attention to me while I was talking. How come you're doing it?"[5]

Eddie Davis turned to Buffett and said, "Well, you remind me of Charlie Munger."[6]

Buffett replied, "Well, I don't know who this Charlie Munger is, but I really like him."[7] Davis's off-the-cuff comment would lead to a meeting between the two that would create one of the greatest enduring business partnerships of the last 100 years. Buffett said of Munger in 1977, "We think so much alike that it's spooky."[8]

Observers have also noted the similarities between Simpson and Buffett. Buffett described Simpson as having "the rare combination of temperamental and intellectual characteristics that produce outstanding long-term investment performance."[9]

Munger said of Simpson that he "fits right in," because "he lives the catechism."[10] Munger further explained, ". . . good stock-picking records are held by people who are a little cranky and are willing to bet against the herd. Lou just has that mind-set, and that's what impressed us:"[11]

Now Lou happens to be very smart but I would say his basic temperament was a big factor. He has the temperament of the kind of investor we like and we are.

It's no coincidence that Greenberg and Simpson, with their similar personalities, are friends. Greenberg says of Simpson, "His headlights go out further than anybody I know. It's like asking Picasso how he does it. He'll explain it and then you still can't put paint on a canvas like that."[12]

Keynes, of whom Buffett said in 1991 that his "brilliance as a practicing investor matched his brilliance in thought,"[13] wrote in his *General Theory* that successful investing relied heavily on an investor having the right temperament:[14]

> *He who attempts it must surely lead much more laborious days and run greater risks than he who tries to guess better than the crowd how the crowd will behave; and, given equal intelligence, he may make more disastrous mistakes. It needs more intelligence to defeat the forces of time and our ignorance of the future than to beat the gun. Moreover, life is not long enough;—human nature desires quick results, there is a peculiar zest in making money quickly, and remoter gains are discounted by the average man at a very high rate. The game of professional investment is intolerably boring and over-exacting to anyone who is entirely exempt from the gambling instinct; whilst he who has it must pay to this propensity the appropriate toll.*

The manifestation of the right temperament—one able to ignore the "[d]ay-to-day fluctuations in the profits of existing investments, which are obviously of an ephemeral and non-significant character," which Keynes said tended to have "an altogether excessive, and even an absurd, influence on the market."[15]—is the ability to think about the long term.

Buffett has said that his favorite holding period is "forever:"[16]

> *In fact, when we own portions of outstanding businesses with outstanding managements, our favorite holding period is forever. We are just the opposite of those who hurry to sell and book profits when companies perform well but who tenaciously hang on to businesses that disappoint. Peter Lynch aptly likens such behavior to cutting the flowers and watering the weeds.*

Kristian Siem describes his long time horizon as central to his success:[17]

> *Industry, by nature, is long term, and the fund management business, by nature, is short term. Financial investors come in and out: They can push a button any day and get out. The principal industrial investors don't have that luxury. They have to think for the long term. I believe indeed the success of industry is that you always think long term, so even if incidents like mergers or takeovers cause you to be out in the shorter term, you take the long-term decision as if you were to be the owner forever, that is healthy for the industry,*

and therefore also for its shareholders. I think that has been the success of our operation.

Keynes favored long holding periods precisely because it allowed him to ignore short-term fluctuations:[18]

There are very few investors, I should say, who eschew the attempt to snatch capital profits at an early date more than I do. I lay myself open to criticism because I am generally trying to look a long way ahead and am prepared to ignore the immediate fluctuations.

Greenberg anticipates holding investments over a two- to three-year time frame, but re-evaluates as the business progresses:[19]

We're not holding them forever. Our time horizon is two or three years. If it turns out the business continues to progress and the valuation never gets high, it will end up being 10 years.

If keeping your head when all about you are losing theirs, and focusing on the long term is so difficult to do, why concentrate? When endeavoring to describe his own investment philosophy, Buffett quoted from a letter Keynes wrote to a business associate, the chairman of Provincial Insurance, Francis C. Scott, on August 15, 1934. Buffett held that Keynes's letter "says it all:"[20]

As time goes on, I get more and more convinced that the right method in investment is to put fairly large sums into enterprises which one thinks one knows something about and in the management of which one thoroughly believes. It is a mistake to think that one limits one's risk by spreading too much between enterprises about which one knows little and has no reason for special confidence. . . . One's knowledge and experience are definitely limited and there are seldom more than two or three enterprises at any given time in which I personally feel myself entitled to put full confidence.

Keynes believed that the other end of the spectrum—full diversification—was the only approach suitable for investors who did not possess skill in value investing:[21]

The theory of scattering one's investments over as many fields as possible might be the wisest plan on the assumption of comprehensive ignorance. Very likely that would be the safer assumption to make.

Buffett agreed with Keynes that some investors—the "know-nothing" investors—should diversify:[22]

> [A] *situation requiring wide diversification occurs when an investor who does not understand the economics of specific businesses nevertheless believes it in his interest to be a long-term owner of American industry. That investor should both own a large number of equities and space out his purchases. By periodically investing in an index fund, for example, the know-nothing investor can actually out-perform most investment professionals. Paradoxically, when "dumb" money acknowledges its limitations, it ceases to be dumb.*

Academics have cast the problem of diversification in terms of seeking to match the return of the market. Modern portfolio theory holds that, as it's impossible to beat the market other than by chance, the investor's best option is the most broadly diversified portfolio, perhaps one based on a market index. In constructing portfolios to achieve this end, they look to strike a balance between holding as few positions as necessary to minimize transaction and monitoring costs, and as many positions as required to diversify away from *idiosyncratic risk*, which is the risk that any given holding encounters trouble. In a 1977 paper, Elton and Gruber showed most of the gains from diversification are enjoyed by holding between 20 and 30 securities.[23] The additional gains beyond 30 securities are minimal, and the costs of acquiring and monitoring those securities likely outweigh the benefits of any further risk reduction.

Munger's rationale for holding few stocks was based more on practical considerations—"How could one man know enough [to] own a flowing portfolio of 150 securities and always outperform the averages? That would be a considerable stump."[24] He gives the academics partial credit. He believes that most securities are mostly appropriately valued, but the idea was taken to an unwarranted extreme:[25]

> [T]*he people that came up with the efficient market theory weren't totally crazy, but they pushed their idea too far. The idea is roughly right with exceptions.*

When Buffett was asked by business students in 2008 about his views on portfolio diversification and position sizing, he responded that he had "two views on diversification:"[26]

> *If you are a professional and have confidence, then I would advocate lots of concentration. For everyone else, if it's not your game,*

participate in total diversification. If it's your game, diversification doesn't make sense. It's crazy to put money in your twentieth choice rather than your first choice. . . . [*Berkshire Vice-Chairman*] *Charlie* [*Munger*] *and I operated mostly with five positions. If I were running $50, $100, $200 million, I would have 80 percent in five positions, with 25 percent for the largest. In 1964 I found a position I was willing to go heavier into, up to 40 percent. I told investors they could pull their money out. None did. The position was American Express after the Salad Oil Scandal.*

Buffett's views on portfolio diversification can be seen as two ends of a spectrum, with the market portfolio at one end, and a concentrated, Kelly-sized portfolio at the other. The efficient market hypothesis holds that, as it's impossible to beat the market, the market portfolio—represented by a low-cost index fund—is the better option. Buffett reaches the same conclusion with a slight nuance, arguing that a low-cost index is best for investors unable to dedicate sufficient time to the markets. For those with the time and ability to identify mispriced securities—those securities for which the market isn't efficient—concentration makes more sense. Do such securities exist? Notes Buffett in his 1988 Chairman's Letter:[27]

Observing correctly that the market was frequently *efficient,* [*academics, investment professionals, and corporate managers*] *went on to conclude incorrectly that it was* always *efficient. The difference between these propositions is night and day.*

Unskilled investors can maximize their long-term return by limiting the risk to the portfolio of any individual portfolio holding. They can achieve this by diversifying into the market portfolio and minimizing costs through a market index-tracking fund. Skilled investors can maximize their long-term performance by maximizing the margin of safety of each stock held in the portfolio, which is to say, by concentrating on the best ideas. To be "skilled," an investor must be able to identify which stocks are more undervalued than others, and then construct a portfolio containing only the most undervalued stocks. In doing so, investors take on the risk that an unforeseeable event leads to an unrecoverable loss in the intrinsic value of any single holding, perhaps through financial distress or fraud. This unrecoverable diminution in intrinsic value is referred to in the value investing literature as a *permanent impairment of capital*, and it is the most important consideration for value investors. Value investors distinguish the partial or total diminution in the firm's underlying value, which is a risk to be considered, from a mere drop in the share price, no matter how significant the drop may be, which is an event to be ignored or exploited. The extent to which the portfolio value is impacted by a portfolio holding suffering a permanent impairment of capital will depend on the size of the holding relative to the portfolio value—the bigger the holding, the greater the impact on the portfolio. Thus the more concentrated an investor becomes, the greater the need to understand individual holdings. Says Buffett of the "know-something" investor:[28]

> [*If*] *you are a know-*something *investor, able to understand business economics and to find five to 10 sensibly priced companies that possess important long-term competitive advantages, conventional diversification makes no sense for you. It is apt simply to hurt your results and increase your risk. I cannot understand why an investor of that sort elects to put money into a business that is his 20th favorite rather than simply adding that money to his top choices—the businesses he understands best and that present the least risk, along with the greatest profit potential. In the words of the prophet Mae West: "Too much of a good thing can be wonderful."*

Keynes would have likely agreed:[29]

> [*My*] *theory of risk is that it is better to take a substantial holding of what one believes in than scatter holdings in fields where he has not the same assurance.*

Munger, using betting on horse races as an analogy for investing, notes that, though horse racing is unpredictable, some bettors consistently beat the house:[30]

> *And the one thing that all those winning bettors in the whole history of people who've beaten the pari-mutuel system have is quite simple. They bet very seldom. It's not given to human beings to have such talent that they can just know everything about everything all the time. But it is given to human beings who work hard at it—who look and sift the world for a mispriced bet—that they can occasionally find one. And the wise ones bet heavily when the world offers them that opportunity. They bet big when they have the odds. And the rest of the time, they don't. It's just that simple.*

John Kelly reduced Munger's admonition to bet-big-when-you-hold-an-edge; don't-bet-when-you-don't-hold-an-edge into a simple mathematical formula, the Kelly Criterion. The formula, which can be simplified to *edge/*

odds, strikes a balance between maximizing return when the probabilities lie in the investor's favor, and avoiding loss when they do not. Crucially, the Kelly Criterion never risks ruin. One implication of Kelly sizing is that favorable odds and a good chance of success lead it to call for huge bets proportionate to the bankroll, and when those bets don't pan out, its downswings can be too much for many investors. The solution for those investors has been the fractional Kelly bet, often simplified to the *half Kelly bet*, which supplies three-quarters of the return with half the volatility. In this context, Kelly should be viewed as the maximum bet size. Bets beyond Kelly don't increase the likely return, but do increase the risk of loss. All of these qualitative features of Kelly's Criterion correspond with our intuition about how to bet. Kelly advanced the theory of betting by bringing to it mathematical rigor. He showed that in the very long run, the bankroll of a Kelly betting investor would eventually surpass the bankroll of anyone following any other strategy.

Ed Thorp applied the Kelly Criterion first as a gambler, and then as a convertible arbitrage investor. In 2011, he examined the application of Kelly theory to value investment. He observed that value investors may be oversizing positions using Kelly because it was intended to be used in series—one bet at a time—rather than parallel—several bets filling a portfolio at once.[31] He noted that this occurred because value investors may be failing to consider the opportunity costs of each position. Thorp offered the example of a portfolio with two opportunities that each required a bet greater than 50 percent of the portfolio's capital. If the optimal Kelly bet for each is greater than 50 percent of the capital, the total capital committed to the positions would amount to more than 100 percent of capital. But this cannot be. Kelly will not allow more than 50 percent of capital in both opportunities because it risks total loss, which Kelly always avoids. The optimal bet in that situation must therefore be less than 50 percent of capital. Thorp argues that the same reasoning applies for any set of opportunities of two or more, and hence, "We need to know the other investments currently in the portfolio, any candidates for new investments, and their (joint) properties, in order to find the Kelly optimal fraction for each new investment, along with possible revisions for existing investments."[32] Thorp suggests that this is one of the most common oversights made in the use of the Kelly Criterion: computing the optimal Kelly bet without considering the available alternative investments.[33]

It's not necessary to employ the Kelly Criterion to be a "Kelly-type bettor."[34] Keynes, for example, embraced the insight, although, had it existed in his time, he may have shied away from such an attempt at mathematical precision because "our existing knowledge does not provide a sufficient basis for a calculated mathematical expectation.[35] The elegance of Kelly's method of calculating optimal position sizing is that it accounts for precisely that risk. Understanding this, implicitly or explicitly, many value investors advocate for concentration balanced by limited diversification on the basis that even relatively safe investments, purchased at a discount to intrinsic value, have some probability of downside risk. In his book *Margin of Safety*, investor Seth Klarman wrote:[36]

> *The deleterious effects of such improbable events can best be mitigated through prudent diversification. The number of securities that should be owned to reduce portfolio risk to an acceptable lever is not great; as few as 10 to 15 different holdings usually suffice.*

Benjamin Graham advocated for limited diversification. In *The Intelligent Investor* (1949), he advocated a minimum portfolio size of 10 and a maximum of 30 holdings. Graham's recommendations approximately coincide with the academic research, which holds that the optimal number of positions in a portfolio is somewhere between 10 and 30. Klarman, Buffett, and Munger recommend fewer positions—5 for Buffett and Munger, 10 to 15 for Klarman—all of which broadly agrees with the research that best returns for value investors can be had at very concentrated portfolios, along with Patrick O'Shaughnessy's finding that 25 positions offered the best volatility-adjusted return.

Permanent Capital

A risk distinct from the risk that a portfolio holding suffers as a permanent impairment in capital is the risk that the portfolio capital varies through fluctuations in the share prices of portfolio securities, either in absolute terms, or relative to the market. Absolute variability, or a swing in price, is known as *volatility*, and deviation from the market's performance is known as *tracking risk*. Keynes's stock portfolios, for example, exhibited high tracking error, and greater volatility than the comparable market index. This allowed him the opportunity to express his skill, and outperform, but the trade-off was periodic underperformance, and portfolio volatility. Keynes's two very different experiences with the boards of the institutions in which he managed portfolios provides an excellent illustration of the risks of outside capital, and the advantages of permanent capital that cannot be withdrawn at market lows. Those experiences demonstrate both the opportunities available to investors prepared to swim against the tide, as well as the perils of doing so, and the importance of having investors prepared to stick through thick and thin. He was the beneficiary of an administrative arrangement at King's College that allowed him to invest for the long term and ride out any periods of market volatility. He had a free hand to make investment decisions, to change his investment approach when necessary, and to construct a highly focused portfolio—all to the benefit of King's performance.[37] This allowed him to take highly unusual positions for the portfolio. Keynes's uncontested authority to invest as he wished as one of the biggest advantages he had as an investor. When King's College's discretionary portfolio suffered its single worst drop in 1938, the college allowed Keynes to continue unmolested in his investment role there. The discretionary portfolio recovered and then some by the end of the following year, and, though it was down again in 1940, it never again touched the 1938 low. From the 1938 low, Keynes compounded the King's College discretionary portfolio at 13 percent per year, twice the rate of the market over that period.

The atmosphere at King's College, so conducive to long-term returns, stood in stark contrast to Keynes's experience in the investment management roles he had taken on along with the chairmanship of the insurer National Mutual Life Assurance Society. Keynes had been appointed to the board of the National Mutual, served as chairman of the insurer, and helped manage its investment portfolio. That portfolio lost £641,000 ($61 million), an enormous sum of money in 1937. F. N. Curzon, the acting chairman of the insurer, called him to account for the loss.[38] Curzon and the board criticized Keynes's investment policy of remaining invested in his "pet" stocks during the decline.[39] With the world on the brink of a second world war, the board wanted Keynes to sell and retreat to "safer" assets like gold or government bonds.[40] Keynes refused to comply, and in October 1938, he resigned the chairmanship in disgust.[41]

His experience at the Provincial Insurance Company, which was a smaller family-run insurer, managed by Francis Scott, was similar to his experience at King's College. He was appointed a director in 1923, and he served until his death in 1946. Through frequent correspondence with Scott, he was able to persuade him of the advantages of remaining invested through the downturn. In May 1938, Keynes outlined his investment policy in a memo distributed to the Estates Committee of King's College. The King's College portfolio had taken substantial losses—down a staggering 40.1 percent—the worst performance in its history. In the letter, Keynes gives the clearest exposition on the rationale of long-term, concentrated value investment. Keynes began by explaining why he no longer believed in market timing:[42]

> *We have not proved able to take much advantage of a general systematic movement out of and into ordinary shares as a whole at different phases of the trade cycle. Credit cycling means in practice selling market leaders on a falling market and buying them on a*

rising one and, allowing for expenses and loss of interest, it needs phenomenal skill to make much out of it.

. . .

As a result of these experiences I am clear that the idea of wholesale shifts is for various reasons impracticable and indeed undesirable. Most of those who attempt to sell too late and buy too late, and do both too often, incurring heavy expenses and developing too unsettled and speculative a state of mind, which, if it is widespread has besides the grave social disadvantage of aggravating the scale of the fluctuations.

Munger was alive to the risks of outside capital. In the book *Damn Right!*, Buffett told Munger's biographer Janet Lowe that Munger was always far more concentrated than other value investors, and this led to commensurate portfolio volatility:[43]

Charlie's portfolio was concentrated in very few securities and therefore his record was much more volatile but it was based on the same discount-from-value approach. He was willing to accept greater peaks and valleys of performance, and he happens to be a fellow whose whole psyche goes toward concentration, with results shown.

Concerned that an investor would withdraw at the wrong moment, Munger eventually wound up his partnership to seek permanent capital to manage in Blue Chip Stamps and eventually Berkshire Hathaway. Simpson found his permanent capital in insurance float of GEICO, and Rosenfield in Grinnell's endowment. Only Greenberg manages outside capital, but his substantial holding in the fund makes that capital permanent. Like Buffett and Munger with Berkshire, Siem's public company balance sheet provided his permanent capital, allowing him to invest for the long term. Siem contrasts the short-term nature of capital managed in a fund to what he calls "industry:"[44]

Industry, by nature, is long term, and the fund management business, by nature, is short term. Financial investors come in and out: They can push a button any day and get out. The principal industrial investors don't have that luxury. They have to think for the long term. I believe indeed the success of industry is that you always think long term, so even if incidents like mergers or takeovers cause you to be out in the shorter term, you take the long-term decision as if you were to be the owner forever. That is healthy for the industry, and therefore also for its shareholders. I think that has been the success of our operation.

Having the right temperament, and the right capital structure makes it possible to concentrate in the best ideas, and to hold them until fruition. But how does one distinguish worthwhile holdings from those that are best avoided?

Finding Targets

While their starting points differed, the investors in this book became increasingly concentrated, long-term value investors as they became more experienced. Keynes and Rosenfield started as speculators. Buffett and Munger were more traditional Grahamite value investors. Simpson and Greenberg were equity analysts, but not necessarily value investors. Siem was an operator. As they gained experience and developed what fashionistas call *taste*, they became increasingly selective and unwilling to sell. Simpson's career gives the clearest illustration of this phenomenon, gradually increasing GEICO's equity holdings as a proportion of the portfolio, while simultaneously reducing the number of positions from 33 to 10. Until See's Candies, both Buffett and Munger had looked for Benjamin Graham–type opportunities—those that traded at a discount to book or liquidation value. At three times book value, See's represented a significant departure from Buffett and Munger's previous investments. It would deliver an important lesson to Munger:[45]

> *It was acquired at a premium over book and it worked. Hochschild, Kohn, the department store chain, was bought at a discount from book and liquidating value. It didn't work. Those two things together helped shift our thinking to the idea of paying higher prices for better businesses.*

See's turned out to be an excellent business, and Buffett and Munger couldn't help but notice how much easier it was to run a business that organically grew at a high rate funded by its own retained earnings. That property allowed it to grow and return cash at the same time, which Buffett and Munger could direct to other purchases. In his 2007 letter to shareholders, Buffett described See's as the "prototype of a dream business."[46] That year it earned for Berkshire Hathaway, Inc. $82 million on just $40 million of capital, generating an extraordinary 195 percent return on capital. The more than sixteen-fold growth in earnings from $5 million to $82 million required only a five-fold growth in invested capital. This allowed See's to return to Berkshire Hathaway all the earnings it generated between 1972 and 2007—$1.35 billion—less the $32 million required for See's organic growth. Buffett and Munger were able to redirect most of See's excess earnings to purchase other high-quality businesses, and Berkshire Hathaway became a financial powerhouse. It taught Munger that some businesses were "worth paying up a bit to get in with for a long-term advantage."[47]

> *[T]he trick is to get more quality than you pay for in price. It's just that simple.*

Through See's, Munger observed that a high-quality business could provide more margin of safety than a purchase price at a discount from liquidation value. They also required less attention and activity from the owners. Stocks trading at a discount to liquidation value typically owned poor businesses. Low-quality businesses took time and energy to right, and often couldn't be helped. See's did the opposite. It not only grew without soaking up capital, but also threw off cash as it did so. How do they identify such opportunities?

Buffett harnessed Philip Fisher's *scuttlebutt method* outlined in the growth investor's bible *Common Stocks and Uncommon Profits.*[48] Fisher advocated the collection of scuttlebutt to identify qualitative factors that might give an investor an original insight into a potential investment. Gleaned from competitors, customers, or suppliers, these qualitative considerations might include the quality of management; the utility of the research and development, or technology; the business's service ability or customer orientation; or the effectiveness of marketing. Fisher used information reaped through the scuttlebutt method to determine the business's ability to grow, and defend its market against competitors through technological superiority, service excellence, or a consumer "franchise."[49] Buffett blended Fisher's philosophy with Graham's. Graham had codified the philosophy of value investment: the concept of intrinsic value as a quantity distinct from price, and the importance of a margin of safety. Fisher showed that the margin of safety could be found in the quality of the business, which would allow it to grow organically. In 1989, Buffett would distill the investment lessons he had learned from Graham, Fisher, and See's into a single sentence, "It's far better to buy a wonderful company at a fair price than a fair company at a wonderful price."[50] It would become a familiar refrain. Buffett acknowledged Munger's influence on his "wonderful company at a fair price" investment process. In 1989, he said, "Charlie understood this early; I was a slow learner. But now, when buying companies or common stocks, we look for first-class businesses accompanied by first-class managements."[51]

At a very high level, Buffett, Munger, Simpson, Greenberg, and Rosenfield have tended to favor these *wonderful companies at fair prices*, while Keynes and Siem have favored more cyclical, higher risk targets. Siem invests directly in the assets or operating businesses of a single sector. Unlike the other investors covered, his focus is buying assets at a significant discount to their intrinsic or replacement value, and then either selling them or using them to generate additional free cash flow. Greenberg is representative of the *wonderful company* clutch, seeking strong franchises. He also seeks growing businesses where not only are earnings rising over time and value increasing, but also where the perception of that growth will lead to a higher multiple.[52]

> *. . . I like sure things. There are some things that are pretty sure—not completely sure—but I like as sure as possible. And a really good business is a much better bet than a crappy business where you're betting that something goes right for it.*

It is striking how often Buffett, Munger, Simpson, Greenberg, and Rosenfield held the same stocks. Buffett and Munger often overlapped, and Simpson and Berkshire have also frequently held the same securities. Berkshire, Simpson, Greenberg, and Rosenfield held Freddie Mac. That doesn't necessarily mean that they always reach the same conclusions. Greenberg and Buffett, for example, diverged on the prospects for cable television. Greenberg says that he won't generally invest in cyclical businesses on the basis that "Making a huge bet on a cyclical business, which turns on the price of a commodity, to me is a reckless way to invest money."[53] In contrast, Siem only invests in the oil and gas and shipping sectors, perhaps the most cyclical industries on the planet. Keynes invested in commodity businesses like gold miners, and bought technology stocks, which in the 1930s, meant the automobile and aircraft manufacturing, electricity generation and electrical engineering, and chemicals and pharmaceuticals sectors. Greenberg has bought Google—a web-based, advertising business—that would once have been considered anathema to dyed-in-the-wool Buffett-style value investors. Keynes was not restricted by geography: He was not afraid to invest in any jurisdiction in which he could find cheap stocks. Recall that his portfolios were filled with overseas companies, which was highly unusual for a time when even stocks in the top 100 firms were regarded as risky investments.

Buffett argued that portfolio concentration would reduce risk only if it raised "both the intensity with which an investor thinks about a business and the comfort-level he must feel with its economic characteristics before buying into it."[54] The investors in this book go to extraordinary lengths to get comfortable with a stock before buying it. Siem aside, the other investors have typically avoided political and regulatory risks, and the risk of financial leverage. Whatever process they employ, it is clear that they think deeply about businesses and investing. For example, though Greenberg and Siem sit at opposite ends of the quality spectrum, both dive deeply into the companies they examine. If Greenberg and his team are excited about an opportunity, he speaks with former employees, directors, competitors, private companies, regulators, and industry experts.[55] He then talks to the company. If he's feeling enthusiastic about the business, he wants to meet management as quickly as possible. The meeting leads to a complete financial analysis, and a model. Greenberg says he prefers to get the valuation approximately right than precisely wrong. He doesn't use large, complicated models, preferring to write down numbers by hand on a yellow legal pad, rather than into a computer spreadsheet.[56]

> *We always did our analysis just on the yellow pad. It makes you much more sensitive to getting something generally right, as opposed to a multi-variant, 600-line model that can get everything precisely wrong. The younger guys from the model generation figure that if it's in the model with all the assumptions, then it must be right. Whatever that mental process is, it's not something you can give to a computer.*

After checking out the business, and the people, and calling unbiased sources, in the end, for Greenberg, it becomes about judgment.[57]

> *There are positives. There are negatives. How do I weigh them? Do I think the negatives hold me back from making the investment or not? Do I think it's priced so attractively that even if one or two of those negatives come to pass, we'll still do okay? That's where the rubber meets the road. It is the hardest thing. You can't put it down in a book or put it down in a list or tell someone, "This is how it's done." This isn't a checklist. I don't know whether the Big Blue computer can replace that part of human beings.*

Greenberg notes that every position attracts "experts who will tell you why you're completely wrong."[58]

> *Most people are plagued by doubts. And if something you buy goes down, suddenly the negative arguments against it [sound] a lot stronger. The further down it goes, the more those negative arguments, the worries and concerns start to get front of mind and they begin to prey on you.*

He says that when this happens, some people have the constitutional makeup to stay with their bets and see them through, while other people panic and get out:[59]

> *Even if you've they've done a lot of homework, you know the things that can go wrong. You know some trends that you're not too happy about. And you do know that there's some risk involved. And in the end you're making a bet with a lot of money that you're going to be right, but you know that you may be wrong.*

Ultimately, it all comes back to temperament. While all of the investors covered here are extraordinarily intelligent, they would not credit their intelligence with their success. Rather, it is a combination of unusual personal characteristics. They are passionate. They simply love what they do, and consequently spend their working lives thinking about investing, and leaving work with bags of annual reports and trade journals to read while relaxing. They are also disciplined, with the ability to do nothing in the portfolio, and hold cash when nothing appears appetizing. And finally, they look to the long term. These personality traits tied to permanent capital have created outstanding long-term returns for investors.

The lesson of this book condensed into a single sentence is: "Bet seldom, and only when the odds are strongly in your favor, but when you do, bet big, hold for the long term, and control your downside risk." As Buffett's lauding of Joe Rosenfield makes clear, it is a rare "triumph of rationality over convention."

NOTES

1. Janet Lowe, *Damn Right! Behind the Scenes with Berkshire Hathaway Billionaire Charlie Munger* (Hoboken, NJ: John Wiley & Sons, 2000).
2. "A Class Apart: Warren Buffett and B-School Students," NDTV, May 24, 2011, https://www.youtube.com/watch?v=4xinbuOPt7c, as discussed in Shane Parrish, "What Makes Warren Buffett a Great Investor? Intelligence or Discipline?" *Farnam Street Blog,* April 19, 2014.
3. Glenn Greenberg, interview, January 2015.
4. Alice Schroeder, *The Snowball* (New York: Bantam Books, 2008).
5. Ibid.
6. Ibid.
7. Ibid.
8. Steve Jordan, "Warren Buffett and Charlie Munger: Billion-Dollar Partnership," *Omaha World-Herald,* May 2, 2015, www.omaha.com/money/buffett/warren-buffett-and-charlie-munger-billion-dollar-partnership/article_2819b16e-1933–51a7-b14b-002d9bb918de.html.
9. Warren Buffett, "Chairman's Letter," Berkshire Hathaway, Inc., 1984.
10. David Barboza, "GEICO Chief May Be Heir to an Legend," *New York Times,* April 29, 1997.

11. David Barboza, "GEICO Chief May Be Heir to an Legend," *New York Times,* April 29, 1997.
12. Ibid.
13. Warren Buffett, "Chairman's Letter," Berkshire Hathaway, Inc., 1991.
14. John Maynard Keynes, *The General Theory of Employment, Interest, and Money* (London: Palgrave Macmillan, 1936).
15. Ibid.
16. Warren Buffett, "Chairman's Letter," Berkshire Hathaway, Inc., 1988.
17. Glenn Greenberg, interview, January 2015.
18. John F. Wasik, *Keynes's Way to Wealth: Timeless Investment Lessons from the Great Economist* (New York: McGraw-Hill, 2014).
19. Glenn Greenberg, interview, January 2015.
20. Warren Buffett, "Chairman's Letter," Berkshire Hathaway, Inc., 1991.
21. David Chambers, Elroy Dimson, and Justin Foo, "Keynes the Stock Market Investor: A Quantitative Analysis," *Journal of Financial and Quantitative Analysis* 50 (2015): 843–868. doi:10.1017/S0022109015000186.
22. Warren Buffett, "Chairman's Letter," Berkshire Hathaway, Inc., 1993.
23. E. J. Elton and M. J. Gruber, "Risk Reduction and Portfolio Size: An Analytic Solution," *Journal of Business* 50 (October 1977): 415–437.
24. Glenn Greenberg interview, January 2015.
25. Ibid.
26. Dang Le, "Notes from Buffett Meeting 2/15/2008," *Underground Value,* February 23, 2008, http://undergroundvalue.blogspot.com/2008/02/notes-from-buffett-meeting-2152008_23.html.
27. Warren Buffett, "Chairman's Letter," Berkshire Hathaway, Inc., 1988.
28. Warren Buffett, "Chairman's Letter," Berkshire Hathaway, Inc., 1993.
29. David Chambers, Elroy Dimson, and Justin Foo, "Keynes the Stock Market Investor: A Quantitative Analysis," *Journal of Financial and Quantitative Analysis* 50 (2015): 843–868. doi:10.1017/S0022109015000186.
30. Charles Munger, "A Lesson on Elementary, Worldly Wisdom as it Relates to Investment Management and Business," transcript of talk to University of Southern California Business School, 1994, https://web.archive.org/web/20060208032616/http://ycombinator.com/munger.html.
31. Leonard C. MacLean, Edward O. Thorp, and William T. Ziemba, "The Kelly Capital Growth Investment Criterion: Theory and Practice," Singapore: World Scientific Publishing Company, 2011.
32. Ibid.
33. Ibid.
34. Leonard MacLean, Edward O. Thorp, and William T. Ziemba, "Good and Bad Properties of the Kelly Criterion," Unpublished, January 1, 2010.
35. John Maynard Keynes, *The General Theory of Employment, Interest and Money* (London: Palgrave Macmillan, 1936).
36. Seth A. Klarman, *Margin of Safety: Risk-Averse Value Investing Strategies for the Thoughtful Investor* (New York: HarperCollins, 1991).

37. Howard Gold, "What Keynes Can Teach Us about Investing," *MarketWatch*, December 6, 2013, www.marketwatch.com/story/what-keynes-can-teach-us-about-investing-2013–12–06.
38. David Chambers, Elroy Dimson, and Justin Foo, "Keynes the Stock Market Investor: A Quantitative Analysis," *Journal of Financial and Quantitative Analysis* 50 (2015): 843–868. doi:10.1017/S0022109015000186.
39. John F. Wasik, Keynes's *Way to Wealth: Timeless Investment Lessons from the Great Economist* (New York: McGraw-Hill, 2014).
40. Ibid.
41. John Wasik, 2013, quoting from Barton Biggs, *Hedgehogging* (Hoboken, NJ: John Wiley & Sons, Inc., 2008).
42. Jess H. Chua and Richard S. Woodward, "J.M. Keynes's Investment Performance: A Note," *Journal of Finance* XXXVIII, no. 1 (March 1983).
43. Janet Lowe, *Damn Right! Behind the Scenes with Berkshire Hathaway Billionaire Charlie Munger* (Hoboken, NJ: John Wiley & Sons, 2000).
44. Glenn Greenberg, interview, January 2015.
45. Janet Lowe, *Damn Right! Behind the Scenes with Berkshire Hathaway Billionaire Charlie Munger* (Hoboken, NJ: John Wiley & Sons, 2000).
46. Warren Buffett, "Chairman's Letter," Berkshire Hathaway, Inc., 2007.
47. Janet Lowe, *Damn Right! Behind the Scenes with Berkshire Hathaway Billionaire Charlie Munger* (Hoboken, NJ: John Wiley & Sons, 2000).
48. Philip A. Fisher, *Common Stocks and Uncommon Profits* (New York: John Wiley & Sons, 1996).
49. Ibid.
50. Warren Buffett, "Chairman's Letter," Berkshire Hathaway, Inc., 1989.
51. Ibid.
52. Glenn Greenberg, interview, January 2015.
53. Ibid.
54. Warren Buffett, "Chairman's Letter," Berkshire Hathaway, Inc., 1993.
55. Glenn Greenberg, interview, January 2015.
56. Ibid.
57. Ibid.
58. Ibid.
59. Ibid.

About the Authors

Allen Carpé Benello, CFA, is the founder and general partner of White River Investment Partners, LLC, a private investment firm based in San Francisco, California, which he founded in 2000. Allen previously worked in the investment management division of PICO Holdings, Inc. Allen graduated with a BA in History from Tufts University in 1988, and received an MA in International Relations from the Paul H. Nitze School of Advanced International Studies (SAIS) at Johns Hopkins University in 1992, where he was an Olin Fellow in Strategic Studies. Allen has lectured at investing seminars and conferences in North America, South America, and Europe. From 1999 to 2003, Allen served on the board of the ICA Group in Boston, Massachusetts. The ICA Group is a non-profit organization fostering employee ownership. He currently serves on the board of GiveSurf, whose mission is to provide surfing equipment for underprivileged youths around the world.

Michael van Biema is the founder and managing principal of van Biema Value Partners, LLC. Michael established the firm in October 2004. Michael was previously a faculty member of Columbia Business School from 1992 to 2004, where he taught value investing, general corporate finance, capital markets, securities analysis, and entrepreneurial finance in both the regular and executive MBA programs. He also served as director of a multi-year, multi-million dollar research project into productivity in the service sector funded by the Alfred P. Sloan Foundation. Michael received his BS in Electrical Engineering from Princeton University and his PhD in Computer Science from Columbia University. Michael is the author of numerous publications, including an article in the Harvard Business Review titled "Managing Productivity in the Service Sector" (Summer 1998), and coauthor of the book *Value Investing from Graham to Buffett and Beyond* (John Wiley & Sons, June 2001), and continues to lecture internationally on value investing.

Tobias E. Carlisle is a founder and managing partner of Carbon Beach Asset Management LLC, and serves as chief investment officer. He is best known as the author of the websites greenbackd.com, and the acquirersmultiple.com, and the books *Deep Value: Why Activist Investors and Other Contrarians Battle for Control of Losing Corporations* (2014, Wiley Finance), and *Quantitative Value: A Practitioner's Guide to Automating Intelligent Investment and Eliminating Behavioral Errors* (2012, Wiley Finance). He has extensive experience in investment management, business valuation, public company corporate governance, and corporate law. Prior to founding the forerunner to Carbon Beach in 2010, Tobias was an analyst at an activist hedge fund, general counsel of a company listed on the Australian Stock Exchange, and a corporate advisory lawyer. As a lawyer specializing in mergers and acquisitions, he has advised on transactions across a variety of industries in the United States, the United Kingdom, China, Australia, Singapore, Bermuda, Papua New Guinea, New Zealand, and Guam. He is a graduate of the University of Queensland in Australia with degrees in Law (2001) and Business (Management) (1999).

Index

NOTE: Page references in *italics* refer to figures.

N

O